THE ORGANIZATIONAL SELF AND ETHICAL CONDUCT

Sunlit Virtue and Shadowed Resistance

THE ORGANIZATIONAL SELF AND ETHICAL CONDUCT

Sunlit Virtue and Shadowed Resistance

JAMES A. ANDERSON
University of Utah

ELAINE E. ENGLEHARDT
Utah Valley State College

Under the general editorship of

ROBERT C. SOLOMON
University of Texas at Austin

HARCOURT COLLEGE PUBLISHERS

*Fort Worth   Philadelphia   San Diego   New York   Orlando   Austin
San Antonio   Toronto   Montreal   London   Sydney   Tokyo*

Publisher	Earl McPeek
Executive Editor	David Tatom
Developmental Editor	Tracy Napper
Project Manager	Erin Gregg
Marketing Strategist	Adrienne Krysiuk

Requests for permission to make copies of any part of the work should be mailed to: Copyrights and Permissions Department, Harcourt College Publishers, Orlando, Florida 32887.

Address for Editorial Correspondence: Harcourt College Publishers, 301 Commerce Street, Suite 3700, Fort Worth, TX 76102.

Address for Orders: Harcourt College Publishers, 6277 Sea Harbor Drive, Orlando, Florida 32887, 1-800-783-4479, or 1-800-433-0001 (in Florida).

ISBN: 0-15-508260-4

Library of Congress Catalog Card Number: 99-056891

Printed in the United States of America

0 1 2 3 4 5 6 7 8 9 066 9 8 7 6 5 4 3 2 1

To Carol and Kirk

PREFACE

The purpose of this text is threefold: (a) to develop a theory of organizational life that speaks directly to the agency of its members and to the organization as the domain of its practical expression; (b) to more thoroughly articulate and integrate the concepts of the self, morality, the organization, power, and resistance; and (c) to provide readers with the analytical tools to consider their own moral conduct as organizational members. We approach this purpose as communication scholars who view organizations as ongoing products of dynamic communicative processes rather than static structures or determinant forces (Conrad, 1994). We use the principle of consequential membership to designate processes as organizational rather than limiting ourselves to corporations, firms, and job sites. Our theory intends to be appropriate to such instances as well as to classrooms, social groups, families, sports teams, or any circumstance of membership in ordered relationships produced and sustained through communication.

Our organizational and ethical analysis is grounded in social action theory. Anderson, (1996) quoting Schoening (1992) and Schoening and Anderson (1995), offers these six principles that define social action theory:

1. The "meaningful world" (i.e., "reality") must both be produced and maintained in consciousness. Correspondingly, the meaning of reality has no autonomous existence and must be brought into being in deliberate ways.

2. The engagement of this reality emerges through the performance of identifiable lines of action that signify "what is being done." Therefore, any material fact will always be made "real" in conjunction with some known and knowable activity.

3. All lines of action are dialogic and improvisationally enacted by local agents as a partial expression of a collectively held semiotic of action.
4. The "decoding activities" produced by signifying lines of action shift as the lines are reinterpreted and performed in different routines (in the same way that a sentence changes its interpretive power by its position within a paragraph). Therefore, the meaning potentials for both content and interpretive practices remain open-ended.
5. "Knowledge" is made concrete in signifying practices and, therefore, is necessarily relative to and contingent on the here-and-now performance characteristics of a given social collective's routine. Any domain of knowledge is a cultural production reproduced in local settings.
6. The social scientist has an ethical obligation to contribute understanding about social practices to the social worlds investigated. The social action researcher, therefore, is obligated to inform social groups about the potentials and consequences of their reality construction practices (p. 216).

Social action theory is epistemologically grounded in methodological holism and places an emphasis on the material practices by which human action is made sensible (instead of relying on physical determinants, biology, or mental states), on the social construction of knowledge, and on the necessary ethical presence of the scholar in society (Conquergood, 1992).

The integrative, holistic character of social action theory leads us to investigate interconnections. Nothing stands alone: no self without other; no identity without subjectivity; no structure without action; no control without resistance; no virtue without vice. Just as sunlight is seen from shadow, so each thing stands in relation to something else. Our principle is that singularities are revealed only through concealment. It is a principle that drives much of our study.

We are also directed by certain postmodern sensibilities. As "postmodern" can mean nearly anything, let us be explicit. We accept the postmodern challenge to objectivity, representation, and referentiality. Objectivity is a rhetorical form, representation is always political, and referentiality is always in doubt. These principles require us as authors to reflexively call the question on our own arguments, which in turn, leads us to a discourse of vulnerability (Mumby, 1997a)—a pursuit of dialogue with our readers rather than a position of authority. As in everyday life, we offer no final text and nothing is put to rest, but we are responsible for what we say and do.

Finally, both our organizational and ethical theory are empirically grounded in material practices. The scenarios, from the simplest to most complex, are taken from field notes made during our observations and participation as organizational members, consultants, mediators, and scientists. They have been fully disguised and, on occasion, pedagogically enhanced, but their factual basis remains authentic. We offer no abstract models of organizations or ethics. We consider what people do.

PLAN OF THE BOOK

Chapter 1 begins with a dialogue between the authors that intends to locate the reader in the problematics of ethical analysis, to raise questions, and to disturb what might be well-cemented ideas of right and wrong. It goes on to introduce the concepts of organization and ethics.

Chapter 2 takes up the study of ethics and reviews the traditions of duties, rights, utilities, virtues, and care in comparison to its own position of obligation. This chapter poses three irreducible tensions across the axes of universal versus cultural values, the primacy of the individual or the community, and the analytical priority of human nature or human action. This chapter challenges the reader to take a position over the several elements that constitute these axes.

Chapter 3 takes the reader from the focal point of the organization to the focus of the organizing processes. In this chapter, we look at these processes as being embedded in a larger culture and as performing cultural tasks of their own across semiotic, epistemic, moral, aesthetic, economic, political, and social systems, considering the individual as a product of these cultural systems.

Chapters 4 and 5 develop the concept of the self as the acting agent within this cultural domain. Chapter 4 investigates the persistent characteristics of identity. Chapter 5 examines the culturally invoked and evoked qualities of subjectivity. Together, these characteristics and qualities present the self as an expression that actualizes the potentials of identity and subjectivity in a continuous state of becoming an action.

Chapter 6 puts the self in action with the domain of agency provided by organizational membership. It begins with a review of the concept of agency and the requirements of the ability to choose. This chapter then demonstrates how the organizing processes modify the conditions of freedom and autonomy to both constrain and enable agency.

Chapter 7 presents what might be a counterintuitive position on power as the reciprocal of the relationship between individuals or cultural subject positions. It takes this stance to illuminate the material practices of control that enforce the ideology and coherence—what is true and what is justified—of member action. This chapter ends by introducing resistance as a necessary counterpart to the practices of control. In this introduction, resistance serves to resuscitate the individual from control's discipline of thought and action.

Chapter 8 provides an extended case study that allows the reader to apply the concepts developed in the previous chapters to a complex ethical problem. This chapter offers suggestions and questions to guide this analysis but no final solution.

Chapter 9 recapitulates the theory of the previous chapters, bringing together in close array the concepts and principles to show their interconnections and interactions. This chapter represents the "academic presentation" of this theory and is offered as a teaching and learning aid to be used in conjunction with the other chapters. Students can turn to this chapter to find "another presentation" of the concepts they may be working with in a prior chapter, to see how those concepts work with earlier ones, and to anticipate what will come.

PEDAGOGICAL FEATURES

We begin each chapter with a "Preview" box that provides a short description of what follows and what the writing intends to accomplish. We also make use of "comment boxes" that reflexively break into the text to work with, upon, or even against the writing. These comments open up a different angle and keep the text from being sealed. Throughout the chapters, we make use of extended narratives in the development of our theoretical arguments. Students should be able to see how the theory works in actual situations. To offset the tendency to "lose the ideas" in these narratives, we provide "Principal Concepts" boxes along the way and at the end of each major section. We have attempted to support readers as they engage what might be unfamiliar terms by bolding the first occurrence in the text and providing a definition in the Glossary. Chapters 1 through 7 end with a case study and questions that allow further work in the application of the concepts.

A NOTE ON AUTHORSHIP

This is a co-authored work that neither of the authors could have written alone, but each author had different responsibilities. Jim was responsible for the theory and its illustrations; Elaine was responsible for the pedagogy and for keeping the arguments centered in contemporary ethics and appropriate for use in ethical analysis. Because at times the writing reflects a single voice, we use the device of "keyboardist" (e.g., "The keyboardist writing this preface") to denote those passages that reflect the examined experience of the person composing the lines.

A NOTE ON CITATIONS

To keep occasionally dense text readable, we have avoided using citations in the main text except where we have directly appropriated work. We have attempted to acknowledge our debts and connections in footnote listings of works that inform the writing. We are, however, developing ideas in particular ways to do particular theoretical work. We make no modernist suggestion that our ideas necessarily follow as conclusions from the work of those cited, but the influences should be obvious to the informed reader.

ACKNOWLEDGMENTS

A number of people have assisted in the writing of this text. Mary Strine, Leonard Hawes, Michael Holmes, Karen Ashcraft, John Armstrong, Jerry Benson, James Fisher, Kara Gould, Kristine Snipes, and Karen Stout at the University of Utah provided good advice and counsel. Joe MacDoniels and his communication students "beta tested" the manuscript at Hope College. Robert Solomon at the University of Texas; the reviewers contacted by Harcourt (Philip Clampitt, Susan Holton, Larry Hugenberg, Pamela Kalbfleisch, Jay Martinson, Pamela McWherter, Darrell Mullins, Lexa Murphy, Robert Schihl, Matt Seeger); as well as Melissa Anderson, Brian Birch, Harriet Eliason, Laura Hamblin, and David Keller all provided detailed feedback. Our thanks to all who helped. The errors that remain, alas, are ours.

TABLE OF CONTENTS

1

AN INTRODUCTION TO ETHICS IN ORGANIZATIONAL SETTINGS

PREVIEW

This chapter begins with a brief introduction to postmodern writing and the differences you might expect to find in a comparison between this textbook and other textbooks. The chapter then enters a conversation that visits the complexities of analyzing ethics and organizational life. From that conversation, it moves to a more systematic introduction to ethics and organizations, providing a "first look" at the ideas and concepts that will be developed in detail in later chapters. It takes these concepts in an actual case study and ends with a preliminary analysis of the case, using the concepts provided. At the end, readers should be aware of their increased responsibilities in postmodern writing and should know enough about our project to move forward in the reading.

This book concerns itself with developing a method of analyzing the ethical conduct of individuals as organizational members. It does this from a perspective of considerable difference. This book does not consider the individual as a secure unity or even as the same person from circumstance to circumstance but rather makes use of a concept called the "**self**" that appears in and is constituted by its action. It does not make use of moral absolutes but explores the character of performance to make its judgments. It does not limit its view of the organization to corporate life but extends it to any social grouping that depends on the recognition of membership. It does not consider an organization to be a thing but rather a set of material practices that are recognized by the members. It insists that every action in which there is **choice** has a moral character.

This book is postmodern, based on postmodern tenets, and written as a postmodern text. **Modernism** has been characterized as the drive toward closure, control, and certainty (Martin, 1993; Berman, 1994). **Postmodernism** avoids closure, seeks openness; is deeply skeptical of certainty, offers standpoints instead; and attempts to reveal the methods and practices of control. Modernist writing is **objective,** its authorship is concealed, its claims are essentialist. Postmodernist writing declares its **standpoint,** reveals its authorship, and reflexively analyzes the constructed character of its claims. Most textbooks are modernist with fixed definitions, declared truths, and no contribution from the reader. Postmodern texts tend to give more than the argument can use, seek other ways of looking—often undermining their own claims, and call upon the reader to bring the work to its conclusion. Postmodern texts are disruptive, dangerous to engage (to quote Harrison, 1991) because they implicate the reader in their project.

This postmodern text on the ethical conduct of organizational members begins with the following conversation between two wannabe authors held in a coffee shop somewhere along the Wasatch front of the Rocky Mountain chain during one of its infamous smog inversions. The scene is bathed in a heavy fog laced with a heady cocktail of noxious emissions.

Fade to Conversation

Wannabe 1:   So are you a foundationalist or a consequentialist?[1]
Wannabe 2:   Well, I'd have to say that I'm not a relativist. I hold certain actions to be fundamentally wrong—like cold-blooded murder.
Wannabe 1:   And so are acts of war, or that oldie but goodie—capital punishment—murder?

---

[1] Foundationalists generally hold to some absolute or universal set of moral principles that are independent of the action or the analyst. Consequentialists look at the results of action as the basis of their judgments, although their criteria for what is good and bad can be equally foundational. Relativists generally hold that the moral character of action depends on some aspect or aspects of its performance.

WANNABE 2:   Oh, you know the answers to that—overriding state interests, principles of self defense . . . .

WANNABE 1:   I see. You wouldn't shoot anyone personally, but it's OK for the state of Utah to have four guys shoot another person in a firing squad execution.

WANNABE 2:   That is a bit gruesome isn't it? But what about you? Let's push your position a little bit. Do you really believe that actions can be justified by the situation? Even rape or genocide?

WANNABE 1:   No, I don't believe that, but I do believe that the situation can change the character of an action. I don't think I could ever justify the Bannock massacre [where 400 Native Americans, mostly old men, women, and children, were cut down by the U.S. Cavalry], but I could justify an individual soldier not questioning the action—mainly on the basis of what did he know and when did he know it.[2]

WANNABE 2:   You mean slicing a saber through an eight-year-old child might somehow not be immediately recognizable as an immoral act?

WANNABE 1:   Talk about gruesome. I guess I have to answer "Yes, somehow," though in this quiet moment I can't imagine how one could do it.

WANNABE 2:   I think you're confusing culpability with immorality. The pony soldier may not be culpable for what he did because he was of diminished capacity, brought on by the discipline of his profession, the persuasion and orders of his superiors, and the fever pitch of the battle. But as a matter of fact, killing an eight-year-old child as if he or she were a combatant is always immoral.

WANNABE 1:   Not to nitpick on an excellent point, but the immorality is much easier to see given the state of weaponry of the late 1800s than it would be now. The situation has now changed to where an eight-year-old could be a very dangerous combatant indeed. If you allow war, killing a child might not always be immoral. Equally to the point, one cannot profitably separate morality from culpability. Action exists only in its performance. To declare that stealing is immoral is to beg the question, "What is stealing?" It is only when we can point to some action and say "that is stealing" that we know it is wrong.

WANNABE 2:   And so the Ten Commandments have no value.

---

[2] In part, the Bannock massacre occurred because of European and European-American belief-sustaining stories that depicted Native Americans as a people to be conquered, subdued, or even exterminated. A massacre of "Savage Indians" is not a *massacre* but a *justified act of war.*

Wannabe 1:   Recruiting the Almighty into the discussion are we? The Ten Commandments and any other lesser text of "shalls" and "shall-nots" pose the same problem. They establish the moral outcome of some action without being able to specify what the actual action is. Consider "Thou shalt not steal." I go to the supply cabinet and take a box of AA batteries to use in my VCR remote. Looks like petty theft, right? But, my employer has required that I watch a video on safe driving so that the company—not me—can reduce its insurance rates. And further, I have to do it on my own time, with my own equipment. Who is stealing from whom?

Wannabe 2:   Why not both?

Wannabe 1:   I object, because you make me out to be a petty thief when all I am doing is appropriating supplies necessary to do my job, which is exactly why they are there. The actual thief in this case is the manager who changed the character of my job without adequate compensation. I'd take this even further. The company owes me a considerable amount for the rental of my machine, the conversion of my house to office space, compensation to my family for their loss of access to their facilities and to me and additional compensation to me for my time. But do I present my manager with this bill?

Wannabe 2:   No, of course you don't. Presuming you have no contractual or collective protection, you run too great a risk of being fired. Given your familial responsibilities, that may be immoral risk-taking.

Wannabe 1:   So, I am to be simply a victim, eh? Not on your life. I am going to find ways to justly compensate for my time, efforts, and facilities. Supplies, software, equipment not in use, time allocated to personal business during the workday, using the company's Internet connection, all become part of this justified compensation.

Wannabe 2:   But there is no standard to govern your actions. You have become just like the manager—taking without proper regard.

Wannabe 1:   Well, that's possibly true and exactly why we need to write this book—because these are contested grounds. Is taking the AA batteries an informal but just compensation for work that was unjustly imposed, or is it stealing in retaliation? And what if my manager is an enlightened person who says, "I expect my people to find the appropriate ways that are available within this organization to compensate for their time"? Is she stealing from the stockholders who presumably own the company? My culpability depends on what the act is declared to be, which in turn depends on who has the power to make the declaration.

In the case of my appropriation with managerial approval, the CEO could make three equally likely determinations: "Yes, it's OK," and we are both absolved of wrongdoing; "No, it's not OK," and the manager is fired, but I am absolved because I was acting with managerial approval; or, "No, it's not OK," and we're both fired.

WANNABE 2: So, might makes right?

WANNABE 1: It could seem pretty close to that, but the might I'm talking about is not coercive force but rather the communicative practices by which the story of *what* was done gets to be told. The CEO who fires two otherwise productive employees over a $2 box of batteries is equally vulnerable to the claim that he is destroying the company to feed his personal lust for power. The story that succeeds in telling the tale succeeds because of the collective efforts of the telling and listening, retelling and confirming—communicative processes all—not because it is true. Remember that the facts of the case are few: a manager, a videotape, batteries, and me. Whether I was ordered to watch or only encouraged, whether I took the batteries or only used them are all matters of discursive interpretation and invention. They are not self-evident. Each shade of talk results in a potentially different consequence. The ethical character of the event is constructed in the story—not in the facts of the action.

WANNABE 2: I am not surprised that you are taking this to a communication ending, but what about your intentions? Did you intend to steal the batteries?

WANNABE 1: Well, that raises the question of whether I can know my intentions directly or if, in fact, I come to know them when they are encoded in **discourse.** If Lacanian analysis[3] is right, we are continuously motivated by unfocused desire that seeks an unfulfilled and unfulfillable completion of self. That desire establishes the relationship between me and the batteries. *What* that relationship is, however, determines its intentional character and that determination can be made only after the relationship is established. Consequently, I don't intend anything except the batteries. Whether I steal, take, or use them is a status conferred by the collective.

WANNABE 2: You mean to tell me that you cannot intend to steal something?

---

[3] Named after French psychoanalyst and author, Jacques Lacan (Lacan, 1968, 1977).

Wannabe 1:   No, I mean that it takes that sort of declaration, something like "I'm stealing these batteries" for me to know that intention. That declaration can be contested as well: It's called struggling with your conscience.

Wannabe 2:   So, unless you say something with "stealing" in it, it's not stealing.

Wannabe 1:   Look, as a living organism I have to act. There is no non-acting condition. We punctuate that continuous acting into bounded fields of action. But what the action is depends as much on the punctuation as the acting, and that punctuation is discursive. It is action that carries ethical quality, not act. I need batteries to run my remote. It becomes stealing when the act to fulfill that need fits the action story of stealing. We do a lot of cultural work to make sure that these stories are in place: value education, moral training, law and regulation, corporate policy. But still action and story have to be brought together before we know the ethical quality of an act.

Wannabe 2:   The story tells the tale.

Wannabe 1:   But wait, there's more . . . .

The Study of Ethics

The "more" is that the stories we tell of right and wrong are embedded in the stories we tell about the self, the **other,** and the organizing circumstances that bring self and other into a **relationship.** We live our lives in relationships—relationships that both produce and are the product of our organizational memberships. From our family, to our friends, to our team, to voluntary and political memberships, to our churches, to the classroom, to the companies we work for, we spend most of our lives in organizational relationships. These relationships overlap, intersect, interact in a complex interplay of discourse and action. Anyone who balances an intimate relationship with going to school and holding a job knows this complexity well.

Ethics concerns the rights and responsibilities, privileges and obligations of our conduct within and between those relationships. The study of ethics does not end up by telling you what is right or wrong. Instead, it provides the methods we can use to arrive at those decisions. Ethics can be considered a system of guidance designed to assist in living within a society. We are social animals. Our species would not survive if each of us lived in isolation.

That we must live together installs the positive requirement of doing good for one another. A primary goal of ethics, then, is to establish appropriate constraints on ourselves. We are asked to curb our inclination to always do what pleases us. These constraints are necessary because we have conflicting interests and selfish desires that can inflict harm on ourselves and others. We would not need ethical guidelines if people lived together peaceably in mutual support without harming one another. The fact that we do not live in this manner is the major condition requiring ethics.

Ethics is not created by each generation. Rather, as William K. Frankena (1963) observes, "Like one's language, state or church, [ethics] exists before the individual, who is inducted into it and becomes more or less of a participant in it, and it goes on existing after him [or her]" (p. 98). We do not get to "invent" our own system of ethics. Justified ethical systems survive the test of public scrutiny and debate.

Ethics is not *just* a coda for individual behavior. It is a social enterprise that consists of a system of rules, ideals, and sanctions that facilitate the basic social functions of accord and cooperation (Gert, 1988). But it also *is* a coda for individual behavior; therefore, ethics continually represents the tension between the person and society.

An important component of our definition of ethics concerns the concept of rational justification. Ethics is located within the discipline of **philosophy;** therefore, work in the field of ethics rests ultimately on reason and its power to justify beliefs and actions. Ethicists generally hold that while reason is not the only guide to "truth," it provides the best direction. Ethics involves our **analysis** of and reflection on moral choices and judgments. When we ask individuals why they believe an action is ethical, we expect more than the answer, "'Cuz." Within ethics and the rubric of rational justification, it is not enough to justify a point by replying, "I feel that way," or "I don't know, but I'm doing it anyway."

To approach a rationally supported answer, we must first separate the question of "Why did you do that?" from the question of "Was it the right thing to do?" The first question (often expressed in that pejorative tone of "What possessed you to think any good would come of that?") presumes we know everything but the reason for action. The second question is far broader, entailing questions of who was the **acting agent,** what motives were present, what resources for action were available, what action was performed, how it was performed, what were the intended and unintended consequences, what resources for further action were sustained or created, and what are the means of our evaluation—our criteria, evidentiary process, the warrants for our conclusions. It is this sort of complexity that demonstrates the ethical character of some action.

Finally, ethics is concerned with what we actually do. Experiences of harm and mutual aid occur because concrete actions are either committed or not committed. Motivation, intention, and character are certainly of interest in the field of ethics, but in the end, what we actually do or don't do is what we must justify ethically.

Ethics, then, concerns judgments about the quality of our actions in terms of their capacity to do harm or provide benefit. This fairly simple definition belies the complexity of work that must be done in making those judgments. For example, both the definitions of harm and benefit have to be achieved—put into place. Consequently, is it "what" (an inherent character of action or a universal value) or "who" (the authorized voice of empowered interests) that determines the definition of harm and benefit? Or, as harm and benefit are often mixed in a single action, what relative terms can be used to determine the worth of the balance? In making these judgments, ethics brings to bear a pantheon of ethical argument about what should and should not be considered as the basis for our actions. And as with the Greek pantheon of the gods, the inhabitants don't always agree.

There are foundationalists versus utilitarians, liberals versus communitarians, categoricalists versus cultural relativists, just to name a few. (These schools of thought and more are explored in some detail in Chapter 2.) Each of these camps start with different first principles to arrive at different instructions on how to live a good life. The question for us to answer here is not in which one of these camps do we wish to pitch our tent, but what is the smallest number of principles from which we can proceed. We argue for three. First, from whatever moment the human species sought its success in sodality, we were immersed in **obligation** to one another. That obligation forces us to consider ethical conduct. Second, ethics itself has to move us beyond the tautology of desire (I want it, therefore it is good; I don't want it, therefore it is bad) to consider the "other," from the person next to me to the rest of the world as well. And third, we adopt the Socratic dictum that an unconsidered life is not worth living. Consequently, ethics provides the means to manage obligation and desire and requires us to explicitly evaluate our choices from the principle of harm and benefit. Those, then, are the three rules of our discussion. The discussion these rules direct examines the ongoing moral judgments we make to justify our actions as well as how we craft and put those judgments in place. As we take up that discussion throughout this book, we will use powerful but often contradictory tools of situation analysis provided by centuries of ethical debate.

PRINCIPAL CONCEPTS

Ethics is the study of morality. It is the study of action in the terms
of its potential for harm or mutual aid. Ethics seeks to resolve the
problems of what is harm and what is help and to unravel the complexities of moral choice. These moral choices concern the rights and
responsibilities, privileges, and obligations of our conduct within
and between those relationships. The study of the choices starts in
our *obligation* toward one another and ends in the careful analysis of
our action. Experiences of harm and mutual aid occur because concrete actions are committed or are not committed. Motivation, intention, and character are of interest, but in the end what we actually
do or don't do is what we must justify.

The word *moral* may make some readers uncomfortable, as it smacks of
sin and things religious, but *value-laden, ethical,* and *moral* are all synonymous terms. They refer to conditions where one set of interests is upheld and another set is denied or deferred. All decisions involve a moral
dimension.

THE STUDY OF ORGANIZATIONS

Our analysis will focus on the study of ethics within the discursive and action practices of organizations. These practices are much more than simply
speaking or acting. Discursive practices refer to any extended language use
that identifies a membership and organizes a world view within that membership. "Management talk," for example, is a discursive practice that marks
people who are (or aspire to be) managers and who "think like managers."
Action practices are more than behavior. **Action** is behavior under the governance of some larger understanding such as "going to work," "doing my
job," "watching television." What is done and why make sense according to
what we understand the action to be. Consequently, we will find that organizations do much more than simply assign us to some position within a
hierarchy and divide complex tasks into units of labor. Organizations are
themselves the product of the recurrent and extended practices of discourse and action of their members. Those recurrent and extended practices not only provide the physical edifices and sociological structures that

we ordinarily think of as organizations, they also provide the basis for much of our understanding and justification of our actions.

Corporate management in multilevel firms, for example, constitutes its own organization with its own forms of discourse and action and criteria of right decision making that are often quite different from the other organizations they legally govern.

Just as there is great diversity in what is considered to be ethical, so too there is diversity in the way we think about organizations. A few distinctions and definitions may be in order. Let's start with what an organization is not. The term *organization* is not synonymous with the terms *business, corporation*, or *firm*. Most often businesses, corporations, and firms are not a *single* organization but rather multiple organizations. More importantly, many organizations look nothing like businesses or corporations. They are families, bowling groups, chat rooms, Girl Scout troops—any circumstance that brings people together as members in common interests. An organization is not a building, a place, a chart, a technology, or even a thing—those things are both the products and the resources of organizations.

So if an organization is not a corporation, place or thing, then what is it? An organization involves three elements: (a) people, (b) membership, and (c) the communicative processes of organizing. An **organization** is composed of people in conjoint communicative action. The idea that an organization involves people seems almost too obvious. But the requirement of "people" is a useful test. It helps us understand that organizations are relational processes. They are understood by studying people jointly engaged with one another, not by looking at structures alone or at individuals alone.

Membership is one of those reciprocal relational processes. **Membership** involves the declaration or claim of *belonging* and the recognition of that claim by others identified as members. Any one of us can claim to be a member of any group, but it takes the other members of the group to acknowledge this claim before it is authentic. For example, the social action of firing is the decertification of membership. It is enforced by the refusal of the membership to grant recognition. No boss can fire without the complicity of the other membership.

True memberships create domains of privileged action and discourse. Your privileges may be as simple as authentically speaking the lingo of a fast-food franchise, putting the "special sauce" on the burgers and collecting your paycheck, but they are privileges we nonmembers are not allowed to share. Unfortunately, many of the privileges of membership are also the demands of membership. Not only do you get to put on the special sauce, but you must put it on to remain a member. (You also must pick up your paycheck but, somehow that seems less onerous.)

The privileges and demands of membership create a particular field of moral judgment. To skip the special sauce on a customer's order has different ethical implications than to do so at home. Membership provides the conditions of both the meaningfulness of an action (tells us what we are doing) and the criteria by which it should be evaluated (tells us how well we are doing it).

The third element in this triad is the communicative practices of organizing. Organizations are, to use Conrad's term (1994), "communicative creations." They are the result of communication practices that provide for and sustain the domain of membership and its meaningful action. These communication practices include the most detailed policy statement to the politically incorrect but effective, "Hey sauce girl, get on the line; we've got 'em hanging out the door." That discursive line recognizes the membership of the employee, defines the field of action, creates an instance of a power relationship, and references one criterion of good performance (serve the customer with no waiting).

When the employee steps to the production line to dispense the sauce, she validates all of the discursive line's organizing force. She confirms her membership, declares the meaning of the work, acknowledges the discipline of her coordinated action, and accepts the criteria of good—moral—performance. She may do so in a naturalized fashion without evaluating the action or with full knowledge and acceptance. She may do so resentfully because she needs the job and is, therefore, subjugated by the action. She may do so but, in a pose of resistance, execute the performance in ways different from those approved. She may do so in appearance only while committing acts of industrial sabotage in actual opposition. All of this potential is brought to one actual performance as she steps to the production line and defines the terms and conditions of her membership. The boss may seek a committed and knowledgeable relationship—and there are those who would argue that she owes the company that sort of relationship—but she may deliver something quite different.

The quality of organizational life may be one of commitment, but there are also lives of **resistance** or downright rebellion in the face of the practical disciplines of organizing required by collective action (Werhane & Doering, 1995). Work, to use one organizational setting, may be just a job where relationships are constituted as mutually exploitative—the worker intends to give as little labor for as high a wage as possible and the employer intends to give as low a wage for as much labor as possible. Given "rational" practices, market forces will ultimately balance these opposing pressures, although each side will continually seek to contain the other. Taking assembly operations off-shore to cheaper labor markets or docking pay for being late are both examples of this containment effort as are unionizing and appropriating supplies. The qualities we assign to any of those actions (good business sense, sweatshop labor, a day's work for a day's pay, mean-spirited policies, union protection, socialist practices, stealing, getting the job done) are ethical judgments informed by what makes sense to us. And much of what makes sense to us is constituted by what we do and say in the relationships and memberships that, as we shall see, constitute the organizations in which we live.

The language choices possible here signal the interests that are being upheld. We could have used "pilfering" to clearly acknowledge the ownership claim of the employer. "Appropriating," the word we used, still does that work but calls that ownership claim into question. "Using" might shift the balance more to labor. Any of these language choices, however, support the principle that managers control and therefore "own" supplies. This principle is a part of the organizing practices by which we distinguish managers from workers and is another example of the way such practices also "organize" our beliefs.

We can bring these thoughts on ethics and organizations into a practical focus by considering them in the analysis of the following scenario. All the scenarios in this text, including the following one, are based on first-hand observations in our research or consultations. They have been modified to protect identities and to achieve pedagogical purposes. They are not, however, made up.

Rightsizing

Bill Rodriguez had been nervous for three days now. On Monday his supervisor, Mary Weber, had published the schedule of employee/supervisor interviews that would bring each member of his department in for review. These interviews have been a standard at ELCO for the twelve years Bill had

PRINCIPAL CONCEPTS

An organization involves three elements: (a) people, (b) membership, and (c) the communicative process of organizing. An organization is composed of people in conjoint communicative action. Membership is a reciprocal relation process; it involves the declaration or claim of *belonging* and the recognition of that claim by others identified as members. True memberships create domains of privileged action and discourse. Finally, organizations are communicative creations; they are the product of communicative practices of organizing. Communicative practices provide for and sustain the domain of membership and its meaningful action.

been employed there, but this year the company was riffing people. This year's interviews were separating the sheep from the goats. A couple of Bill's friends in the department had completed their interviews. "Short and sweet," one described the meeting. "She just said my performance evaluation looked good and that she looks forward to working with me next year." But Bill had heard of others who had not been so lucky. Those folks didn't seem to be around to talk to, though. "Guess I wouldn't want to be coming into work if I had been told I was to be *rightsized*," Bill thought, with a bitter emphasis on the word.

Bill took one last look at his performance dossier. He wanted to make sure he had his facts in case he had to argue for his job. It had been a pretty good year. He figured he had saved the company about $50,000 by shifting consignors for the heat-treatment process. There had been some problems getting the finished gears at the right hardness and some early customer complaints, but Bill had stuck with it, got the process corrected, and received a rebate for the defective parts. "Initiative, follow-through, net savings, what more could they want?" Bill thought. He touched the photograph of Josie, Bill Jr., and Carla for good luck and moved purposively to his supervisor's office. Weber's secretary was professionally friendly but impassive. Told Bill to go ahead and knock on the door.

Mary Weber was going over the script one more time. This was her seventh interview; nonetheless, the whole thing still felt very awkward. The consultants and her supervisor had been very clear. "First of all, understand that this is a business decision, not a personal one. It has to be handled in a business-like way: fair, direct, equitable. Whether it's a retention or a reduction, follow the script. There is to be no deviation. No adjustment. You say this for the retention, that for the reduction. We want the treatment to be the same across each action. No chance for anything from EEOC or other legal action. Remember this is happening everywhere in the company—top to bottom. We all have the same risks. This is not the time to screw it up."

Mary thought the script made her sound cold, hard, unfeeling, even when the news was good. That was not her style. She took an interest in her "associates," learned about their families, felt that had made her department more productive. "We're more of a family than a work group," she was fond of saying. "We look out for one another and do the job well." She knew that other departments had lost more positions than hers had, so maybe her group did do the job better.

The soft knock on the door signaled that her next appointment—"Who was it now, ah, Bill Rodriguez"—was at the door. She crossed to the door, opened it and ushered Bill in. "Come in Bill, have a seat." Mary gestured toward a chair on one side of a small round conference table. At Mary's place at the table was a reading easel with some papers on it. The angle of the easel made it hard to see what was there, but Bill thought he recognized his performance dossier. Bill relaxed a little bit. "These are all good signs," he thought.

"Bill," Mary started, "as you know the parts and supplies purchasing departments are being merged. . ."

"Wait," Bill thought to himself, "this is not how it is supposed to start." He felt the panic start to rise.

". . . positions have been cut and good people, even some of my best people, have been asked to leave. Bill, you're one of those people. I'm sorry. Here's what the company's going to do for you . . ."

Bill could hardly hear Mary as she went on about severance agreements, job counseling, and references.

"It's all in this brochure, Bill, but we certainly recommend that you check with your attorney," Mary said as she rose, went to the door, and beckoned someone in.

Bill looked dumbly at the brochure. It was brightly titled *Performance Benefits for the Future*. The first line said something about, "This is not about closing a chapter, but opening all the new ones of the future." Bill swallowed hard and started the defense he had rehearsed as insurance. He turned in his chair saying, "Look Mary, I've been very successful . . . ." He saw Mary standing with George Rieckhart, whom Bill knew vaguely as a security guard.

Mary interrupted his sentence by saying, "George here will help you with your things. We greatly appreciate your years of service, Bill, and know with your skills and the help of this company, your future looks bright."

Bill started to extend his hand, but George stepped between him and Mary and, with a hand on Bill's elbow, moved him through the door. As they crossed through the door, George switched sides to be between Bill and the secretary. George was carrying on in a respectful manner. "I think we have everything prepared for you, Mr. Rodriguez," George was saying as he led Bill directly to his office. Bill stepped into his old office to see several open boxes, some with carefully wrapped objects in them. Tape and more tissue paper were on the desk.

"We took the step of wrapping all the things the company included in the benefit package but thought you would want to wrap your own things yourself. It might be best to start with the top drawer. It shouldn't be more than a couple of minutes to clean this all up." Bill started to do what he was told. "Hey," he realized, "where is my computer? I've got stuff on there I've got to get." "Sorry, Mr. Rodriguez, the computer and all the files stored on it are company property. If there is some personal item that was stored there by mistake, you can file a request for a copy. They're real good about that." "Oh, I bet they are," Bill growled. "Yep, these sure are tough times, Mr. Rodriguez, but you'll get through them." Bill just glared.

Bill emptied out the desk drawers, not bothering to wrap anything. Now he just wanted out of there. The disbelief and shame were oppressive. "Oh god, I've got to tell Josie and the kids," he thought. "What am I going to do?" His hand felt the computer disk that he had taped under the desk. Earlier that morning he had made copies of some sensitive material that might help him get another job, just in case. It wasn't much, but it was a set of procedures he had devised and was proud of. He had felt like a school boy—watching too many spy movies—taping it in place, but here it was. It had worked, it was useful, and he felt smart.

He handed George a box and asked him to tape it up. "Oh, I'm not really supposed to touch anything, Mr. Rodriguez." "Well, the box and tape are the company's, George. I think you can do that," Bill offered in his management voice. George bent to the task. Bill retrieved the disk and slipped it into his pocket. It felt huge, he was sure everybody could see it. He finished packing up the contents of the desk drawers and started to take the pictures off the wall.

"George, there's a picture missing. It's a Deluca painting. That painting is mine. Where is it?" "Yeah, I've got a note on that," George said. He picked up a clipboard from the table. "It says here that the painting was framed at company expense. They'll have the painting itself at the door waiting for you." "Whaat?" Bill started, but George interrupted. "Oh don't worry; they've done this for lots of people." Just then two guys pushing dollies came into the office. "Well, we've really got to go," George said. "I've got another appointment in 20 minutes." Bill looked at his watch; 40 minutes since his meeting with Mary. Twelve years of service and out the door in 40 minutes, and some other sap is about to get it too. "You sleep well at night, George?" "Oh sure, I'm just helping people, you know."

George escorted Bill down the back elevator. Bill was grateful that no one seemed to be around, "Oh, yeah," he thought, "the staff meeting. How convenient." The painting was at the parking lot door, as promised, carefully rolled into a tube. The security guard handed it to Bill and said to George, "He OK?" "Yeah, I've been with him the whole time," George answered. He smiled and turned to Bill, "Good thing you didn't slip away to the men's room or something. He'd have to do a body search on ya, if I hadn't been with you." Bill caught his breath and pushed through the door, "Well, see you guys around." "OK, Mr. Rodriguez." Bill led the two dolly men to his car. They put the boxes in the trunk. One looked hard at Bill when he nervously patted his pocket. Bill finally released his breath as he drove off the lot. He felt excited, dangerous, free. He was at the top of the roller coaster ride waiting for the long drop.

"You know Mr. Rieckhart, I think he probably had something. He kept patting his pocket while we were putting the boxes in his car," one of the dolly men reported. "Well, he did set me up by giving me a box to tape. You guys need to get in there a little bit earlier. Anyway, it couldn't have been much. He wasn't that high up. Boy, you should have seen the look on his face when I told him we had him spending company money on his personal stuff. I love catching those guys at that."

A Preliminary Analysis

This scenario brings two sets of interests into conflict—the corporate interests of ELCO and the interests of Bill Rodriguez. One of the things we see in the narrative is Bill's movement from an enactor of those corporate interests to a defender of his personal and familial concerns. In that movement, part of Bill's **identity** also changes. At the end of the interview, Bill is effectively denied the means by which he can be a "corporate advocate."

He is no longer a member of the corporation and is not permitted to act as one. As that identity changes, his understanding of his own actions change as well.

In the scene before the interview, Bill tapes a computer disk with some proprietary files—ones he developed himself but still arguably the company's—in a hidden place under his desk. The scenario's description of his behavior recognizes the questionable character of the act. It was a violation of his commitment to the company, against company policy, and against the law. He would have been deeply embarrassed had anyone come in on the process. After the interview, however, the presence of the security guard repudiates Bill's commitment and demonstrates that the company expects him to retaliate in resistance or sabotage. Taking the disk, Bill merely complies with that expectation.

The moral significance of the two acts can, therefore, be considered as quite different. It is the prior act—collecting the files and taping that disk to the desk—that is the more culpable of the two. This is the point where Bill clearly chooses one set of interests over another at a time when the chosen interests should have had less standing.

Is Bill's act of disloyalty justified in the firing? If we argue that, then Bill and each of us could always act on the presumption of being fired. No reason for Bill to wait for the last day to begin to collect things useful in his search for a new job. He might just as well start on the first day of work as people are fired all the time. The likelihood, or even the increased likelihood, of separation would not seem to justify acting against the interests one has agreed to uphold, though certainly rightsize-seasoned workers may well have a regularized practice of collecting information useful for the next job.

So, is Bill justified in taking the disk after the firing? Ethicists would probably be in more disagreement about the answer to this question. Foundationalists would point to the act as a categorical representation of stealing—a violation of a moral foundation such as the Seventh Commandment, or more globally, Judeo-Christian standards or even our heritage of British property rights. But if the disk is actually his, then what has Bill stolen? He has taken a copy, not the documents themselves. He intends no injury to the company, but only to show his ability. It is his work. What Bill has stolen is the company's exclusive right to those documents. Bill has legitimate access to those documents only as a representative of the company. When Bill loses the right to be a company representative, he loses the right to those files. From a foundationalist viewpoint, then, Bill has clearly stolen the files.

The consequential view is different. Bill is not guilty of stealing because Bill has taken nothing of value. He is simply making a reasonable effort to protect his own interests. He is justified in not asking permission to take the files because he assumes all risk in the asking. There is no good reason (at least that we can see) to deny Bill those files, but the company might still say "no." The act remains against company policy and even against the law. Bill would have to pay the price of being caught. But it's the referee's dictum: No harm; no foul. Bill has violated no practical ethical standard. Don't ask; don't tell, but taking the disk is reasonable.

A phrase like "there is no good reason" should raise an instant red flag, because it is the discourse of speaking for another. Power is managed in this discourse. If John can speak Mary's interests, John has power over Mary. For example, when the U.S. government determines that it is in the best interests of women not to serve in ground combat, then the government exercises power over women's ability to determine their own best interests. This is a subjugation move because it implies that women are not capable of determining their own interests and demonstrates this lack of capacity by denying them the opportunity to do it. The formulation changes, however, if the military decides that it is not in its best interests for women to serve in combat. Such a decision is rightful exclusion or improper discrimination, but not subjugation. Speaking for another is a common discursive practice: "All of us here want . . . ," "Most women prefer . . . ," "Generation X'ers are . . . ." When appropriate, such statements should be challenged.

What allows the consequentialist to make this claim is Bill's change of identity. When Bill is a corporate member, he is the company within the domain of his corporate **agency.** Bill, Mary Weber, George Rieckhart, the unnamed supervisor, the unknown other supervisors, workers, board of directors, and stockholders are all the company within their domain of corporate agency. It is their conjoint membership—their commitment to coordinated action in the name of ELCO—that brings ELCO into existence. Without that common membership, ELCO is simply a set of letters.

When Bill acts within the domain of his corporate agency, he is responsible for the interests of the company as he knows them. When Bill goes home, he is in a different field of action with different interests to uphold. (Marriages and partnerships flounder because this change is not managed well, although the company's continued success may be in the home site's interests too.) In the scenario, Bill is deprived of his corporate membership.

PRINCIPAL CONCEPTS

This example of rightsizing briefly demonstrates the study of ethics within the discursive and action practices of organizations as a domain for actions, justifications, and ongoing moral judgments. The case allows us to see how we craft and put in place those actions, justifications, and judgments. We find that the organizing processes that produce organizations participate in the questions of who (am I?) and what (am I doing?).

He is freed of his responsibilities to represent the company's interests and becomes an outsider, negotiating his best outcomes. Even as covert as it is, the disk is part of that negotiation. Bill can presume that the company is competent to safeguard its own interests. If the files were vital, they would have disappeared from his LAN terminal long before.

MORAL JUDGMENT IN ORGANIZING PRACTICES

Moral judgment comes into play when an acting agent (person or legal entity) has the opportunity to do otherwise. The "opportunity to do otherwise" simply refers to the case where there are alternatives of consequential action recognized by the acting agent who has the means to accomplish them. The problem with this simple statement is that every element is up for grabs: Alternatives have to be present ("nothing else could be done"); the action has to have consequences that implicate ethical issues ("nothing happened when I did that"); the alternatives have to be recognizable by the agent ("I didn't know I could do that"); the agent has to recognize those alternatives ("I just didn't think that was possible"); and the means have to be available ("my car broke down, and I couldn't get there").

All of these items—alternatives, consequence, acting agent, recognition, and means—are put into place within the social processes in which we are engaged. The alternatives for action, the consequences of that action, the identity of the acting agent, the recognizability and recognition of alternatives, and the means of accomplishing them are all under the influence of collective practice. Mary Weber may determine that the rightsizing script is insensitive and callous, but she is not justified in making a change because she has no alternative that has been tested as reliably better. Her personal choice is not an authentic alternative to a well-thought-out script. That choice may make her feel better, but it is also likely to cause damage to the organization and possibly hurt Bill more. The ethical choice for her is to enact the script. The conditions of that ethical choice occur because of the actions of others—because others have set the stage for her moment in a particular way. She was not a party to the consultants' actions, but she is held in the consequences of them.

We spend much of our lives in organizational settings. Being at home, in the office, at school, or even our recreations typically requires us to enter into the social practices of organizing. The myth of the rugged individual— free to do whatever she pleases—quite to the contrary, those practices create the conditions from which we can act. We are, therefore, bound in social action that is both made meaningful and meaning making through the processes of organizing. Far from self-made, each of us presents an organizational self that must find its ethical conduct within the sense-making processes of organizing.

In our search, the postmodern, deep skepticism of revealed and discovered knowledge and of any sort of universal ethical truths will force us to consider the social processes by which knowledge is created and ethics constituted. These processes are communication processes: Communication is at the heart of knowledge production and at the center of morality. But communication itself is neither simple nor given. It too is a set of constructed processes that have different characteristics and consequences. In fact, we will see that differences in communication processes most clearly mark organizational membership. The practices of organizing assemble the communication processes that provide for the organization, just as the processes of communication provide for the practices that constitute the means of organizing.

In the interplay of organizing practices and communicating processes, we come to recognize the organization as a domain of action, of knowledge construction, and of moral judgment. Our organizational memberships make a difference in what we do, know, and hold to be right.

Transitions

This chapter focused on assessing the quality of our organizational life. One of the methods used to assess that quality is the study of ethics. Ethics can be simply defined as "First, do no harm." A more sturdy definition of ethics

PRINCIPAL CONCEPTS

Much of anyone's life is constituted (not simply happens) in organizational settings under the governance of organizing processes.
Much of the answer to *who* we are is given as we, each using joint resources, enact a self appropriate to those processes. And much of the
answer to *what* we are doing is given according to the sense making
of organizing. We will find communication processes central to these
answers as such processes constitute the organizational setting in
which we perform who we are, what we are doing and judge the quality of both.

includes the study of morality and moral behavior. In the discipline of organizational communication, ethics can be used as a vehicle to assess what
actions and practices may be helpful and harmful to individuals, memberships, and the entire organization.

Ethics involves the practice of rational justification. As part of the ethics
enterprise, every member of an organization must be able to rationally
justify why a particular action or event is ethical or unethical. Given that
organizations contain multiple ethical standpoints, we would not expect organizational members to agree on the quality of any action, though each
member can reason to a conclusion.

This chapter also focused on the definition of an organization, which
must include three elements: people, membership (or a boundaried domain
of action), and the communicative process of organizing. Organizations are
best understood by studying people jointly engaged with one another, not
by looking at individuals or structures separately. We constitute much of
our lives in organizational settings, and we are bound together in the social
processes that produce them. These social processes are preeminently communication processes. Communication is the center of the organization. It
is also the center of postmodern understandings of knowledge and moral
judgment. Communication is the central line through action, knowledge,
and judgment.

The work of this chapter, then, has been to strengthen our understanding of ethical practices in organizational action. The work of the next chapter is to develop in more complete detail the tools and resources of ethical
analysis.

Case Study

While working as a representative of a small pesticide firm, a young man was called into an emergency meeting. All employees, other than clerical and shipping personnel, were in attendance at the meeting. The owner reported they had discovered one of the chemicals they were using could be harmful to humans. He went on to explain that it met all current federal and state guidelines, was highly effective as a pesticide, and was used by every major pesticide firm in the area. He wanted to warn the handlers of the chemical of the potential danger and have them take special precautions.

Then he asked for a vote of everyone present to see if they should continue using the chemical. After a great deal of debate, the vote was taken, and only the young man dissented. He felt the company should cease all use of the chemical and try to publicly warn consumers of the potential hazard to health.

Based upon the overwhelming expression of support, the owner decided to continue using the effective chemical, only include those warnings required by law, and ask his own employees to take extra precautions to protect themselves.

1. What are the young man's options? What should he do? What are the long-term consequences of his actions?
2. In the utilitarian perspective of "greatest good for the greatest number," is the company correct in their vote? Explain.
3. What are the cultural and historical implications involved in this case? How would you vote? Explain.

2

OBLIGATION, ORGANIZING,
AND THE TOOLS OF ETHICS

PREVIEW

This chapter begins with a brief examination of *obligation* as the foundation for postmodern ethics. It then presents a story to demonstrate what the practice of ethics analysis looks like. But this is just warm-up for the main act of the chapter, which will take the reader through four traditional systems of ethical thought, plus the newer ethics of care, to a set of analyses that shows the range of decisions that the ethicist must make to conduct a truly informed inquiry. Readers are encouraged to find their own position along these lines of tension that might more fully articulate the basis of her or his analysis.

In beginning his book on ethics (aptly titled *Against Ethics*), John Caputo (1993) puts us in the midst, in the middle, of obligation already given. We encounter this obligation in even the simple moments of acknowledging a passing greeting, going to the end of the line, or making space in a crowded elevator. These, and hundreds like them, are obligations we recognize and feel obliged by, but cannot identify the time or action in which we accepted them. We are immersed in obligation—I to myself, I to you, we to others. Indeed, we trust in it (Baier, 1985, 1986). Obligation is the sodality by which we can come together, live together, work together, care for one another.

The principle that we are born into obligation is deliberately contrary to the notion that we are essentially free and autonomous and accept obligation as a rational act. At some point in our prehistory, we surrendered the fullness of freedom and autonomy for the disciplines and benefits of communication.

Like Caputo, we begin with the principle that obligation is given[1]—that it pre-exists any effort in the study of ethics. Ethics arises because we are obliged to avoid harm and to do good, and in that obligation there appears the questions of what is harmful, what is helpful, and what are the means of avoiding one and seeking the other. Ethics is the study of the terms and conditions of our obligation—the means by which we can do good and not harm. Or in more postmodern terms, it is the effort to explain, contain, and direct our sense of obligation in line with particular ideological and political ends (Foucault, 1994). Ethics works in the service of obligation.

It is not easy work. The evidence of the effort required to achieve ethical practice appears in the persistent performance of contradictory (or at least competing) lines of thought as to what constitutes the fundamental principle(s) of ethical conduct (Railton, 1996). For some it is justice (Rawls, 1971); for others it is love (Gilligan, 1982); for some it is the utilitarian principle of the greatest good for the greatest number (Mill, 1897); for others it is enlightened self-interest (Hobbes, 1921/1651); for some it is the success of the community (More, 1516/1964; Bellah, et al., 1996; Kymlicka, 1989); for others it is the success of the individual (Nietzsche, 1886/1969; Thoreau, 1849/1960). For some, the guiding ethical principle is universal (Wilson, 1993); for others it is keyed to social relations (Harman, 1977, 1995; Harman & Thomson, 1996); for some we must be monists, selecting a single system for guidance (Wong, 1984); for others we are to be pluralists, selecting systems appropriate to the question (Clark & Lattal, 1993).

Whatever we would do, it would seem, we will find comfort from some line of argument and, at the same time, be vulnerable to attack from another. MacIntyre (1988) aptly puts it as:

> So those who had hoped to discover good reasons for making this rather than that judgment on some particular type of issue—by moving from the arenas in which in everyday social life groups and individuals quarrel about what it is just to do in particular cases over to the realm of theoretical inquiry, where

---

[1] For a wide spectrum of discussion on obligation, see DeMarco, 1996; Fischer and Ravizza, 1998; Gilbert, 1996; Jacobs, 1995; Kamm, 1988; Kagan, 1998; Rainwater, 1996; Rawlins, 1992; Ross, 1994; Wong, 1984; Zimmerman, 1996.

systematic conceptions of [ethics] are elaborated and debated—will find that once again they have entered upon a scene of radical conflict (p. 1).

It is a conflict that MacIntyre wishes to end, but does not, although he claims to have done the hard part by finding the place to start. We will not end it either but will acknowledge the traditions in ethics that we continue to rehearse both in organizational practice and in academic debate (and equally those we ignore or suppress) provide a variety of means for understanding, elaborating, and managing obligation.

Jim notes: My father's undergraduate philosophy text (F. Ueberweg, *History of Philosophy, from Thales to the Present Time*, 1896) begins its reporting with the comment:

Philosophy as science could originate neither among the peoples of the North, who were eminent for strength and courage, but devoid of culture, nor among the Orientals, who, though susceptible of the elements of higher culture, were content simply to retain them in a spirit of passive resignation,—but only among the Hellenes, who harmoniously combined the characteristics of both (p. 14).

No one today would, of course, make such an ethnically limited comment, but the 8th edition of *Great Traditions in Ethics* (1996) contains no representative Asian, African, Arabic, or Judaic texts and only Kierkegaard "from the North." It is clear from a quick review of several such readers that the "great" traditions rehearsed and recycled in our universities are Western European traditions on the British-French-German axis. Therefore, it is not surprising, given this operation of the ideological apparatuses, that these traditions should regularly appear as thematics in the processes of organizing and that the thematics of, say, Zen or Gaia would ordinarily be absent or contested if presented. Further, we would not expect the current push for diversity in liberal education to change the center because such efforts are usually considered "enhancements" of the core. The ethics diversity text *Beyond the Western Tradition* (1992), for example, touts itself as "an excellent supplement" to the standard works.

The diversity in the field of ethics arises out of the diversity in human practice. Ethical theory starts in what people actually do. And just as there is disagreement over how something should be done, there is disagreement on how those actions should be evaluated. Some seek deontological answers concerning universal duties; others seek **teleological** answers concerning universal ends; we will develop an empirical approach evaluating the quality of actual practice.

PRINCIPAL CONCEPTS

Ethical theory develops out of the systematic study of what people actually do. The diversity of theory follows the diversity of cultural practice. Ethical theory provides a variety of means of analysis and judgment rather than *the* answers to questions of right and wrong. Ethics itself is the science of conduct. As a science, it is the rational inquiry into human conduct with the intent of ascertaining what ought to govern our action and the goods we should seek in life.

The complexity of moral writings we will encounter develops out of the complexity of our **culture.** One of the first tasks of a culture, according to David Wong (1985), is the development of an "adequate moral code" (p. 44) that will provide an action guide "that pertains to interpersonal relations" (p. 217). Unfortunately, the texts of a culture's moral code are not inscribed in any *one* place. They are the nominated and rehearsed texts of moral philosophy, religion, literature, and law. But they are also the rhymes and reasons of politics, policy, judicial action, bureaucratic regulation, popular culture, and common practice. That a moral code speaks adequately as an action guide means that the resources are there to solve the problems of obligation that living in the culture gives rise to. It does not mean that those resources will be readily apparent, internally consistent, or rationally coherent. Consequently, we are not going to find *the* answer by studying the various theories of ethics. We *will* develop the tools and skills of analysis that deepen our understanding of what we consider to be right and wrong.

MacIntyre (1988) again phrases it well by writing:

> Philosophical theories give organized expression to concepts and theories already embodied in forms of practice and types of community. As such they make available for rational criticism and for further rational development those socially embodied theories and concepts of which they provide an understanding (p. 390).

DOING ETHICS

It is important to understand what we are doing when we "do" ethics. For centuries thinkers have tried to define the best way to live a moral life. Their practice typically begins with an act of questioning. Socrates, whose questioning greatly disturbed an Athens at war and ultimately cost him his life (ethics is not a bloodless exercise), justified his approach with the phrase, "the unexamined life is not worth living." But contemplation is not enough; the contemplation must form a platform for action. John Finnis (1983) helps define the practice of ethics through the following:

> One does ethics properly, adequately, reasonably, if and only if one is questioning and reflecting in order to be able to act, i.e., in order to conduct one's life rightly, reasonably, in the fullest sense well (p. 1).

The "doing of ethics," therefore, involves reflection, analysis, and the reasoned application of the means of ethical practice.

The need for reflection emerges because first we are required to act. There is no non-acting state. The doing of one thing always involves the not doing of some other thing. Whatever is done always entails what could have been done. Second, action is a real-time activity that demands our attention and uses our resources in the performance. We can be denied the opportunity to consider the larger view of quality and consequence that ethics requires. Third, action may have multiple enactors and be motivated by multiple intentions. Sorting through risk and responsibility is often very complex. For example, our intentions may not be visible even to ourselves. And last, there is an essential difference between the doing and the done (Ricoeur, 1991). "The doing" is an expression of our being in the world (Heidegger, 1996); doing is a becoming. It is not available for our analysis until it is the text of what has been done. We have, for example, different responsibilities for the consequences of failed performances (we call them accidents) than for those of the expertly concluded, but we will not know which is which until it is done.

Analysis is called for because action is the sign of what is being done and no sign is self-evident, but rather each sign must be read and interpreted. The analysis that is called for is of two types: First, there is the primary analysis of the action. What was done (the sensibilities of time, place, and context; the in-place rules of conduct)? Who did it (the enactors, their intentions, foresights, capabilities, and skills)? How was it done (the quality of performance, skillful or not)? What results occurred (consequences, intended or not, foreseeable or not)?

Second, because nothing can be granted as self-evident, there is the reflexive analysis of the primary analysis. From what set of assumptions (standpoint) do we make the claims about what was done, who did it and so forth? What are the ideological positions, intentions, performances, and consequences of the primary analysis?

Finally, there is the application of this reflection and analysis in the practice of the ethical life. The "doing of ethics" cannot be without consequence. It is not a set of propositions to be posted on the wall. Rather it is implicative knowledge (Harrison, 1991). It is knowledge that changes the knower. To demonstrate the effect of implicative knowledge, we offer an analysis of a story common to everyday life.

A Parable

It has been a tough day at work. Sandy heads to his new motor pool car and thinks of the promotion that put him in the driver's seat. He starts the ignition and begins to back up while trying to find a radio station. He fails to account for the car parked closely to his left and suddenly hears the sickening sound of metal on metal. He immediately pulls back into his parking space and assesses the damage. There is no damage to his motor pool car, but the car he hit has a large dent in the front door panel. Sandy looks around to see if anyone has witnessed the accident. He is alone. Sandy's first thought is that he doesn't want to admit to the company that he has damaged someone's vehicle while in a company car. What are Sandy's options? Should he drive away? Or should he leave his name, phone number, and driver's license number for the owner of the damaged vehicle?

Sandy drives away, justifying his actions by thinking, "It was only an accident. That person parked too close to me and is just as much at fault as I am. It's a nice car, and I'm sure they have the insurance to pay for it. I could have my motor pool privilege suspended because of this accident. The price on my side is just too high."

Analysis

Our story starts with Sandy doing what he thinks is "going home from work," but it doesn't end that way. He doesn't see the car parked close to his side. Was he distracted? Inattentive? Was the car positioned out of his sight lines? The "doing" is finished. It is now time for Sandy to make sense of what was done. He declares it an accident for which he is only partially responsible and from which more harm would accrue to him rather than the other owner. He applies his analysis consequentially by driving away.

But Sandy fails to reflexively consider his analysis. From what set of beliefs has he allocated responsibility? How has he determined harm? How has he established the facts of "parked too close" and "they have insurance"? Clearly, Sandy has developed an analysis that serves only his interests. Sandy could have taken the view of the other driver and asked, "How would I react had my car been damaged? Would I want the person to drive away and figure my insurance would pay for the dent?" Sandy also knew (his looking around gives that away) that under the law, he was responsible for his actions. If he moves either of these standpoints—the view of the other or the rule of law—to the primary position or even uses them to balance his self-interests, he would no longer simply drive away. Sandy's action has intersected another person's life. In so doing, Sandy has incurred an obligation to that person. It is an obligation he fails to discharge.

Ethics, then, can be considered as a systematic reflection on the practical accomplishment of obligation that, in turn, provides the means of performing, analyzing, and evaluating those accomplishments. This chapter is charged with discussing selected ethical traditions that we have found as common themes in organizing and as useful in understanding the practices of organizing. We now turn to that discussion with fair warning to the reader to be prepared for the complexity, uncertainty, and equivocality that accompanies any such effort.

SELECTED DIMENSIONS OF ETHICS

Many decisions within ethics can be based on five systems or constructs of ethical analysis—the theoretical systems of duties, rights, utility, virtues, and relationships. These theories each seek to define what it means to act morally. These theories are not flawless, and sometimes a theory does not perform well when used in a professional or practical ethical situation. Further, through analysis of these theories, we will find that these systems of ethics can and do conflict with one another. It is important to understand the similarities and differences with each of these systems. We will attempt to approach this understanding by explaining each theory, drawing on those works most closely associated with the theory, and comparing their differences in examples.

DUTIES

Duty is concerned with the obligation of the individual to the generalized other—the collective. The duties one has are usually seen as natural, revealed, rationally self-evident, or in some other way universalized across humankind. One of the first examples of a duty ethics is found in **divine command theory,** in which the participant makes an ethical decision because it is based on a law of God. Consider the Judeo-Christian text of The Ten

Commandments. In this text, a god tells his followers they have a duty to obey these commandments. The followers are to obey these rules because their god said they have a duty to obey these rules. As part of these moral guidelines, there are punishments and rewards given by a god for performance or nonperformance of these morally defined behaviors. Divine command theory is just one form of foundationalism and does not depend on any particular religion. Most other ethical systems rely on rational justification, consequences, or individual moral knowledge.

Some readers may not be aware that the wording and enumeration of these commandments are not the same across different religious traditions, although the sense of them remains much the same. One common translation (*King James*) is provided below; another version combines the first two commandments and splits the object of coveting into property and person. Even common traditions have enough differences to be confusing.

- Thou shalt have no other gods before me.
- Thou shalt not make any graven images.
- Thou shalt not take the name of the Lord thy God in vain.
- Remember the Sabbath day, to keep it holy.
- Honor thy father and thy mother.
- Thou shalt not kill
- Thou shalt not commit adultery.
- Thou shalt not steal.
- Thou shalt not bear false witness against thy neighbor.
- Thou shalt not covet.

Outside the West, theories based on duty may not follow the style of Western moral theories but appear to be duty based nonetheless. Often, ancient wisdom literature fits into a duty ethic; this includes some proverbs, rules, and codes. *Instructions* from Egypt and 'Abba Mika'el's *Book of Philosophers* are two examples of non-Western duty theory. And an ethical text, *The Autobiography of Harkhuf*, which dates from about 2300 B.C.E., seems to presuppose a duty approach to ethics.

There are differences between ethics and the fields and customs of religion, law, and etiquette. For example, religions have made contributions to ethics, but because something is termed *religious* does not mean it is ethical. Recent examples include the cyanide poisoning of Jim Jones's followers and the problems with the Branch Davidians in Waco, Texas. Conversely, because something is ethical doesn't mean it is religious.

Another approach to duty ethics is to refer to them as *moral rules,* meaning that one performs a particular action because there is a moral rule that says it is so. Not all duty theories, however, trust universal rules to portray the moral truth accurately. For some thinkers, ethical truth also depends on the details of individual situations. The Sufis and Seung Sahn, for example, believe we have duties that must be performed regardless of the consequences and moral knowledge results from the special insight granted by the analysis of their application in particular situations. The rule is not enough; one must also know its application.

The ethicist most known for duty theory is Immanuel Kant (1785/1959). Kant, a German philosopher (1724–1804), is best known for defining duty ethics through a system of thought known as *deontology.* **Deontology** bases its argument of right and wrong on the intrinsic character of the act rather than on its consequences. To understand Kant's concept of duty, consider this scenario:

A panhandler approaches you, and you give the individual $5. What made you give that individual the money? Was it to impress other people who were watching you? Was it because you didn't want the fellow to starve? Was it because you feared this individual would attack you if you didn't hand over the money? Was it because you considered it was the right thing to do? For Kant, only the last reason meets the standard of duty. He believes we should make moral choices based on what one ought to do from a non-consequentialist perspective; we have a duty to humanity to do so. Kant states that we do something because it is the right thing to do, not because it appears the consequences will be favorable. One makes a choice and follows through with an action out of a moral sense of duty.

To specify the universal character of duty, Kant states his theory in terms of the **categorical imperative.** This principle states that you should always act so that your personal principle of behavior would stand as a universal for all rational beings. Kant wants us to move from a self-centered way of making decisions to decision making that could be universalized, such that anyone could make the same decision, and it would be right or desirable for all humanity.

As an example, Phil has found a nifty way to make his co-worker Jerry look bad. He schedules meetings and fails to inform Jerry of the meetings. When Jerry misses the meetings, Phil immediately notifies Jerry's boss of the missed meeting and of Jerry's overall incompetence on the job. Kant's categorical imperative wouldn't allow for this deception, unless everyone else could act in a similar manner. Basically, Phil shouldn't deceive because it is not a behavior we can universalize. As a deontological theorist, Kant would ask if this is the right thing to do in all cases. Since the answer is "no," we are guided by Kantian theory that we have a duty not to deceive because we "ought" not act in this manner.

Kant gives three tests of lawfulness for his categorical imperative. They are similar and even repetitive in some respects. (Kant is sometimes called a dense theorist and takes small steps as he moves us forward in this theory.) In *Fundamental Principles of the Metaphysics of Morals*, he defends in detail these tests of lawfulness (Kant, 1785/1959). Succinctly they are:

- ◆ Act always that you can will your maxim (personal principle of action) to be a universal for all humankind.
- ◆ Never treat an individual merely as a means to an end but always as an end in and of themselves. (Don't use anyone.)
- ◆ Act as if you were a legislating member of the universal kingdom of ends (pp. 16–17).

Kant is an Enlightenment philosopher. He seeks the moral power of the individual intellect. Although he did have a religious background, his enterprise was to prove that individuals could make decisions without relying on religion. For Kant, one shouldn't make a decision because a religious leader required this behavior. One should make a decision because this is the action that ought to be done—one has a duty to do so. Kant's theory is not concerned with consequences. Kant would not support an action by arguing that "if you do this you will go to heaven" or "if you do this you will get a promotion." Kant's theory requires that we make a decision because of duty—that we have a reverence for moral law.

Kant sought to find universal laws in morality by insisting that if it were right for one, it had to be right for all. One of the most clear but seemingly most difficult to actually achieve was that of always telling the truth (see Mieth, 1997). Kant held that it was never acceptable to lie. His proof of this maxim came by trying to prove the counterfactual maxim: "It is permissible for everyone to lie when it is in their best interests to do so." His proof showed, at least to his satisfaction, that the whole institution of truth collapses if the maxim of permissible lying is universalized.

Kant concluded that we have a duty to tell the truth to others in all cases. Through this principle, Kant believed we could develop a perfect civilization where other moral problems would disappear as well.

Kant's ethical theory has many strengths; however, weaknesses are also apparent. Critics accuse Kant of rigid absolutism. His critics question, for example, whether we have an absolute duty to tell the truth. If by lying to a

> **PRINCIPAL CONCEPTS**
>
> In duty ethics, one adheres to a moral practice because of a duty to a moral law. Depending on the philosophical theory, the moral law is universal as created by a god or discovered through rational self-evidence, or revealed in general practice. However, it can also be relative as to a culture or particular circumstances.

mob hit squad, one could save the life of an innocent co-worker, should that person do so? Kant's answer is simply and profoundly, "No." Kant believed the duty to tell the truth always prevails since lying cannot be universalized. This stance, however, seems to violate moral common sense. Perhaps one answer to this **paradox** is that in Kant's perfect world, there would be no mob hit squads seeking the life of innocents.

RIGHTS

The theory of **rights** looks at the obligation between self and other from the standpoint of the duty of the collective toward the individual—what every individual is owed. Again, one's rights are usually universalized by declaring them natural, divinely conferred, or rationally self-evident. For example, in 1776 Thomas Jefferson wrote in the Declaration of Independence, "We hold these truths to be self-evident; that all men are created equal; that they are endowed by their creator with certain unalienable rights; that among these are life, liberty, and the pursuit of happiness. . . ." Jefferson undoubtedly had an understanding of the writings of Thomas Hobbes, John Locke, and others who had previously written theories that all humans had the same basic nature and as such were to be treated as equals.

Thomas Hobbes believed that humans should be able to establish a social compact in which members of a society could covenant to keep certain agreed-upon practices. Hobbes based his theory on *egoism*, meaning that individuals would keep their covenants out of a sense of self-preservation. More importantly, however, Hobbes established through theory that individuals should have rights in a society. These rights can be determined by the members of a society and then sustained by the society. Hobbes believed, as did Aristotle, that humans are capable of rational thought; therefore, the laws of society would be derived from natural laws. Natural law is knowable by human reason, applies to all human beings, and is grounded in human nature. The natural law grounds the moral law because moral law must fit the necessary consequences of who we humans are. What we ought to do according to natural law theory is determined by considering some aspects of our nature as human beings and then seeking that action that best fits that nature.

Not everyone agrees on what rights are encompassed in natural law. The 1948 "United Nations Declaration of Human Rights," listed rights to food, clothing, shelter, and basic security. These are known as basic "welfare" rights. Other philosophers argue for rights well beyond these. There are liberty rights such as the right not to be interfered with in our daily life, rights of self-expression such as freedom of speech, and rights to political action such as the right to vote.

The contemporary philosopher John Rawls (1999, 1971) helps define rights by placing moral agents behind a veil of ignorance or in what he calls "the original position." In the original position, individuals have no concept of their past history, their present circumstances, or future worth. Behind this veil then, they cannot personally benefit to any greater extent than anyone else. From this position, moral agents determine what basic rights all should have to maintain a minimum level of dignity. Through this concept of rights, Rawls believes that fairness can be attained.

For Rawls, in working out the conception of **justice** as fairness, one main task clearly is to determine which principles of justice would be chosen in the original position. His effort at the task generated two principles:

> First: each person is to have an equal right to the most extensive scheme of equal basic liberties compatible with a similar scheme of liberties for others. Second: social and economic inequalities are to be arranged so that they are both (a) reasonably expected to be to everyone's advantage, and (b) attached to positions and offices open to all. (1999, p. 53)

Rawls believes that a society organized on such principles will accord the right to each individual to maximize happiness and to achieve the greatest good that each individual can justly attain. One's fullness of happiness may not happen, of course, but it will be chance or personal failure and not the action of society that will be the cause.

UTILITY

The ethics of utility concerns the outcomes (the usefulness) of a moral proposition. It is a *consequentialist* theory. Consequentialist theories attach

PRINCIPAL CONCEPTS

An ethic of rights considers what is due the individual from society. Rights may be universal or relative, but they must be sustained by the action of society rather than by an individual.

value on an act's ultimate consequences, which is the opposite of Kant's deontological view—a nonconsequentialist theory. Deontologists generally make decisions for actions and intentions that are quite independent of their consequences.

Consequentialist theories declare that an action, intention, or principle of social organization should be judged by its consequences. Something is good if and only if it has, or tends to have, good effects. Although what is defined as good can be universalized, consequentialism does seem to open the door to actual situations of enactment, something not readily apparent in Kant's categorical imperative or in Rawls's veil of ignorance.

Not all consequentialists are utilitarians because consequentialists can seek to find the greatest good for the individual or for the collective. Consequentialism itself does not resolve the issue of the primacy of the self or the collective. **Utilitarianism,** however, resolves this issue by taking the good of the collective as primary. (Self-interest forms of consequentialism would, of course, resolve it by selecting the good of the individual.) Jeremy Bentham and John Stuart Mill were both consequentialists and utilitarians. They held the view that we should always maximize good. The more moral action is one that produces the greater good for the greater number of individuals. As in many other consequentialist theories, utilitarianism rests on an independent characterization of good results. It can also be termed a strong collectivist theory because it concerns only the total amount of good; it makes no difference who enjoys this good or where the good is found.

The non-Western utilitarian tradition may include Mo Tzu, in a philosophy that doesn't strictly state utilitarian ideals but does bring up notions of harmony, peace, and prosperity as a part of ethics. Ethical consequences would be to both the individual and society. The Akan of West Africa have a moral code based on utility for the community. Actions that are seen as moral are those that promote a greatest good for the entire community, where good for the community involves harmony and cooperation.

Mill refined utilitarian philosophy to take on the concept that the moral action would be that which brings about the greatest good for the greatest number of people. In stating this principle, he stressed that the good of an individual may be sacrificed for the good of many.

Assume with us that you are part of a county planning commission, and you are asked to rezone a piece of land for an individual so that he can put a rifle shooting range on the land. The individual tells the commission that he is tired of farming and now wants to use his land for a rifle shooting range because he can make more money this way. Your planning commission is subject to other voices as well—the folks who own land that surrounds the shooting range. The neighbors are strongly against the shooting range. They fear stray bullets, an increase in traffic in their area, or that inadequate fencing would allow a toddler to wander onto the range.

After listening to the neighbors' concerns, the planning commission may find themselves prepared to vote against rezoning for the shooting range. The basic rationale is that they are acting in the interest of the greater good for the greater number of individuals.

But then other folks appear; they argue that many could be helped by the shooting range. They ask the commission to consider those who would be employed, the local sporting goods stores selling equipment and supplies, and other local businesses that could benefit. Perhaps the list of those helped is longer than the number of neighbors.

There may be greater numbers, but the question of the greater good remains. If good is defined as the absence of harm, then in this case the property is not an appropriate site for this type of activity because the potential dangers outweigh any potential economic benefits.

The farmer's rights to use his land to support a change of career are denied because a greater good needs to be served. In our society, we often make utilitarian decisions. One individual may be harmed in the equation; however, it is generally determined that the health and welfare of the community have been preserved.

Mill also advanced the controversial notion that moral action does not require useless self-sacrifice, the heroic gesture. Consider this actual example:

A sign company was using a crane to install a new electric sign. While making the installation, workers inadvertently maneuvered the crane into a power line that electrically shocked the two individuals working the crane and its load. The two men were alive but remained in mortal danger from the current. Paramedics were immediately called to the scene to help the two individuals. When the paramedics got to the scene, however, they found that the electric power had not yet been turned off at the site. They called in an emergency order to shut off the power.

In the meantime, a crowd gathered around the scene vociferously questioning why the paramedics were not attempting to rescue the two downed workers. The paramedics explained that the power was still on and that anyone who entered the electrical field could be severely injured or killed. One bystander could not believe that the rescue had not taken place and, in a heroic effort, ran to the workmen. The "hero" was blasted by the electrical charge and suffered injuries even worse than the two workmen. The hero's brother witnessed the incident and demanded that the paramedics save his brother. The paramedics literally sat on the brother so that he could not enter the electrical field.

Finally the power was shut off, and the rescue took place. The three injured individuals were rushed to the hospital. The two workers recovered from their injuries. The hero died.

This example demonstrates Mill's concept of a useless self-sacrifice. The example is not meant to be cruel. Instead, it is intended to emphasize the point that one must always survey the long-term consequences of an action before pursuing that action. It is important to understand that critically thinking through reactions to emergency situations before they actually happen could save lives—even one's own. If you see someone drowning in a raging river, and you don't know how to swim, it is senseless for you to dive into the current in an effort to save the life. If you did, two lives would most likely be lost, not one. Mill is not stating that risks should be avoided, but that the risks need to be appropriate to the good to be gained and the likelihood of success.

Mill's philosophy would have you do any moral action which will bring about good or desirable long-term consequences. You would avoid those actions that produce the opposite results. This philosophy is in direct contrast to Kant's moral guideline, which is nonconsequentialist. Kant would have you do an action because you "ought" to do it—because it is your duty. A large part of Kant's philosophy is based on pure, rational thought. He believes an individual should make the decision that has universal properties and could be reached by anyone using right reason.

In opposition to Kant, Mill states that we always make decisions based on the consequences and on what makes us happy and that decisions based on utility are most natural.

As an example, let's consider the marriages of Glen and Wade. Glen is very happily married. His wife is wonderful to him, his children bring him much joy, and he enjoys the entire family association. Next we have Wade, who is unhappily married. However, he continues to stay married because of a sense of moral duty. He has made a commitment to marriage and stays married because he "ought" to perform his duty.

For Kant, Glen's marriage is an example of consequentialism. Glen stays married because the long-term consequences are good. (Kant terms this a *hypothetical imperative:* one stays married because of the positive outcomes.) Wade is a nonconsequentialist or follows the doctrine of deontology. He stays married because of his moral duty. (Kant terms this a *categorical imperative:* one stays married because it is one's duty.)

As a further example, Bob and Peter each decide to open respective tire businesses. Bob decides that he is going to be honest in business because it is the right thing to do. He doesn't care if he goes out of business as a result of his honesty. Bob will be honest with all his customers because he *ought* to be honest with them. Peter decides that he will be honest in his business because "honesty is the best policy." If people know that Peter is honest, it will bring in repeat business and also new clients through word of mouth. Peter bases his decision on consequentialism, a position like Mill's. Bob bases his decision on nonconsequentialism or Kantian thought.

On the surface the outcomes appear to be the same; it is the pressure of a crisis that will bring out the differences. Given increasing economic pressure, Bob may decide that one cannot be honest in serving dishonest customers because his honesty is used against him. He may insist on his right to make a living, regardless of its effect on honesty. Peter may find that it is not "good enough" to be honest, one also has to be a sharp entrepreneur. Both will remain in their nonconsequentialist and consequentialist camps, but Bob will abandon duty for his rights and Peter will change his notion of the greater good.

The nonconsequentialist philosophy of rights and duties and the consequentialist philosophy of utility will, perhaps, be the most commonly used in your moral deliberations. They each offer a different perspective. They each offer a look at morality, but you must supply the intellectual and moral justification for action. We now turn to two additional systems, virtues and relationships.

VIRTUES

Virtue ethics can be seen as a combination of duty and rights where one has the duty to self-actualize and the right to accomplish that self-actualization. A virtue is generally seen as an internal quality—a mark of character—that leads to right action. The four classic virtues were prudence, temperance,

---

PRINCIPAL CONCEPTS

An ethics based on utility is consequentialist in nature. Action is justified through its long-term consequences. The criteria of justification include the long-term pleasure or pain that might result, as well as the extent of those consequences. The criterion for judging these consequences is often expressed as "the greatest good for the greatest number."

---

fortitude, and justice. The Christian tradition added three theological virtues of faith, hope, and charity. Virtue ethics does not, however, depend on this list, as the system itself must establish the appropriate marks of quality. In establishing that list, the focus of virtue ethics is on the individual as a fully vested member of a collective (rather than the suborned individual of duties or the rugged individual of rights). The virtues themselves are most often universalized, although in the relationship ethics that follow, virtues might be a cultural production. The moral philosophies of David Hume, Aristotle, Socrates, Plato, Augustine, and Buddha are often classified as virtue ethics. Further, some elements of virtue ethics are present in the writings of Confucius: "The rule of virtue can be compared to the Pole Star which commands the homage of the multitude of Stars without leaving its place" (*The Analects*, book 4:4).

The ancient Greeks were far more concerned with the virtues and character of individuals than an ethics emphasizing rules or principles. For the Greeks virtue was not just attached to individual attributes, such as happiness, integrity, charm, and honesty, but to society as well. A Greek citizen was honest not only as a virtuous individual, but also because it made for an honest society. A citizen was not just honest once in a while, but a citizen was to make a lifelong habit of honesty. Therefore, it would follow that a person would not have to debate over whether or not to be dishonest, because honesty would be the natural character trait developed through habit.

The term *virtue* can become confused with the idea of moral purity or sinlessness. An ethics that focuses on virtues as the necessary qualities of human life has a very different emphasis than an ethics that takes virtue to be synonymous with moral purity. Ethical virtues focus on realizing one's intellectual, social, and spiritual potential, and on cultivating those habits that are deemed most important by a given society. Virtue is a carefully developed character trait that is important to a given society.

The great virtue ethicists include Socrates, Plato, and Aristotle. Since Socrates did not write down his lectures and discussions, they come to us from others who were involved in the dialogues. Plato was Socrates' student and is credited with writing the "dialogues" of Socrates. Socrates lived in Athens from 470 until 399 B.C.E. He was a brilliant thinker and teacher, often living off only the gifts from his students. Plato lived from 427 to 347 B.C.E. He was with Socrates through his fated trial and execution. Following Socrates' death, Plato founded the famous Academy in Athens. He recorded Socrates' dialogues and often used Socrates as a model in his own writings. Sometimes it is difficult to distinguish which theories are Plato's and which belong to Socrates (for example, in works such as *The Republic*). Plato's top student was Aristotle, who was born in 384 B.C.E. in northern Greece. His father was physician to King Philip of Macedonia. Aristotle studied with and tutored the king's son Alexander, who later became known as Alexander the Great. Aristotle studied with Plato for eighteen years but parted company with him because of differences in theory. Aristotle's description of the parting is, "Dear is Plato, but dearer still is truth."

In this book we will use the writings of Aristotle to encapsulate the thinking on ethics and virtues. Aristotle makes the point that virtues should be connected to the good of humankind. This means that all human activities should aim for the ultimate good of happiness. Happiness, he points out, can be defined in many ways, such as wealth, health, pleasure, or honor. He believes that the ultimate human happiness must come through reason; the best life for a human is the life of reason. Aristotle defines virtue as, "a rational activity, activity in accordance with a rational principle."

Although Aristotle is currently in vogue, for years an ethics based on virtues was omitted from college ethics classes and texts. Aristotle was omitted because philosophers focused on finding a single guiding principle to help us identify moral choices so we can avoid acting immorally. Aristotle offered no help in this search. For Aristotle right action does not result from knowing and following the "right" principle. Rather, right action results from living a harmonious life. Living that balances all aspects of life is the state of happiness. Aristotle explains we can achieve this by living virtuously.

Happiness, for Aristotle, is the state when our actions accomplish their goals. We need all of our characteristics together to help us accomplish our goal. So happiness is in the harmony of all these characteristics that allow us to act in accord with our human character, and happiness includes living a successful moral life, among other things.

How did Aristotle think we get all the activities of our lives working together in harmony? First, he looked at the different activities of the mind or

PRINCIPAL CONCEPTS

Ethical virtues focus on realizing one's intellectual, social, and spiritual potential, and on cultivating those habits that are most important in a given society. Virtue is a carefully developed character trait that is important to society.

soul, since they are the most important for happiness. The activity of the soul is rational and in two parts: moral and intellectual. Aristotle describes intellectual and moral virtues as those that help us perform the activities of the soul well; so there are moral virtues and intellectual virtues.

In general, a moral virtue is the characteristic of avoiding both excess and deficiency in moral action. Activity that is neither excessive nor deficient but seeks "the mean," is virtuous action. For example, courage could be selected as the mean between foolhardiness (an excess) and cowardice (a deficit). When Aristotle advises we seek the "Golden Mean," he is advising we seek that which is reasonable, not mediocre. And Aristotle thinks we must choose the mean relative to us. By "relative to us" Aristotle means according to the particular situation we are in and who we are. If I am extremely generous by nature, then giving away ten percent of my income may not be virtuous. The mean relative to me may require I give thirty-five percent for virtue's sake. Giving any more might be excessive, but giving any less would be miserly. The mean depends on the concrete circumstances and the person.

Another important feature of moral virtues, according to Aristotle, is that they cannot be taught as propositional rules. Aristotle said we learn moral virtue only by performance. Learning moral virtues, the characteristics that let us perform the moral function well, depends on training, upbringing, and practice. Our need for training is why Aristotle thought it so important that nations (city-states) develop good laws; good laws habituate good practices in its citizens. Without good laws and without a good city, Aristotle held that people cannot live the moral life well (if at all). In the same vein, Aristotle declared that the primary duty of a friend is to help the other achieve a moral life.

RELATIONSHIPS

An emerging theory of ethics currently in the spotlight is a theory based on caring, sharing, and relationships. **Relationship ethics** can be seen as a form of virtue ethics in which the virtues that celebrate justice are associated with the cultural production of the masculine and those that celebrate love are associated with the feminine. Men and women, therefore, tend to reflect this gendered difference. Much of the work on this moral theory has been done in the field of psychology through the research and writings of Carol Gilligan. Gilligan believes that through psychologists such as Freud and Erikson and particularly through the work of moral developmentalist Lawrence Kohlberg moral research has focused on male patterns of decision making as the only or the superior pattern of making decisions. According to Gilligan, Kohlberg's six stages of moral development were based on male models of maturity. These models privileged autonomy and independence, while female moral development is often based on the strengths of relationships and the caring and sharing that can take place among others. Gilligan's work, *In a Different Voice* (1982), develops the theory that women and men may make moral decisions based on different cultural preconditioning and that neither is inferior nor superior to the other but combined they create a different voice (Gilligan, 1999).

According to Gilligan, our culture and our values create a discrepancy between "womanhood" and "adulthood." In traditional definitions, adulthood is a masculine maturity equated to personal autonomy that would read concern for relationships as a weakness rather than a human strength. Gilligan makes the following observation:

> Women's place in man's life cycle has been that of nurturer, caretaker, and helpmate, the weaver of those networks of relationships on which she in turn relies . . . . When the focus on individuation and individual achievement extends into adulthood and maturity is equated with personal autonomy, concern with relationships appears as a weakness of women rather than as a human strength (p. 17).

Gilligan explains that since the primary caretaker is female, the interpersonal dynamics are different for boys and girls. Girls identify with mother while boys separate themselves. In the process, boys curtail primary love and a sense of empathy. She further explains that since masculinity is defined through separation, and femininity is defined through attachment, the male gender is threatened by intimacy while the female gender identity is threatened by separation.

In the different voice of women, however, lies the truth of an ethic of care—the tie between relationship and responsibility. For Nel Noddings, we make moral choices based on an ethic of care. One of her primary examples focuses on a mother picking up a crying baby. She does not pick up the child because of a sense of duty or because she is worried about the consequences

PRINCIPAL CONCEPTS

A relationship ethics is emerging in contemporary scholarship. Its major claim is that it is appropriate to make moral decisions based on caring, sharing, and relationships. Appropriate moral decisions can be made based on the network of relationships in our lives and how others in that network are harmed or helped by our moral decisions.

TABLE 2.1 **Moral System**

	DUTIES	RIGHTS	UTILITY	VIRTUES	RELATIONSHIPS
Terms	Obligation of individual to moral rules	Obligation of community to individual	Obligation to maximize happiness	Obligation to self and community	Obligation to the relationship
Basis	Based on universal, self-evident requirements	Universal, self-evident prerogatives of the individual	Based on consequences of action	Based on integrity of character	Based on the social practices of care
Action	Moral action discharges duty	Moral action preserves individual rights	Moral action produces favorable consequences	Moral action improves the individual & state	Moral action produces caring relationships

of not picking up the child. Noddings theorizes the mother picks up her baby out of a sense of care based on their relationship.

Relationship theorists reinforce that this is not a gender-based ethics or an ethics system to be used in exclusion of other systems of analysis. They believe it is an important way of thinking that should be included within an overall analysis of an ethical dilemma.

SUMMARY OF THE FIVE SYSTEMS

The five moral systems of duties, rights, utility, virtues, and relationships can be compared across the terms of their obligation, the basis for their standard of moral action, and the criteria for what moral action is. Table 2.1 provides that comparison.

Analytical Tensions

As Table 2.1 demonstrates, the different moral systems lead to quite different conclusions regarding what constitutes moral action. These competing systems, plus others and those from the Eastern traditions, exist side-by-side in the world of moral philosophy. When moral philosophy is even briefly examined as we have done here, the diversity of positions is striking. Issues raised some 2,500 years ago in the Greek academies have a freshness and currency, a vitality of argument, even today. Nothing has been put to rest; issues addressed in past times sustain their importance in today's deliberations.

No small part of the reason for this diversity and unrest is that any area of human studies, including those of science and ethics, rests on a set of tensions that we have not been able to reduce. Anderson (1996) has suggested seven such lines of tension: (a) the character of reality; (b) our engagement of reality; (c) the nature of the individual; (d) the constitution of knowledge in the justified claim; (e) our distribution of knowledge through the practical argument; (f) the relationship between epistemological claim and epistemological method; and (g) the role of scholarship in society. Basically, Anderson argues that any truth claim requires the claimant to adopt some position along these lines of tension. That adoption permits the claim but does not resolve the underlying tensions that remain to position the next effort. For example, if you believed that we encounter the reality in which we live directly and that your experience of that reality is trustworthy, you would be considered an objective empiricist (i.e., realist) and might be on your way to being a scientist of a certain sort. If, on the other hand, you believed that same reality is engaged in some part through some symbol system such as language and that your experience of it is culturally mediated, then you would be considered an hermeneutic empiricist (i.e., social constructionist) and might be on your way to be a scientist of a different sort. To be a scientist of any sort, however, you have to make the prior decisions (or have them made for you), including these about the nature of reality and its engagement.

Since the Anderson of the quote is one of authors of this text, we can—and will—appropriate his arguments here to consider the irreducible tensions of ethics. To do so, we will pose the world of moral philosophy as a sphere trisected by three axes that round up Anderson's seven tensions into the traditional oppositions in solutions to ethical problems

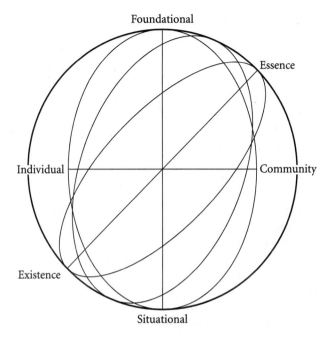

FIGURE 2.1   *A model of the oppositions in moral philosophy*

(Figure 2.1).[2] The three are: (a) foundational/situational; (b) individual/community; and (c) essence/existence.

THE FOUNDATIONAL/SITUATIONAL AXIS

The foundational/situational opposition appears in Plato's answer to Protagoras in the debate whether values are foundational with a set common to all humankind, or values are a cultural production with different sets possible across cultures. If value is foundational, then ethics can rest on certainty; if it is cultural, then ethics is situational. And yes, this issue is still being debated after more than two millennia.

---

[2] The model and the ones that follow are heuristics—aids for thinking. They should not be read as representations of all moral scholarship.

A current position is that value sets are composites of both foundational and cultural values (Christians, 1997; Elliott, 1997; Traber, 1997; Wilson, 1993). Foundational values persist (although they may be subjugated to cultural values); cultural values wax and wane. This is a typical—even favorite, have it both ways—solution to irreducible polar opposites because it is the least restrictive on the claims scholars wish to make. For example, if analysis shows that a value—say, truth telling—has been around a long time, then it must be foundational. If some other value—say, chastity—seems to wane, then it must be cultural (even though the argument permits it, as a foundational value, to be weakened or even temporarily disappear under the dominance of some cultural value). One of our problems here is that any value finds its worth in its opposite. Truth is a value because of the shadow utility of lying. If lying wasn't valuable to us, we would not have to celebrate truth. Consequently, the value of truth and of lies as well as chastity and promiscuity all seem to persist.

In our analysis here, it is only the particular belief in universal values that also present themselves in self-evident ways that makes a difference for us, however. If such a belief is true, then a set of universal rules can be written to define the right thing (the action of greatest good) to do in every situation. If cultural values are admitted in any way in the equation or if the values of whatever kind do not present themselves in self-evident ways but offer different configurations in different circumstances, then the rules must be historical, local, and situational. For example, we might all support the value of honesty, even for different reasons as Bob and Peter did. But if what honesty means changes from situation to situation or if honesty is not always the best choice in social relations, then the foundational quality of the value disappears as it did for our two radial entrepreneurs.

Two other tensions are connected to this foundational/situational axis. The first of these is an elaboration on the self-evidentness of reality. Does all of reality simply present itself to us as the early British empiricists have claimed? Or must we interpret reality in forms of discourse and action? An element in this question is the nature of reality as constituted—that is, materially given to us or as constructed—that is, socially produced (at least in part) by us. To continue our example, is the quality of honesty self-evident? Does it have hard and unmistakable boundaries that clearly distinguish it from everything else? Or does honesty depend on time, place, or even culture of presentation?

The second of these tensions is about whether our claims about reality—as self-evident, interpreted, constituted, or constructed—can represent reality

---

PRINCIPAL CONCEPTS ─────────────────

The central questions of this tension consider whether ethics are culturally or universally constructed and whether action is self-evident or must be interpreted. If moral principles are social or cultural products, then social practices set moral codes. If action must be interpreted, then an action can have different moral standing depending on the political or social circumstances of its interpretation. Your authors would affirm each of these conditionals.

---

in universal, neutrally-objective, rational statements, or do those claims always co-construct reality in ideologically encoded statements directed toward some political end?

If reality is not self-evident, if it must be interpreted, then values like honesty have no fixed or final character. Rather, the character of honesty will be constituted in the interpretation that is fashioned in the process of understanding what honesty is in a given context. Under these circumstances, any claim about the presence of honesty is disputable and can be resolved only by political rather than objective processes that move a particular agenda forward. The recent impeachment trial of President William Clinton is an excellent example of this tension in action.

THE INDIVIDUAL/COMMUNITY AXIS

Another set of disputes persist across the axis of the individual and community. This tension appears today in libertarian (primacy of the individual) versus communitarian (primacy of the community) arguments. These arguments pit the primacy of the individual against the primacy of the community. There are three dimensions of interest to this opposition. The first considers whether the advancement of the individual is to be preferred in the particular to the advancement of the community, holding that the good for the individual will ultimately appear as good for the community or that the interests of the community are to be advanced to provide for the good of its individuals.

The second considers whether the individual is the ultimate source of moral probity (the Enlightenment ideal), or the collective wisdom of the community (generally as expressed in its leadership) is the basis of moral judgment.

The third appears across the balance of justice and love. Generally libertarian views emphasize equal justice without compassion as the way to achieve the greatest good. Communitarian views, while concerned with justice, hold that justice without love cannot flourish.

For a corporate manager, the decisions that must be made in distributing salary raises give good examples of all three of these tensions. In most corporate settings, salary raises come out of a pool of money made available from some limited source (e.g., increased profits, reduced costs, sequestered funds). As the pool is finite, the raise game is a zero-sum game: giving more money to one means less money for another. Does the manager give equal raises to all (and therefore less to the most deserving) to maintain the morale of the community? Or does the manager give significantly higher raises to some, thereby dividing the community? (Which is more important, the community or the individual?) Is the manager able to determine the relative merit of each individual objectively and, therefore, justly? (Is meritorious action self-evident and decisions about it objectively rational?) Must the manager disregard need and distribute funds only on the basis of merit? (Is justice the only basis of the decision?)

THE ESSENCE/EXISTENCE AXIS

The third (and last) of these fundamental oppositions occurs across the axis of essence and existence. The basic question is whether the condition of human existence is derived from some prior essential character or the condition of human existence provides for an essential human character. In moral terms, the question positions, for example, duty ethics, virtue ethics (Foot, 1958), and feminist ethics (Walker, 1998) on the essence prior to existence side and **existentialism** (Sartre, 1956) and consequentialism (Raymond, 1991) on the existence prior to essence side. In duty and virtue ethics, for example, it is the universal duty or virtue that establishes the character of action in its name. The essence of duty and virtue precedes its existence in action. Hence, it is our duty not to lie that makes being honest ethical.

Modernist ethics and social science are heavily biased toward the essence leads to existence formulation. Modernist ethicists, for example would be heavily invested in intentions as setting the quality of an act. For these ethicists, we act for some reason and that reason has implications for the character of the action. Similarly, modernist social scientists would be heavily invested in cognitivism, a form of explanation where prior mental states hold the key to subsequent behavior.

PRINCIPAL CONCEPTS

Some analysts argue that essence precedes existence, or that the human condition is the result of pre-existing determinants. For others, existence creates essence, or the human condition is the product of ongoing human action. In moral terms, these translate into global principles (essence) for human action (existence) or the local performance (existence) of a moral practice (essence).

Postmodernists often undercut this linear progression by insisting on agency (the ability to choose without prior cause) and on the improvisational character of action. (Action is a process—not an instant—and must be made up as we go along.) Postmodernists, then, are likely to give priority to existence as enactment (the process of becoming) over essence.

POSITIONING ONESELF

It is our contention that an initial task in the practice of ethics is to come to a self-understanding concerning one's own position across these lines of tension. We call them "lines of tension" because one's position is always dynamic along them. One way to think about this positioning is to consider oneself as a decision-maker at the center of these axes in Figure 2.2. To help you in this process, we present these axes in three sets of pairs and then go through the decisions that are called for.

FOUNDATIONAL/SITUATIONAL ACROSS INDIVIDUAL/COMMUNITY

Figure 2.3 presents a slice of moral philosophy that intersects the foundational/situational and individual/community axes. We have designated the center as the neutral point—the point of silence where no claim can be made. We have heavy inked the major axes that offer a selection of opposition that would appear in this slice. The decisions that have to be made concerning the primacy of the individual or the community and the question of whether ethical premises are foundational or somehow under the governance of the situation (culture or other domains of sense making) divide the circle into useful quadrants. The lower left sets the ethical world as rational, material, and self-evident. The upper left sees this world under the

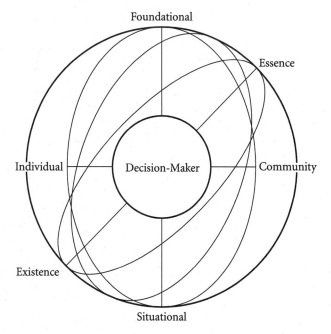

FIGURE 2.2   *Positioning oneself on the lines of tension.*

governance of justice, universal rules, and in the hands of the essential, willing self. The lower right puts the emphasis on love, action, and the self discovered in the other. This dependent self operates in a world, as shown in the upper right quadrant, that must be interpreted, made visible through the social processes of the constitution of reality, and understood through cultural ideologies rather than a self-correcting, universal rationality. While the quadrants are broadly useful, they do not deny our ability to be creatively selective. One can certainly hold to an ethics of care as a foundational requirement of human life, for example.

Foundational/Situational Across Essence/Existence

The issues across these two axes (Figure 2.4) have to do with prior assumptions about the character of human nature and values and about the notions of the self as the acting agent. Again, useful quadrants appear that contrast fixed priors in the upper left, and stable conditions of action in

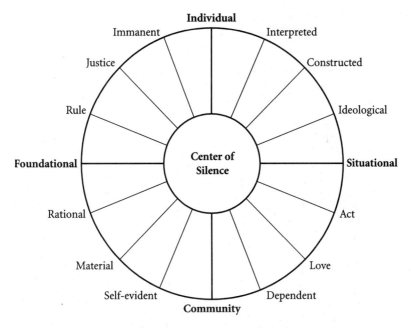

FIGURE 2.3   *Foundational/situational across individual/community.*

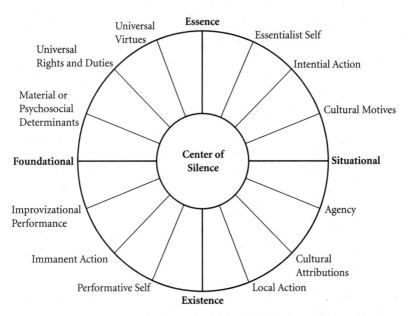

FIGURE 2.4   *Foundational/situational across essence/existence.*

FIGURE 2.5   *Individual/community across essence/existence.*

the upper right with agency, action, and performance in the lower two quadrants.

INDIVIDUAL/COMMUNITY ACROSS ESSENCE/EXISTENCE

In the final comparison (Figure 2.5), we find the Enlightenment ideals of individual rationality, knowledge, and goodwill contrasted with the person as a cultural production in the upper quadrants, and the person as an independent, active agent contrasted with the person as an element in collective action in the lower. Diagonally from left to right are the conceptions of knowing and choosing, and from right to left the independence of the individual from culture.

IMPLICATIONS

For us, these circles of ethical tensions represent the struggle in which we as a scholarly community, a society, and as individuals are immersed as we attempt to make good decisions and take right actions. We call the question,

"Where do you stand?" We recognize the need to take a stand somewhere on these lines to evaluate those difficult decisions, such as when a father makes a promise he cannot keep to sustain hope, when a teenager lies about where she has been to keep peace in the family, when a manager uses the terms of rational economics to cut a workforce for more profit, when a legislator accepts campaign funds from companies whose products sicken and kill. For ourselves, we stretch these lines of tension toward the situational, community, and existence poles, finding our answers in cultural processes, community practices, and social action. You, dear reader, make moral judgments every day in the actions you take, advice you give, evaluations you make. To be blunt, if you have not taken the time to systematically consider the positions—and the often changing positions—from which you make those judgments, you will have little insight into their quality. The rest of the text will encourage this analysis, but our encouragement will celebrate the struggle for understanding rather than declare it complete.

TRANSITIONS

There are traditions in ethics that we continue to rehearse in academic debate as well as organizational practice. In this chapter, we have been looking at ethics from the principle of obligation. Obligation comes into existence the moment self recognizes other. Ethics, then, concerns the methods that manage and discharge the obligations of constituting self in the presence of the other. We have looked at five major systems of ethics: rights, duties, utility, virtues, and relationships. Each leads us to consider the issues of the interpersonal from different perspectives. Duties ask us to formulate our ethics in terms of what is owed the other; rights focuses on what the collective must give to the individual; utility finds its value in good outcomes for the many; virtue seeks the perfection of the collective member; and the ethics of relationship or caring puts the emphasis on the virtues of love.

The differences we studied were not just limited to these five systems. We examine the multiple tensions that must be accommodated in any ethical judgment. These tensions are resolved only momentarily, held steady for us to speak what we consider to be true about some action. But any sense of a final resolution is simply illusory, for when we reflexively analyze how we were able to make our claim, we see the braces and anchors that hold the enterprise in place. That any solution to these tensions is a temporary one, a particular one among many, does not relieve us of doing the work. It should lead us to a deeper understanding, a greater sense of the struggle, and more modesty in claim.

Case Study

In preparing for a major exam, a group of three students decided to get together for a study session. At the meeting, one student said his brother had taken the same class the two years previously and had the test used that year. The student suggested the group use the old test as a barometer to see how they might do. After studying for some time and discussing a number of issues from their class notes and the textbook, the group went through the old exam. They found they did pretty well, but identified some areas which needed a little more study. All in all, it was a great study session and they felt confident about the exam the next day.

When they got to the testing center, they discovered the professor was using the identical test used two years earlier. Feeling guilty, one student quickly glanced to see what the other two were doing. They were busily writing away on the test.

1. What are the students' options and their respective cost and benefits?
2. Why does this case involve ethics? What are the long-term implications of each choice?
3. Who are the unethical persons in this case? Justify your answer.
4. How would ethicists from the five moral systems discussed in this chapter differ in their answers to question three?

3

ORGANIZATIONAL CULTURE AND FRAMEWORKS OF AGENCY

PREVIEW

This chapter takes up the detailed analysis of organizations as frameworks of agency and action. It offers a definition of the organization centered on the material practices of organizing that allows us to view organizations as processes rather than as objects. It then immerses the organization in the culture that sustains it to examine how the seven major systems of culture—semiotic, epistemic, ethical, aesthetic, economic, political, and social—constitute organizational life and are interpreted within it. It concludes with the individual as the cultural/organizational agent acting within, upon, and in the name of the cultural/organizational practices that are the repertoire of daily life.

Ten people have been waiting for the cross-town bus that is now more than twenty minutes late. It is an experience that these ten have had on all too many a workday morning. They stand singly or in groups of twos and threes, chatting about this or that. In one such group, Josep remarks to Luann that something really has to be done, and maybe they could do it better if they joined together. Luann, a formidable and take-charge sort of woman, agrees. "You're right," she says, "and we're going to do it now." "Hey," she calls out, "let's say we form a riders' support group!" Shouts of "Good idea," "Count me in," are heard as eight people move to form a group around

Luann. Two people hang back and, when one is encouraged to join, answers, "Nah, it's not for me."

In that moment of commitment, the Cross-town Riders, now a non-profit organization with more than 400 members, was formed. All organizations start in some similar moment of join-up. It is the commitment to a relationship, a form of common identity called membership, that makes organizations possible. All the other characteristics of organizations—terms of relationships, divisions of labor, hierarchies of control, economies of rights and responsibilities, systems of value and meaning, and characteristic ways of thinking, speaking, doing—will all develop over the history of this membership.

It is rare, however, to be present for that initial moment of join-up. In most of our organizational experience, we join the already ongoing activity of organizing as a new member (Clegg & Hardy, 1996). For the new member, the view can be intimidating what with the imposing physical, cultural, and communicative structures of the well-developed organization. It is hard to believe that all of it develops out of the communicative practices of people in relationships. But as Karl Weick (1987) notes:

> Communication is the essence of organization because it creates structures that then affect what else gets said and done and by whom. Structures form when communication uncovers shared occupational specialties, shared social characteristics, or shared values that people want to preserve and expand. The structures themselves create additional resources for communication such as hierarchical levels, common tasks, exchangeable commodities, and negotiable dependencies. These additional resources constrain subsequent contacts and define more precisely the legitimate topics for further communication (pp. 97–98).

Weick is describing the duality between communication and relationship. Communication and relationships depend on one another. Communication provides for relationship and, at the same time, occurs under the governance of relationship. Relationship appears in communication and defines the terms of—makes sense of the how, what, where, when, with whom, and why of—communication. We can apply this concept of the duality of relationship and communication to two people standing at a bus stop, to an instructor and a class, to a vice-president, and to a corporate division. All conjoint human endeavor starts in this duality. The different **structurations** that develop out of it—Weick's "additional resources"—provide for the two strangers at the bus stop, the instructor and the class, and the vice-president and the division.

Our detailed study of organizations and of the practices of organizing begins at this point. We will define an organization as a set of ordered relationships and communication processes that is both meaningful and meaning-making. This ordered set of relationships and processes is meaningful in that the organization is an ideational site. Regardless of its material attributes or lack thereof, the organization serves to make sense of both the objects of its domain and the persons who inhabit it. The ordered set is meaning-making (the semiotic term is significant) in that within it, the means for the constituting appearance of the self are produced. We—the members of those relationships and enactors of those processes, not some structural or material force—provide those constituting means through the process of organizing.

Organizing is a process that disciplines individual performance to be accountable to and understandable within a coherent ideological framework of member-to-member relationships, practices of discourse and action, rules of performance, and the judicial procedures of each. This discipline is produced through the reproduction, modification, specification, and enactment of culture. We see culture as that grand system that provides for, mediates the process of, and is reproduced by human interaction.

We will, at least somewhat, unpack this dense, theoretical language at the start of Chapter 9. In this chapter, we want to quickly establish the organization as a set of ordered relationships and communication processes that is the product of the processes of organizing. We also want to remind you that we are writing about organizations of every sort—not just corporations—in order that we can move on to an overview of culture.

CULTURE EXPLORED

The thorough examination of the concept of culture is well beyond the scope of this text, but from a social action perspective, culture is something significantly greater than some simplicity of shared values and meanings.[1] Culture involves major systems of ideology and practice that constitute the conditions of our daily affairs. Traditionally, these systems have been seen as:

- the *semiotic*: the system of meaning in language and action
- the *epistemic*: the system of truth-making

---

[1] A comparison of Frederick, 1995; Scott and Hart, 1989; and Sackmann, 1991 would demonstrate this difference.

- the *ethical*: the system of right and wrong
- the *aesthetic*: the system of beauty
- the *economic*: the system of value exchange
- the *political*: the system of allocation
- the *social*: the system of self, other, and relationships

Every culture that can claim to be a culture will have these systems in place. On the other hand, no culture in this postmodern world operates independently of every other culture. We borrow, poach, steal, and are enmeshed and embedded in each other. The United States may currently lead a worldwide economy, but it is also disciplined by that economy as disturbances in markets thousands of miles away cause our stock prices to tremble.

Organizations, too, to the extent that they provide a membership identity and a framework for action, must somehow mark or color the cultural systems in which they are embedded. But that marking and coloration does not discharge the configuring force of the larger culture. The effect of organizing on cultural processes is mainly one of re-tracings and erasures that sharpen certain lines of action while softening others. Organizations do not have the resources either to resist larger cultural forces or to create wholesale substitutions. The effects of organizing are ones of extension, redirection, distention, contraction—modifications but not inventions. Organizational women and men may be recognizable as members, but they are always also recognizable as women and men. To state that a corporate organization constitutes a unique culture is to commit a massive error of scale.

Nonetheless, organizations, be they corporate, political, familial, or whatever, do have particular ways of doing things, speaking about things, thinking about things. To the extent that those ways are the product of the organizing processes of that organization, then that organization creates a particular framework of agency for its members. It is the terms of that framework that are important to an ethical analysis.

Culture, however, is not some transcendent monolith, but rather a set of adaptable and changing (through both learning and accretion) systems that must be put into play to make their appearance. The totality of one's culture comes from the multiple shadings that it can support, just as visible light is constructed of the spectrum of color but not of infrared or ultraviolet. Different organizing processes do not produce a new spectrum but contribute different colorations to the existing mix. The spot on which

PRINCIPAL CONCEPTS

Culture is something significantly greater than notions of shared values and meanings. It involves major systems of ideology and practice that constitute the conditions of our daily affairs. Today no culture in this world is able to operate independently of every other culture. We borrow, poach, steal and are enmeshed in each other. Organizations color the cultural systems in which they are embedded. Organizations, however, do not have the resources either to resist larger cultural forces or to create wholesale substitutions. The effects of organizing are ones of extension, redirection, distention, and contraction.

we stand, to continue this metaphor, is bathed in the full spectrum of this light. We are all, therefore, multiply illuminated in culture, but we return those values we reflect. Culture, as color, is a potential that appears in the particular.

THE CULTURAL AGENT

This last point about the multiplicity and potentiality of culture being materialized in the particularity of performance leads us to the cultural agent. Each of us, rather than being self-made, is a cultural agent. We understand the term *agent* as both the enactor—the one who brings about—and the representative—the one obligated to the cultural understandings that constitute meaningful enactments. The agent achieves agency (the ability to act as one-who-makes-a-difference) under the terms of her or his cultural representation. For example, what one can do and how it will be evaluated as a student in a classroom are defined by the terms of being a student.

Agency always involves the struggle for meaning. That struggle is not the fight between one preconceived meaning and another. Rather, it is the **Heideggerian** struggle of becoming, the struggle for a recognizable existence, the struggle to find the space to be between the enablements and constraints that the cultural domain of interpretation provides.

Organizations as Cultural Modifiers

We have been led by the writing to this point to see culture as a set of interlaced systems that provide for the meaningfulness of self and other and to see the cultural agent as an improvisational actor within that domain of interpretation. Now we want to move to consider the means by which organizing activates and modifies those cultural systems in the particular methodologies that create the boundaries of the organization through the enactment, reproduction, and sedimentation of some part of the cultural potential. We will do this by examining exemplars of organizational activation and modification within each of the seven systems of culture: semiotic, epistemic, ethical, aesthetic, economic, political, and social.

It is important to note the heuristic rather than the ontological quality of these systems. We would expect little argument that a culture must somehow do what we have assigned to these various systems. We would expect much argument over whether, say, epistemology is a cultural invention or over the relative primacy of one system or another. Such arguments are paradigmatic.

The Semiotic System

The semiotic system manages significance and meaning in the processes of language and action. **Significance** is the referential and expressive potential of the sign—word, symbol, icon, sound, melody, odor, color, action, anything that stands for or connects to something else—what the sign can come to mean. **Meaning** is the consequential result of using a sign—word, symbol, icon, action, etc.—in a particular time, place, and process. Language works in sentences and discourses and action in routines and practices. The sentence is the sign of what is being done in and through language (Searle, 1969); discourse is extended language use that is identified with and identifies a cultural position. The routine is the sign of what is being done in instrumental and expressive action; practices are extended action and are identified with and identify cultural positions (Anderson & Meyer, 1988; Crespi, 1994; Sigman, 1987).

Although **language and action** are each minutely decomposable, one does not understand language by moving from the morpheme up to the sentence or action by moving from the muscle contraction to the routine. It is the sentence that makes sensible the morpheme and the word, and the routine that makes sense of the contraction and the act.

If humans did not have the resource of **semiotics,** we would be limited to the eternal present of sense data and direct response. Our brains would have only the immediate sensory data available at that moment. Everything else—every memory, every projection into the future—is a sign: a something (be it a word or an electro-chemical state of a neuron) that stands for something else. Further, every action would have to be hard-wired in instincts or invented anew each time we acted. Finally, without the collective effort of developing and maintaining common signs, no one could communicate and no one would recognize what was going on.

But we do have a past and a future; we can communicate; and we do recognize what ourselves and others are doing. We have those things because of the semiotics of language and action. We turn to a more detailed examination of those semiotic systems.

Language

Organizations mark and modify the language side of the semiotic system by such activities as activating vocabularies, formulating specialized syntactical rules, and importing and crafting discourses. As a result, organizations with high cultural identity have recognizable ways of using language. Members speak and write in identifiable ways. There are a number of levels operating here. An accountant has to sound like an accountant to other accountants no matter where they work. For the accountant and most other such professional memberships, the organizational influence is first from the profession and then from the specific site. Further, organizations of any size are never unidimensional; consequently, we would expect language use to be differentiated even within the organization. Accountants in sales use different terms from accountants in production.

This differentiated language use is more than the substitution of a preferred local word or phrase over one in more general use. It represents a different way of parsing the world into its parts and may represent particular constitutions not available elsewhere. Every profession, for example, gets criticized by nonmembers for its use of "jargon." That jargon, however does important work for the membership and may index concepts not otherwise available. Nonmembers are right in their complaint that specialized language use "shuts them out." The identification of members and nonmembers is a consequence of differentiated language use (and an important one), but what shuts the nonmembers out of the conversation is that nonmembers do not view the world in the way that the member language indexes.

Action

The division of labor that even the simplest of organizations undertakes assures that specialized ways of doing things—the routines that contribute to the constitution of the self—will develop. Some of these are stylizations of widespread cultural forms, such as the way "we do business letters here." But others are finely-developed action knowledge held by the relatively few. This action knowledge brings different understandings to the same issue. Mechanics and design engineers are often at loggerheads because engineers want to achieve an elegant design that mechanics complain cannot be serviced. The truths of the practices of design are different from the truths of the practices of repair.

A cabinetmaker offered this interesting example of how practices intercept the world:

> The most helpful apprentice I ever had was a nurse who was on furlough from her career. Yes, a woman is unusual in the shop, but thankfully less so these days. We got by the man/woman thing pretty quickly. What I thought was uncanny was her ability to—what's the word—diagnose, dissect, anyway, break down an operation to anticipate what was needed. She would watch a task a couple of times, ask about the names of the tools and what was being done, and then when an extra hand was needed, it was there; when there was a change of tool it was there; when there was some preparatory work that had to be done, it was done. I asked her about it and she said it was her nurse's training. I sure appreciated her help, but it made me wonder what would happen when she took over the job. I was embarrassed by this thought when she did that well also.

Action is the performance of our being in the world. Action is the expression of who we are in the moment-by-moment constitution of the self. When organizations provide us the means of doing, they provide us that part of the means of existence. The apprentice is a surgical nurse in a cabinetry shop. Bill Rodriguez's downsizing is a crisis of the self. The organizational imprint on action imprints the agent.

Management of Significance and Meaning

It is our position that the semiotics of language and the semiotics of action are both socially constituted. They are both human inventions, actively managed, supervised, and reproduced in daily exchanges in both their significance and their meaning (Saussure, 1910/1959; Peirce, 1960).

Organizations are a prime field in which active management, supervision, and reproduction occur. Organizational media systems—white papers, reports, memos, performance review sessions, voice mail, e-mail, meetings, hallway conversations, on- and off-task performances, family dinners, even the refrigerator door and corporate commercials—circulate and reproduce the signs of language and action. Our critiques of such content forms supervise our uses of them. And our responses to them as organizational members consensually validate the meanings we make of them (Manning, 1992). It is an everyday fact that language and action, on which the facts of the case are ostensibly the same, have great consequential differences across organizational sites. It was at least once true that we could expect a profanity on the shop floor to have a different result from that profanity at the dinner table.

The significance of a sign is its reality constituting character held in the ideational object that it signifies and in its potential for meaningfulness. The meaning of a sign is first its recognition as a sign and second its consequences for whatever action in which it is embedded (Anderson & Meyer, 1988).

Organizations produce, maintain, distribute, supervise, and evaluate the signs and symbols of local significance and meaning. Much of the organizing processes is taken up by these activities. If organizing is to have any instrumental effect, it must first make sense of our coming together to achieve it. It makes that sense in the vocabularies and discourses, routines and practices of language and action. The local governance of these vocabularies, discourses, routines, and practices is clearly evident when we attempt to export what we say and do from the ordinary site of their performance. Others simply do not understand in the same way we do.

THE EPISTEMIC SYSTEM

The semiotic system and the epistemic system are closely allied (as are all cultural systems). The alliance is forged out of the reality constituting function of language and action. Once we adopt the position that speaking and acting are constituting and not simply referential, we are forced to accept the simultaneity of meaning and knowledge. The **epistemic system,** however, does not focus on what you and I know. It is actually not at all concerned with individual knowledge. Its concern is with publicly-authenticated

PRINCIPAL CONCEPTS

Language use is more that the substitution of a preferred local word or phrase over one in more general use. It represents a different way of parsing the world into its parts. Action is the performance of our being in the world; it is the expression of who we are in each constitution of the self. When organizations provide us the means for action, they provide us that part of the means of existence. Within organizations, language and action are actively managed, supervised and reproduced in daily exchanges in both their significance and their meaning

knowledge. The study of this system focuses on the means by which proposition and practice are declared to be true.[2]

> As postmodernists, we reject the position that there is a foundational basis for truth—that there is any basis other than social processes for declaring what is true. We may be wrong here. There may be foundational truth that impresses itself on each of us in self-evident splendor. But as postmodernists, we are dedicated to finding the social processes that support its universal declaration (and they are readily apparent) as true. That is, of course the point of this section—that even the most realist of empiricists have to have some method of moving a claim into authentic knowledge.

Organizationally, it doesn't matter that an individual has a special insight into what is true, if that individual cannot validate her claim in the social processes of authentication. She may be able to perform an "I-told-you-so" at some later date, but if her claim is dismissed, it will not be acted upon. On the other hand, the timely enactment of a bid for what is true can rapidly move through the organization. Again our consultant notes give us an example:

> Who has the right to speak for whom is one of those practical rights of truth-making. I [Jim] was sitting in on a meeting of section managers who were trying to decide on the order of work in preparation of the work

---

[2] This section on epistemics is informed by the work of Stephen Toulmin (1950), Thomas Kuhn (1970), Bruno Latour (1987), and Stephen Prelli (1990). See also Burrell, 1993; Chisholm, 1982; Castañeda, 1989; Clark, 1990; Harré, 1986, 1991, 1992, 1995; Lears, 1985; Lyotard, 1984; Searle, 1995; Spivak, 1988; Taylor, 1982.

floor for the coming sequence of production. The discussion seemed to be at a pivotal point where it could have gone one way or the other, when a hitherto fore silent "worker-representative" spoke up and said "the workers on the floor want to do it [this way] because it saves time." "Well, if they want it that way . . .," one of the managers opined and the decision was made. The worker-observer was in a privileged position to speak for the workers. She also managed her rhetorical position well, choosing to speak when the decision was palpable but in doubt—a point where there was no "good managerial" reason for deciding one way or the other—and claiming no more than that she had spoken to "many of the workers but not all" and that her expression covered "only those she had spoken to." Her comment was timely and credible.

She was also there precisely for that moment. Practical rights impose responsibilities of practice (the duality of structure and practice). Structural components—the requirements for a worker representative— had made her voice available. But now her voice must be used in that role. If she consistently fails to speak, she may well be considered useless by managers and workers alike. If she speaks inappropriately, she may be considered a poor representative. She is to speak for the workers, but only when the workers' voice is to be heard. The practices of others create her right to speak, but her agency is clear in this critical instance of performance. The organization created the framework for her agency and she chose to act within it. Her action was true to the framework, which in turn may make her statement true to the others at the meeting. This is not to say that a decision would not have been made without her because the structural demands of the meeting required one or to say that the decision made is a better one (or even ultimately different) because of her effort. It is to say that the process permitted the act that she chose to perform and that her action had consequence because of the process.

The "agency framework" put in place by the organization created the conditions by which the representative's voice could be heard. The managers also created the impetus to accept her claim as true. By committing organizational resources to the space of "worker representative," managers incur a responsibility to treat that space legitimately. This is not to say that they cannot fail to discharge that responsibility. It is to say that they do not have that responsibility elsewhere. A most common failing of bureaucratized organizations is the lack of the ability to pass authentic knowledge from lower levels of the hierarchy to the higher. What is common knowledge for the worker is often commonly unknown by the manager, or worse, deliberately excluded from their common knowledge. This case is all too typical in corporate America, where we have absentee ownership and

PRINCIPAL CONCEPTS

The epistemic system is concerned with publicly authenticated knowledge. This system focuses on the means by which proposition and practice are declared to be true. Within the organization there are methods by which organizational members authenticate or confer the status of truth on propositions and practices.

professional management, neither of whom necessarily knows the work to be done.

One of the primary functions of organizing is the reduction of uncertainty (Alvesson, 1996). Uncertainty is reduced through the production of knowledge. What one knows to be true in the venue of the organization is produced in the epistemic methods held as authentic within that organization. The method in the particular may be the single, timely voice, a committee report, the vested base of practice, or even a passing conversation between those authorized to speak the truth. These are the methods by which organizational members constitute the conferred status of truth on propositions and practices that are consequential. We may not approve of them rationally or scientifically, but they are instrumental and effective. They provide the justification for member performance.

THE ETHICAL SYSTEM

The relationship between the ethical—what is good—and epistemic— what is true—systems has been contentious in Western thought since the fracture of the universal church into its reformist parts and its subsequent political decline. When a catholic God was the single location of the true and the good, there was little dispute. It was the arguments of British **empiricism** (Hume 1748/1961) that split the good from the true for modernity. Given the split, one was free to argue that good results can come from false premises, that the true cannot guarantee the good, that the good cannot be verified empirically or even reached through a perfected rationality. What is right, the empirically enlightened claimed, cannot be reached through the true because what is right depends upon society rather than the phenomenal world. Postmodernists make a move back to our catholic history to unite the true and the good as social processes that provide for one another. For postmodernists, the true is a particular good we seek. We work to authenticate its claims because they *ought* to be true (it is good that they be true). In the absence of foundational truth and in the presence of uncertainty, every claim of *what is* denies *what could be*. A claim to knowledge, therefore, always entails a choice, and choice always entails the moral.

We can see the interrelationships between the true and the good—between the knowledge that justifies and the values that qualify—in the allocation of resources toward particular knowledge productions, in the constraints we place on efforts to speak the truth, and on the boundaries of what is true for us. Organizations demonstrate this relationship in mission statements and policies; in their control of knowledge and information; in the measures of success and effectiveness they put into place; in their grants of access to resources; in promotions, awards, and recognitions; in codes of craft, conduct, and dress; and in the decisions and judgments by which we know what is true and good of us and them.

In the families we study, it is not unusual to find a simple rule used as the standard for moral character. It may be getting good grades, keeping a clean room, or meeting a curfew. As long as some simple rule is met moral rectitude is granted to the rule-keeper. It is a form of moral metonym where when one part of the action meets the moral standard, the rest of the action is presumed to meet it also. (This is the sort of belief that nothing immoral can happen before 11:00 P.M. If circumstance ever reveals the whole of the action, as in the confessional tales of some far-removed family dinner well out of harm's way, plenty of surprises can result.)

Organizational rules and policies generally function in this way. As long as one stays below the horizon of the rule, that person stands within its grace and is morally unassailable at least from that vantage. But if one rises above that horizon, say in filing "difficult" travel expenses or generating repeated customer complaints or failing to meet target sales, then the rule becomes a resource for punishment or privilege, a tool for justice or love.

The implicit and explicit policies, rules, codes, and judgments of an organization formulate the local moral standard of membership—are you good enough to be one of us. A friend writes:

> [When] students in our Ph.D. program complete their coursework, they are required to take comprehensive examinations. These examinations extend over 18 hours of written work and an additional 2 hours of oral defense. Students are typically mystified by what this process is. Their mystification comes out of our organizational deception about the controlling

PRINCIPAL CONCEPTS

An ethical system within the organization establishes rules and their associated practices of enforcement to determine the worthiness of the members.

narrative. Students accept the narrative as one of knowledge. Do they *know* enough to become one of us. But any faculty member on the supervising committee could write an authentic question that the candidate would not be able to answer satisfactorily because the committee member is the one to declare the answer right or wrong. Start a question with "Speculate on" or "Consider the implications of" and the field is yours to command. So the issue of whether the candidate passes or fails is first decided in the questions chosen. The operative narrative is not about knowledge. It is about worthiness. Are you *good* enough to be one of us? Passing is not an act of justice; it is an act of love.

Examinations, tests, sales contests, production goals, targets of all sorts are the means by which organizations determine the worthiness of their members. The celebrated scholars, winners, top guns, million-dollar members, good daughters and sons are held up as the personal standards for our conduct. If only we were like them, we could be good people too. But these are games of a zero-sum morality, where your success is my failure. It is, nonetheless, the typical moral system of organizational meritocracies.

AESTHETIC SYSTEMS

Aesthetics consider judgments of beauty, but these judgments are more than skin deep. Aesthetic judgments about one's person, one's space, one's fashion, one's work are an integral part of judgments concerning merit, competence, trustworthiness, leadership, honesty, and the like. Organizations, from corporations, to schools, to families, routinely govern the aesthetic expressions of their members through standard furnishings and rules about office and other personal space decoration, design requirements for reports, forms, memos, letters, cards, notes etc., dress codes (including casual Friday and proper dinner wear), personal appearance codes (make-up, hair length, facial hair), and diplomatic codes (the aesthetics of action from political correctness to birthday gift thank-you notes).

These aesthetic standards are considered the emblems of the underlying quality of the bearers. For example, a recent fashion article distributed by *The Washington Post* (*Salt Lake Tribune,* May 17, 1998, p. J4) held forth that the button-down collar in men's shirts was a symbol of followership while real leaders (e.g., General Colin Powell) wore spread-collared shirts. When Jim reported this article to his organizational communication class, there were general hisses of scorn and derision. Who would ever think that a shirt collar would make a difference? Exceptions were quickly noted—Herb Kelleher, CEO of Southwest Airlines; Bill Gates of Microsoft (who took to spread collars during the antitrust investigations); even Col. Sanders of KFC (Is he real?). On the other hand, most of the students agreed that they would "dress up" for a job interview, an "important report," an evaluation meeting with their boss, or a significant social engagement. But does that really change who we are?

This newspaper article is a good example of the social management of meaning. Its widespread distribution provides a general resource for many to use. It makes a bid for a difference between objects (shirt collars) to become a *différance* (to use Derrida's term of effect) in judgments about the wearers of those objects. That *différance* must still be enacted by decision makers who make a difference. It may not happen.

Our answer is "of course it does" to the extent that such aesthetics provide the resources for certain facets of identity to be activated and/or the conditions that provide for invoked or evoked **subjectivity.** These resources and conditions lead to the constitution of the self in that moment. The "who" of each of us is a joint production. We use aesthetics to distinguish ourselves, to mark our territories, to find solace, inspiration, pleasure; but, as our choices speak to us, they speak to others about us as well.

Our cultured environments form the other major aesthetic component in the constitution of the self and moral action. Nearly every space we occupy is a cultured environment. Even our wildernesses are marked by boundaries to designate them as *wilderness* and then crossed with trails and dotted with campsites. Our wilderness experience and our expression as a wilderness person can be fully contained in these sedimented markings. (In the mountain West, forest rangers are called "land managers" who provide "customer service" in "one-stop shopping" for all one's primitive experience needs.)

The functional aesthetics of cultured environments considers the meaningfulness of objects and space in the performance of action. It examines

PRINCIPAL CONCEPTS

Aesthetic systems set the codes of beauty, elegance, and style. Organizations from corporations, to schools, to families routinely govern the aesthetic expressions of their members through practical rules governing appearance, personal space, and requirements for performances and products.

subject position (who occupies what cultural space); locations as emblems of status, power, and competence; objects as symbols (what achieves local significance); and even what is unused, unrecognized, or ignored. It looks at the relationship between site and action, considering how the site provides for the action as well as what is evoked, facilitated, permitted, possible, contravened, prohibited, and taboo. Aesthetics investigates how the action relates to the site, noting the allocation of value to features and locations as well as what is sacred, cherished, sacrificial, or profane. It considers the consequences of action for the site, determining what is expended, modified, and accounted for as well as how the action reproduces the structure of the site.

When we step into a site, we are called to work, to play, to challenge, to comfort or to do whatever the site promotes as we are moved aesthetically to action. In that action, we materialize the self. Mary Weber, sitting in her office, *is* Bill Rodriquez's supervisor and her execution of the rightsizing script is facilitated by the aesthetics of her subject position. It would be incredible and an outrage if she accosted Bill in the supermarket to fire him there. That is not the place of her power. In form and function, aesthetics count.

ECONOMIC SYSTEMS

Posters appeared last week in the management classroom building, declaring "Econ, it doesn't suck so bad." Its reputation notwithstanding, economics is morally important because it studies the methods of valuation and exchange. **Economic systems** are the methods by which we sort objects and utilities into categories of greater or lesser value and, in conjunction with political processes, establish the rights to and distribution of such objects and utilities (ownership rights) and set the procedures of value exchange.

Economic systems, therefore, are composed of units of value, qualified participants, the distribution of valued elements (objects and utilities), exchange rates, and methods of exchange. A unit of value can be an hour of labor, a dollar bill (money is a rationalized system), a luxury car, a handsome escort; value is expressed generally in terms of its worth as a object— a luxury car, a handsome escort—or its worth in use—an hour of labor, a dollar bill. Participants are qualified through a number of means, some of them inexcusably exclusionary, such as in race and gender, while others are protective, such as prohibiting minors from entering into contracts. Any economic system turns on the distribution of value. If we all have everything we need and desire, there is no economy. Exchange rates establish the relationship between units of value—the how much of this for the what of that. Finally, the methods of exchange establish the means—do we exchange goods and services or currency, is the price fixed or negotiable, and the like. We speak of different economies as those composition elements change. We have such economies as subsistence, consumer, labor, political, sexual, and so forth.

Why do economies count in issues of morality? Economies generate justifications for action. For example, we justify paying someone less than a living wage by pointing to the "invisible hand" of a market economy as if that economy were somehow an inevitable, objective force rather than a cultural construction. There is no "natural" value for labor, as those values are set in the social practices of an economy. Similarly, in understanding the changing character of gender relations, it is helpful for us to recognize the traditional cultural attribution of *object* value to the feminine and *use* value to the masculine and then to consider the manner in which that economy is being transformed.

Every organization is embedded in the worldwide market economy and is subject to the requirements enacted by its participants. But organizations also develop their own specific, local economies as well. It is the local system of give-and-get: I give you X and get Y in return. These local systems can get quite complex and involve multiple payoffs. A friend writes:

> Your argument about economies in action started me to reflect on my experience on the assembly line at FoMoCo. I was working in a subassembly area where we put together automobile instrument panels. Our assembly was synchronized with the mainline—we were making panels for the cars which were actually coming at us down the motorized track. In those days, a car came down the line every 54 seconds, so each of us in our three-person group had a little less than 3 minutes to put each panel together.

PRINCIPAL CONCEPTS

Economics is morally important because it studies the methods of valuation and exchange. Economic systems are composed of units of value, qualified participants, the distribution of valued elements, and methods of exchange.

There were three different car models on the line and each unit could have options within the model style. Our subassembly group had to keep the panels in strict order, otherwise the line worker would grab the wrong one off our delivery table. In theory, we three were each to do every third panel off of the order sheet.

This scene looks like all response and no expression, but our work was quite different. Subassembly groups like ours had learned well before I punched a clock that the 54-second tyranny of the mainline could be broken if the prior shift would *leave a gift* of units assembled, which would not be used until the new shift came on the clock. We, of course, recognized that the work we did for them was not *ours* and that it was a gift with comments like: "Let's knock off; those guys won't have to start work for hours for all we've done." We also griped when the night shift was less than generous. (We built for the afternoon shift but expected our build-ahead to pay off, which it usually did.)

The build-ahead might put us 30 minutes to an hour ahead of the line. That build-ahead and our own ability to assemble the panels in 90 seconds if we had to (the reported record being under a minute) opened up some free-play space that made the job bearable. I don't recall ever meeting a worker from one of the other shifts, but I was connected to all of them in this economy.

The economy of the "build-ahead" returned good size blocks of leisure time for coffee and conversation in the otherwise relentless progress of the assembly-line for the efficiencies of labor. The return came not from the line system but from workers twice removed. That return also established an interesting moral order. If the night shift "cheated" and did not leave enough, the afternoon shift might be punished as well to get the message to those "night bastards." It was the various shift foremen's job to police this exchange system. Somehow the word would come down, our writer notes, "the line broke down last night" or "we'll let 'em know they messed up."

Economies entail obligation, and obligation entails morality. The complication is that we play in multiple economies simultaneously whose obligations may compete, conflict, or contravene one another. Duties, rights, utilities, virtues, and relationships may all be invoked to resolve the issue, but generally we hope to finesse the situation. We delay, defer, keep it all in the air, promise more, give less, overpay in return, and every so often we pay the price, but that doesn't keep us out of the game. We are economic players of various sorts and are bound to respect the games we play.

POLITICAL SYSTEMS

Politics is the system of allocation—the distribution of rights, privileges, entitlements, duties, responsibilities, requirements, rank, status, and position. The particular political processes that are authorized to perform these distributions are clearly a hallmark of the society, organization, or social grouping in focus. Such processes run the gamut from tyrannical demands to **Habermasian** consensus. The lessons from the 1985 dissolution of the Soviet hegemony to the most recent incidents in Serbia demonstrate forcefully that any such political process involves the complicity of its members. Even the coercive will falters without complicity.

In organizations, we see the imprint of these processes in the hierarchical structures in use—the practical rights of command and duties of service. We see them in the access rights to information and resources, the rights to speak and act, the requirements to be and to do, the responsibilities to one another. The keys to the executive washroom, to the supply cabinet, to the special entrance, the passwords to the financial books, the personnel files, the secret recipes, the titles, territories, reporting lines, the computers, desk sets, and furniture pieces are all corporate emblems of these processes. But we also see these processes in the dispositions toward makeup, body piercing, dating, use of the car, drive-bys, curfews, chores, drugs, allowances, sex, grades, moving back in, Dad's chair, and house rules on which so many households turn.

Organizational political processes can be profitably analyzed by considering the component processes of decision making, enactment, enforcement, and adjudication. We do not want to suggest by this list any sort of linearity or necessity. We see enforcement without rule-making and decisions that have no conditions of enactment (most "worst-case" scenario rules are of this sort of decision making), adjudication that makes new law and, of course, rules of action that have never been decided.

PRINCIPAL CONCEPTS

Politics is a system of allocation—the distribution of rights, privileges, entitlements, duties, responsibilities, requirements, rank, status, position, and the like. The particular political processes that are authorized to perform these distributions are clearly a hallmark of the society, organization, or social group in focus.

If, however, one wishes to constitute a rule that has organizational consequences, then attention will have to be paid to processes of complicity (consequential decision-making is the acceptance of the terms of obligation), the action means of its performance, the methods of supervision and discipline, and the procedures by which breaches will be repaired. Further, any evidence of the presence of one of these process sets calls upon the investigation of the others. The observation of a practice (enactment), for example, motivates the study of its rules of performance (complicity), criteria of excellence (enforcement), and means of correction (adjudication).

It is obvious that these processes participate in morality. We cannot steal what we have the rights to or readily dishonor in what we have permission to do. Organizations, from corporations to families, morally entangle their members in mission statements, policies, and rules. The character of these entanglements establishes strong likelihoods of moral outcomes. Despotic testing procedures, difficult restrictions on necessary supplies, impossibly early curfews, arbitrary reporting requirements all morally endanger those subject to them by promoting cheating, stealing, disobedience, and lying. Such rules are set-ups and they often deliver what they encourage. We have seen corporations spend several times the loss to police supply pilferages when most of the materials were being used for legitimate purposes anyway. We have also seen families expend enormous emotional energy on issues that disguise their true purpose (as in rules that enforce a child's status long past the age of the child). Such incidents are examples of political failure. Morally appropriate political processes within organizations do not endanger their members. They make clear and provide for the means of moral success.

Social Systems

The last of these systems we consider is the social—the system of self and other, the person and the relationship. We will spend Chapters 3 and 4 carefully examining the force of the micro practices of the social system on the constitution of the **domain of agency** for the self. Here, we wish to expand our view to its widest scope by examining a triumvirate of concepts from cultural studies: disciplines, apparatuses, and hegemonies.

Disciplines

Disciplines are systems of practical training that provide for coordinated action. We discipline the body to conform to standardized working conditions—three meals a day, breaks every so many minutes, the ability to stand, sit or be in other action for long hours, meet contemporary demands of an integrated workforce. We discipline semiotic activity—sign usage—to coordinate meaning. We discipline talk in conversational turn-taking, in connecting one turn to another, in topic selection and presentation so that we can communicate. We discipline action according to rules of the job, the road, the game, propriety, and good manners in order that we can jointly recognize what is going on. The self is a disciplined product of the relationship with the other. Its freedom of expression is limited in the act of becoming.

We cannot achieve any relationship and therefore any organizational form without disciplining potential into actual. As with all the elements in the domain of agency, disciplines structure potential into both what is likely and what is possible. They establish the ordinary in what is likely, but do not exclude the extraordinary in what is possible. In fact they allow us to recognize this difference.

Apparatuses

Apparatuses are the resources and practices of social structures. Political parties, class structures, government bureaucracies, industries, churches, and schools are all social apparatuses that go about the business of producing the society in which we live. The constitution of the family you were born into, what made it normal or not, its rights, privileges, and obligations in regard to its members, and so on were all established by some part of these apparatuses. Every other organizational arena is similarly under their influence. One cannot start a business without a license from a bureaucracy, submitting to some system of taxation, meeting work and safety rules, and the like. These apparatuses set many of the taken-for-granted terms of both organizational and individual action.

> ## PRINCIPAL CONCEPTS
>
> The constitution of a recognizable self, the ability to communicate, the coordination of action all require the discipline of potential into actual. The cultural resources of discipline establish what is possible, ordinary, extraordinary. Apparatuses are the sites and practices that provide for and maintain cultural and social resources. Hegemonies are the location of cultural truths and social practices that result in the distribution of control to different segments of society. Hegemonies contain the codes by which we distribute resources across the polarities of gender, class, ethnicity, race, age, and so on.

Hegemonies

Finally in the widest view of all, **hegemonies** are the social contracts by which apparatuses, disciplines, and the other systems are organized and maintained. Hegemonies are the location of the grand cultural truths and social practices that result in the distribution of authority and control to different segments of society. Hegemonies are the agreements by which we recognize the dominates and subordinates of a social system. They contain the codes by which we distribute resources across the polarities of gender, class, ethnicity, race, age, and so on. It is still true, for example, that in U.S. culture we expect—and indeed find in the vast majority of cases—a white male as the CEO of any major corporation. This distribution of power does not happen by chance. It happens because—liberating rhetoric to the contrary—at every level we agree to make it happen. Hegemonies, then, are the cultural processes of **complicity** and **implication** by which more and less are defined and sustained.

Working at this grand cultural level is a bit like a fish trying to discern the water in which it swims. Cultural processes such as these serve to naturalize action and belief. These processes remove what is constituted as normal from our view. We can get to what is naturalized in a society only by what it nominates as different, a danger or a threat. What is considered news—the unusual, the extraordinary, the noteworthy, for example, varies from culture to culture. U.S. news represents the conditions that affect the dominant interests of U.S. society. (We were quick to defend Kuwait with its oil; slow to aid Bosnia that had none.) While those dominant interests may extract value from us, we, nonetheless, agree. It's the American (or Russian or Indonesian) way.

Table 3.1   **Summary of Cultural Systems**

System	Area of Governance	Cultural Domains	Organizational Expressions
Semiotic	Significance and meaning	Language, action, symbolic forms	Discursive practices, action routines, interpretive practices, icons, emblems, marks
Epistemic	Truth	Systems of truth making such as science and law	Structurations, protocols, policies, myths, stories
Ethical	Good	Systems of moral judgment such as religion, the courts, police work, education, the media	Praise, censure, awards, punishments, grades, promotions, supervision, special privileges/restrictions, membership grants, firings, divorce
Aesthetic	Beauty	Art, literature, music, the body, fashion, popular culture	Space, furnishings, decor, dress, accouterments
Economic	Valuation and value exchange	Commodities, capital, labor, information, sex	Salary, access to resources, transaction rules, division of labor
Political	Allocation	Caste system, representation system, privileges and prohibitions, legislative processes	Command structure, authorizations, discursive and actional repertoires, decision processes
Social	Self, other, and relationships	Paradigms, syntagms, subject positions, disciplines, apparatuses, hegemonies	Titles, roles, membership and other boundary practices, relational forms

Summary of the Seven Systems

Table 3.1 provides a quick overview of the seven systems that constitute culture, indicating their area of governance (the topics they control), the cultural domains in which they are active and some typical organizational expressions. It is important to remember that the boundaries of the chart are not actual boundaries. Real life is messy. If we were to take some major topic of a society, we would find voices from all of the systems speaking out. For example, modes of production (e.g., should art be produced in a capital based, factory system or a skills based, craft system) would appear to be an economic issue but it would register in every system.

THE INDIVIDUAL AS THE SUBJECT OF CULTURE

Every individual constitutes an intersection of the systems of culture. We are shot through by their influences. They provide our means of being in the world, of engaging the world, of understanding the world. A colleague writes:

> I have a friend who is a professor at the University of Malaysia. He has helped me conduct a thought experiment on the consequences of culture. We start with the fact that my father was the son of a cowboy who inherited some land from his father late in his life. According to Adnan, my father, assuming he successfully maintained the honor of the family, would have been a landed peasant. He would probably know how to read, write, and cipher at least well enough to participate in the government sponsored programs of rice farming and livestock. To remain successful, he would have to be well-connected locally to play the games of political patronage that set quotas and funded supplies.
>
> We assume that I would appear in this scene with the same genetic material as I now have and as the fourth and last son of the family. The culture would start to write on my body immediately. The different diet and living experiences would actualize my genetic potential in quite different ways affecting stature, strength, longevity, even my intestinal flora and the antibodies in my blood. Language would give me a different way of conceptualizing the world, of speaking it into my existence. The cultural routines of action would give me a different way of being in the world. I would not, could not be, nor would I think it proper to be the boy of the American mid-west or the man of Texas. What it meant to be a man, a son, a husband and a father would be different. The foundational beliefs of what was true, right, proper, and beautiful would be different. And even if I went on to be the Western scientist that I now am, I would understand even the most universally validated proposition differently because of those foundations. I would be practiced in economic and political systems equally arcane as those of Texas, but nonetheless quite different. Finally, if the American me were to stand in front of the Malaysian me, we might both be struck by some resemblances—the genetic marks of brown eyes, facial features, hairy knuckles, longer second toes, but at the level of identity—our persistent sense making and naturalized practices—we would be as different as any other two strangers in the world. There is potential but no "me" in that genetic material. The "me" of myself is a cultural production.

Our colleague's conclusion is startling. The man we know would disappear and we would be faced with a stranger. The stark comparison helps us understand the constituting force of culture. But it also helps us understand the sense of consistency we feel about ourselves. We may each be the product of cultural enactments, but they have a long history of performance. They are well-practiced, deeply sedimented, fully naturalized. We do not have to invent ourselves anew each time we step into a different set of organizing processes. There is more to each of us than any organization can declare. Nonetheless, the each of us is a moment-by-moment performance—an expression—not a soul. The self is always in the process of becoming within the enablements and constraints that are mobilized at the moment. Any moment is a lamination of discourses and cultural resources that speak us into the actual.

That changing lamination, however, is a source of knowledge for each of us. Both Elaine and Jim recognize that they cannot be professors in their own homes. Their respective families will not allow it. They can compare these separate texts from some other reading position. That reading allows us to investigate why choices available in one place are not available in another. So we learn by reaching across the boundaries of the individual settings of the mosaic of our lives.

TRANSITIONS

The struggle-to-be within the enablements and constraints of dominant interests is central to notions of social control. And while such notions emphasize the discipline of constraints, we also need to recognize that without cultural enablements there would be no human self to express. We also celebrate the free play spaces of improvisation and the spontaneity of indeterminancy that are inherent in expressiveness. Every moment of control has its shadow of resistance. In this cultural and organizational play of light and shadow, we find the organizational agent and the topics of the next chapter.

CASE STUDY

Pat is employed in a male-dominated shop. As a new employee, Pat is shocked to see that many of his co-workers, as part of their work stations, have photos of nude women in suggestive poses. Pat mentions to his boss that he finds these photos offensive and sexist. His boss says there is a historical and cultural precedent for the photos and they will stay. If Pat so chooses, Pat may leave.

1. Is historical and cultural precedent a logical reason for keeping the photos in the shop?
2. What is rational argument in asking Pat's co-workers or boss to remove the photos?
3. Is Pat's only option to quit? What other choices would someone have in similar circumstances? Is it necessary to invoke sexual harassment laws? Explain.

4

THE ORGANIZATIONAL AGENT
Part I: Identity

PREVIEW

This chapter begins a two-part sojourn (that continues in Chapter 5) into the self as the source of ethical conduct. In this chapter we lay out the covering principles of our discussion, that the self is not some internal, essentialist character but a sign of our identity and subjectivity and that organizations provide the domains in which the actual expression of the self can appear. We then take up the specifics of identity—those persistent characteristics of the individual—and tour quickly through four identity components, the instrument of the body, naturalized practices, identity images and relationships and memberships.

Ethics concerns the quality or value that is attached to or is inherent in the action of some agent-who-could-do-otherwise. One place to start an analysis of ethical action is to consider the constitution of the acting agent. The acting agent, then, is the focus of this and the next chapter. In this chapter we first consider and reject the traditional view of the acting agent and then begin the task of building a different conceptualization by investigating the concept of identity. The next chapter will complete the reconstruction of the acting agent by exploring social processes of subjectivity.

THE TRADITIONAL VIEW

In traditional forms, most ethical arguments are founded on a vision of the acting agent as a fully-realized, rational intellect who can accurately read the world around it. This vision made use of an ideal Cartesian mind that was ultimately capable of right reason and a material reality that would ultimately yield its secrets to empirical methods. It was the good man thinking well after careful study of the world he was in. And, indeed, it was a man, good by Western cultural values, thinking well in the lines of Aristotelean logic as only a man could, according to prevailing thought, whose careful study was in the mold of European masculinist science. For example, Rachels (1993) writes:

> The conscientious moral agent is someone who is concerned impartially with the interests of everyone affected by what he or she does; who carefully sifts facts and examines their implications; who accepts principles of conduct only after scrutinizing them to make sure they are sound; who is willing to "listen to reason" even when it means that his or her earlier convictions may have to be revised; and finally, is willing to act on the results of this deliberation (p. 14).

CHALLENGING THE TRADITION

This traditional vision is still very much with us, but it is no longer unchallenged. The first of these challenges has been directed toward the Cartesian mind—that unitary intellect that if sufficiently trained and disciplined could reliably reach truth. The work of Freud and Jung and more recently Lacan have thoroughly destabilized the concept of a single, rational faculty. We are left instead with an often squabbling multiplicity of mental faculties thoroughly inhabited by desire. Further, the training and discipline by which the mind would work have been shown to be a particular cultural invention rather than a gift from God or nature. There is, consequently, no *right* reason, no Archimedean standpoint of impartiality, but rather a disputed set of conventions by which reasoning is done and contested territories from which we can state our claim.

The second set of challenges has been directed toward the idea of "a good man" as an internally secure and persisting identity. This identity has been considered to be some essential character that uniquely carries the mark of the person. That mark has been called the *soul* or the *enduring* or *essentialist self*. The challenges to the essentialist self have come in two major forms: The first has been from work in psychology that has atomized the soul into attributes, aptitudes, attitudes, and personality traits. There is no unitary force of action, only a kaleidoscopic composite of probabilities. The second challenge has come from sociological work that has shown that much of identity—much of who we are—is the product of social action, not internal character. It is social action that creates the identifying marks of gender, ethnicity, age, and caste that would have allowed us to recognize—in 1637—the 41-year-old, white, male, French intellectual, René Descartes, under those terms. These socially derived identities are more than just a descriptive badge, however, because social action also establishes a common understanding of what it means to be 41 years old (well past middle age in 1637), white, male, French, and an intellectual and specifies the status, activity, dress, discourse, and so on, appropriate to such a person. Neither Descartes nor any of us can simply be whomever we want.

THE COLLECTIVE AGENT

The final issue that we wish to raise concerning the traditional view is that cultural and organizational studies have pointed out that the acting and, therefore, accountable agent, is often not an individual but a composite of self-other relationships such as parents, a leadership group, or a corporate committee (Ricoeur, 1992). It is the composite and not the individual members that is empowered to act. Consequently, it is quite possible for an individual member to enact her membership in a fully justified manner as the composite agent reaches a morally unjustified decision. This consequence can occur because no single member can control the action of a genuine composite. The knowledge of the membership is greater than the knowledge of its members, and the effect of the composite agent's actions is not the result of any individual member.

Let us work a simple example: Say, Joan, Derek, and Albert are appointed to a committee to develop a policy for purchasing supplies. In the process of writing the policy, Joan proposes a particular sentence because it will control a set of conditions common to her sector. For Derek and Albert, the sentence Joan proposes seems to have no relevance to their particular sectors, so that they have no reason to object. But they do have substantial reasons to support Joan's request—the committee works by agreement; to refuse Joan's request may be read as being obstinate or obstructionist, and so on. At the same time, Joan cannot act (add the sentence) on her own. Subsequently Derek and Albert each propose a sentence appropriate to their respective sectors. The result is that, although Joan knows the value of sentence X and Derek knows the value of Y and Albert knows Z, no member knows X, Y, and Z equally well. The composite knows more than any member. Further, no member could act on his or her own; each has to act in a

PRINCIPAL CONCEPTS

Postmodernism challenges the traditional concept of the individual as an essential unity that exhibits autonomy. In its place it offers a *self* appearing in some self-other relationship as the acting agent.

relationship. And finally, the acting force of the policy is not the sentence from Joan or from Derek or from Albert, but the paragraph from the composite. If the paragraph turns out to be an unethical purchasing policy, one cannot blame Joan or Derek or Albert. They each represented their own sectors as best they could. But can we hold all three responsible? And what would be the terms of their culpability? This circumstance is often read as a failure of the committee and the terms of its creation rather than of its members. At least, it is clear that the moral standing of the committee is different from the moral standing of the individuals.

The Situated, Enacted Agent

The work of these preceding paragraphs has been to undermine the proposition of "the good man thinking well" as the natural description of the acting agent. Nothing of "good," "man," "thinking," or "well" is simply natural; each is thoroughly inoculated with social and cultural practices. The acting agent is not an unproblematic natural unity but rather an historicized construction, brought into the fullness of its existence at the moment of its action.[1] For some readers, this view may seem strange or even objectionable, but we are all familiar with the explanations used for acting in particular ways: "I was tired." "I forgot." "I was too excited." "I didn't make the connection." Each of these explanations notes the contingent bases for our action. Each of them recognizes that *who* we are depends on *when* we are. They also determine the moral implications of an action.

Peter Manning (1992) describes a mark of the contemporary condition of postmodern societies as the search for who we are. The reason for this

---

[1] For more developed arguments along these lines, see Anderson, W. T., 1998; Anderson and Schoening, 1996; Benhabib, 1992; Gergen, 1991; Shotter, 1993 a and b; Taylor, 1989.

condition has been a destabilization of the structures that held us to a clear identity. We no longer have a common education, religion, secure work-life or sociopolitical system in which we could dependably enact a consistent self. Much more is now required of us as we are forced into a diversity of relationships where our fundamental understandings and naturalized actions may be called into question.

ORGANIZATIONS AS FRAMES OF MEANING

Most of us spend our lives moving among organizational fields of action. Elaine, for example, meets with her co-workers as an assistant vice-president and is called upon to express the rights and responsibilities of that position. She *is* the assistant vice-president. But when she steps into the classroom, that expression of her self vanishes because now she is the instructor. Even if she wanted to be the assistant vice-president in the classroom, she couldn't because her students are not in that corporate relationship with her. When Elaine goes home she is in a new set of relationships bounded by the cultural terms of wife and mother. But those relationships disappear as she meets with others as a member of the county conservation board. In each of these callings, Elaine enacts who she is according to the demands of the situation. The requirements for action and the standards by which we judge the quality of action change as she moves from one domain to another. Yes, justice governed by compassion is required in each situation, but the equation of the classroom is not that of the boardroom. There is no single algorithm that we could devise that would stand unchanged across Elaine's many domains of action.

Our conclusion leads to an increased interest in understanding the organizational settings in which our agency or our freedom of action appears. From family, to friends, to classroom, to the workplace, we are rarely outside of some set of organizational process. This process includes instructions as to who we are and directions for what we can do.

The organizational settings, in which we act and are an agent in and of, are often described as *frames of meaning* (Goffman, 1974).[2] A **frame** is first of all a practical achievement of the individuals for whom the frame has

---

[2] The literature on framing is large, but the following is an interesting selection: Bateson 1972; Giddens 1979; Laing 1971; 1982; Rawlins 1987.

meaning. It is built up over time through negotiation, training, rehearsal, repeated performances, characteristic language use, and other actual practices of the membership. When we are situated within a frame, our action and discourse, relationships and notions of self all take on particular values. These values are established by and serve to constitute and maintain the frame of meaningfulness. For example, when Jim steps on the field as a collegiate soccer referee, the individuals at the field location take on particular identities and are entered into specific relationships with him. No longer are there just people there; now there are players, coaches, trainers, timers, scorers, maintenance people and even fans. Each takes on their persona for Jim—and Jim for them—by virtue of his being in the frame of the game as an official. Each has a set of rights, privileges, obligations, and responsibilities established by rule (rules which must themselves be negotiated, written, and interpreted) and common practice as does Jim. The reality of who is at that field has changed. A friend, for example, is no longer simply a friend, and, in fact, friendship obligations recede and may even be rendered inappropriate in the face of the other identification that individual carries. Situated as he is, Jim cannot rightfully enact the ordinary performances of friendship for a player, coach, or fan.

The frame by which we understand Jim's professional behavior toward a friend is a product of the organizing processes by which we bring a soccer game into existence. (A frame, therefore, sets the terms of action but is itself a product of and is sustained through action.) The soccer frame allows Jim to enact the performance of a game official, something that he cannot be anywhere else, but the frame also requires Jim, when there as an official, to *be* the game official—all of what he does will be interpreted accordingly.

The central truth about organizations, then, is not about buildings or products or titles, but about the realities that are produced in the organizing processes. What we organize in the framework of organizations is the meaningfulness of who we are in what we say and do. Organizations, as the product of our organizing efforts, provide the conditions for a particular expression of ourselves to appear. They situate our potential to be someone in a material expression of the self set in motion within a set of relationships, rights, and obligations. That self—that expression in action—is the postmodern equivalent of the Enlightenment's self. The postmodern expression, however, is a goodly distance from the unitary essence of Descartes' argument.

> ## PRINCIPAL CONCEPTS
>
> When we are situated within an **organizational frame,** our action and discourse, relationships and notions of self all take on particular values. These values are established by and serve to constitute and maintain the frame of meaningfulness. What we organize in the framework of organizations is the meaningfulness of who we are in what we say and do. Organizations bring about a material expression within a set of relationships, rights, and obligations.

The Self as Identity and Subjectivity

With some 350 years to rehearse the idea, it would not be unusual for us to persist in believing that we are not only the same material object but also somehow the same person when we are an employee at our workplace, the president of a volunteer group, a parent in one home, and a child in another. In the Enlightenment notion, those roles are simply things we take on; the center of our self remains unchanged. In more contemporary terms, there is no center: We are a living organism always involved in varying rates of change that must manage its self-expression within a socially produced framework of performance requirements. The parent-self appears within a framework of understanding of what is true and, therefore, right that is different from framework in which the working-self appears. It may be appropriate to tell a child that a package will arrive "soon," but wholly inappropriate to tell that to a customer standing at the counter even though the time may be the same. The value and character of time is not the same in those two cases. And, therefore the value and character of statements about time are not the same.

Answers to questions of right and wrong, consequently, depend on the answer to the question of who we are. The answer to who we are, in turn, depends upon the particular circumstances in which the self appears. We will define the self as the acting agent—the entity we would point to in answer to the question, "Who did this?" When we talk about an agent, as we have noted, we use the term simultaneously in two ways. First, the agent is a particular and identifiable *agent of* action, providing some impetus, some momentum, some resource of the action. This is the **identity agent.**

Second, the agent is an *agent for* some recognizable intersection of cultural signs. This intersection is also called a subject position. It denotes a recognizable model of action or Weberian ideal type—such as parent, child, adult, worker, manager, customer, tourist, teacher, student, friend, and on and on. This is the **subjective agent.** Identity and subjectivity appear together as the self. It is the self that acts; not identity alone; not subjectivity alone.

The self acts within some domain of agency. Agency has been defined as the ability to do otherwise. Agency requires some degree of freedom. Freedom involves the availability and recognizability of alternatives of action and some degree of autonomy—one's self-governance. The absence of choices or of the ability to choose negates agency.

The relationship between freedom and autonomy is sometimes difficult to see. Try this example: A parent has received consistent medical advice from competent and reputable practitioners that her child undergo a difficult, risky, but potentially life-saving procedure. There is freedom, here, in that there are alternatives of action, but there is little autonomy because the parent is wholly dependent upon outside advice. She is not in a condition of self-governance, having surrendered that governance to a culture of experts. She still has to make the decision, but there is little room for choice. Her agency is nearly absent. On the other hand, that same parent living under conditions without medical support may be entirely self-governed in her choice but without recognizable alternatives. She has autonomy but no freedom and, therefore, once again little agency.

Intellectually we hold a conflicted position about agency. Traditional human sciences resist the idea of agency and any other form of a self-caused cause in their bias toward determinism. Some traditional studies in morality, however, are founded on the principle of free will—that Cartesian intellect we saw earlier. We will take a position somewhere in between these extremes. We will hold that people make choices that in the end make a difference and that also have no other explanation than the choice itself. Those choices, however, will be in an agency domain that will define the limits of freedom and autonomy for the acting agent. As living entities, we must act. There is no condition of non-acting. As semiotic entities, our acting must make sense in action. It is the meaningfulness of our self in action that sets the domain of agency.

There are, then, three elements to consider when evaluating the acting agent. First, there are the particular and **persistent characteristics** of *iden-*

PRINCIPAL CONCEPTS ─────────────────────

The three elements of the acting agent are identity, subjectivity, and agency. Identity is taken to be to persistent characteristics of the individual. Subjectivity is invoked or evoked according to the cultural meanings of one's subject position. Identity and subjectivity provide for the self, the sign of the person. Agency puts the self in action.

---

tity that provide us with the particular agent—this individual rather than that. Second, there are the cultural meanings by which we enact our *subjectivity* in the paradigmatic values of ethnicity, gender, age, caste, as well as relational and member roles. Identity and subjectivity provide for the *self*. The self is the sign of the person, the answer to who we are. And third, there is agency. *Agency* puts the self in action as the acting agent—a *one-who-makes-a-difference*.

The next several sections of this chapter take up the further explanation of identity, subjectivity, and agency to enable us to reach a deeper understanding of the acting agent.

IDENTITY

Our writing to this point in this chapter has emphasized the contingent nature of the self. Who we are comes into its fullness in our action, action typically made meaningful within frames of organizing. These ideas write against any notion of a central principle of the individual that carries itself mostly unchanged through life and whose rights, privileges, obligations, and responsibilities are in ready view. These ideas promote the concept of a situated, enacted self that will necessarily change across time and occasion and whose rights, privileges, obligations, and responsibilities will change also.

Clearly, however, there are characteristics of the self that do persist across the times and occasions of performance. We call these persistences *identity*. In examining identity we start with (a) the corporeal reality of the body as the instrument of our identity, (b) move to the naturalized practices by which we ordinarily express our self, then (c) consider the practiced images or self interpretations by which we describe our self to our self and

(d) finally take up the **relationships and memberships** that provide substantial resources of identity.[3]

Identity: The Instrument

The first of these persistences we call identity is the **instrument of action**— the material, biological, and semiotic configuration that occupies space and exists across time. This language is necessarily an odd way to talk about the Jim or Elaine who stumbles out of bed as they prepare for yet another round of self-presentation. The point of it is not to be obtuse but to allow us to think about the elements of identity in a new way. The body, for example, is a material object, and it is most often that material object by which we recognize the person. We also use the characteristics of this material object for cultural purposes. We value color of hair, eyes, skin; the size, shape, and proportion of the body and its parts; the luminance, texture, and pliancy of its surface; and so on. The material object of our body archives the markers of these values and presents them at every turn. Our daily recognition of these markers come in the way we cover, drape, paint, dye, assist, augment, and otherwise modify and call attention to this material object.

The material persistence of the body is a key element of identity. If I am 5' 10", I do not suddenly become 5' 3" or turn dark skin to light. I can count on the material presence of your body being pretty much the same tomorrow as it was yesterday. The body, however, is not only material; it is also biological. As a biological entity, it carries a genetic code that allows us to distinguish aspects such as sex, age, and ethnicity. When Jim walks into a room, he is white, male, slightly taller than average, of medium build (but in fantastic shape) older, of vague European ancestry (but apparently more southern than northern), bearded, with greying dark brown hair and brown eyes. He may wish that you not know any of this identity, but his body presents it. Jim's body carries the signs of this identity. The significance of those signs, however—what it means to be white, male, and so on—is held in the company of others. These culturally derived meanings are expressed in self-other relationships. His maleness, for example, may be of no reference in the company of men, but may be a serious issue for his female boss or subordinate.

---

[3] This discussion draws on Anderson and Schoening, 1996; Bateson, 1958, 1979; Bohm, 1980, 1994; Johnson, 1987; Levin, D., 1985; Levin G., 1992; Luhmann, 1990; Maturana and Varela, 1980, 1992; Varela, Thompson and Rosch, 1991.

The reader might consider the response of the press to the apparent changes in skin color effected by Michael Jackson, the popular music recording star. It has been widely condemned as a weird manifestation of his personality, a denial of his race, and a refusal of his identity. We support none of this criticism, but simply point out (a) the value placed on this marker and (b) the overwhelming moral role played by the media.

The last element of the instrument that we consider is its semiotic configuration. We take a social action approach in this text. This theory finds its explanations for the mental states of individuals in observable, social processes such as language, discourse, and action. Action, therefore, provides for cognition. Other theories, such as cognitivism, would speculate on internal mental structures such as attitudes, values, or schemata. Cognition, therefore, leads to action. Most of the practical distinctions between these theories revolve around this outside/inside difference. For example, given the need to explain the actions of an individual, social action researchers would look for the explanation in cultural and ideological memberships, active relationships, and **naturalized practices** of discourse and action. Cognitivists might test the individual for personality traits, aptitudes, and value structures. In talking about semiotic configuration, we are writing about the mind as a persistent element of identity. We will do so by considering its positioning within the processes of sensemaking that are inherently social and necessarily dynamic. Social action theorists agree that there is an individual, cognitive instrument, but the human mind is a collective invention and cognition is a social process not simply interior mental computing. This social process depends on signs.

For example, one does not lose his or her mind. One loses his or her collective standing as a human mind. The loss of mind is the failure to think like others due to physiological or other reasons.

The world of humans is one fully populated by signs. We are born into a language community. We are taught characteristic ways of acting, ways of being—being a woman or a man, an American or not. We are taught characteristic ways of speaking and writing—using language; what are called discursive rights and obligations. All of these signs are culturally and socially managed and are the principal methods by which social reality and our knowledge of material reality are socially constructed.

Consider this scenario: Joan is walking along and sees a five-dollar bill on the sidewalk. (It is, of course, only a green piece of paper upon which we have conferred additional value in the sign of our actions toward it.) "Hey," Joan thinks, "my lucky day." She picks the bill up and puts it in her pocket (generally an illegal action, by the way). Again: Joan is walking along and sees a five-dollar bill on the sidewalk. It is in front of her neighbor's house. "Hey," she thinks, "Mr. Hutchins must be losing his money again." She picks the bill up and puts it in his mailbox (against federal regulations, by the way). Finally: Joan is walking along and sees a five-dollar bill on the sidewalk. A person standing nearby is fumbling in her purse, looking for her keys. "Hey," Joan thinks, "that woman must have dropped that bill." She picks it up and hands it to her. The woman says, "Das ist nicht meins."

All the permutations of this scenario make sense to us because we jointly participate in the same semiotic configuration. We recognize a five-dollar bill and its "lost" state. We recognize the probability of ownership by location. We recognize a sphere of influence, a territory of action, that surrounds a person. We recognize the "foreign-ness" of a language and act accordingly toward a "foreigner." It isn't our choice to make these recognitions. We make them because we were born and assimilated into a culturally governed, societally managed semiotic system of language, action, and discourse. We are simply one of the nodes on this great web of meaning.

Our sentience—our ability to knowingly manipulate signs—is entirely colonized by these systems. We think, speak, and act in the signs and symbols provided us. Here is our consciousness, history, dreams of the future, and articulated desires. Here, in the meanings we declare, is our sense of right and wrong. Though it is the same 5 dollar bill on the sidewalk with the same information value, Joan of the three versions declares the 5 dollar bill to be (a) lost, (b) belonging to Mr. Hutchins, and (c) under the authority of the nearby woman. She acts differently under each of these declarations. Her sense of the right thing to do changes with the meaning she attributes to the object.

Joan's understanding of what it means for something to be lost, belonging to, or under the authority of, is neither of her making nor is it the product of some natural force. Rather it is the product of the processes of ideological apparatuses, as they have been called, such as our governments, schools, churches and media that circulate—and supervise—meanings in society. Those processes configure us semiotically, configure the way we

> ## PRINCIPAL CONCEPTS
>
> The components of identity begin with the instrument of action—the material, biological, and semiotic configuration that occupies space and exists across time.

make meaning. Most certainly we can manipulate this configuration—enrich, suppress, resist, the supplied interpretations of the world around us. But like the materiality of our body, we cannot deny this semiotic contribution to our identity.

IDENTITY: NATURALIZED PRACTICES

Cultural and societal processes provide us with a rich system of discourse and action. But just as our speaking and writing use only a small part of the potential of our language, so our characteristic ways of being use only a small part of the potential of those processes of action and discourse. Each of us is situated in a culture, society, time, locale, as well as sets of organizational memberships and interpersonal relationships as both a given and a produced instrument of action.

As we noted, Jim is white, male, slightly taller than average, of medium build, older, of vague European ancestry, bearded, with greying dark brown hair, and brown eyes. He is also marked by a U.S. culture of both Midwest and western varieties, living in a democratic society as expressed in Utah (which is different from that expressed in California or Maine as they are different from each other) on an April morning in the late twentieth century, working at a keyboard as a member of an academic community and specific state institution in a home office (as defined by the IRS) located in a house that is shared with his wife and that is the place for a number of other activities including family celebrations. Although he participates in all of them, he is the author of none of these circumstances. Those circumstance conspire, however, to produce both the boundaries of his actions and the meaningfulness of what he does.

If he is to sustain himself as a professor, writer, husband, father, he has a limited set of choices of what can be done on this April morning. Those boundaries are not rigidly deterministic—he went skiing yesterday, but they do impose obligations that ultimately must be met. We respond to that constant pressure of circumstance by organizing our environment and actions to accommodate it. This organization constitutes the naturalized practices of our identity.

In order to be the assistant vice president, Elaine must *act* as the assistant vice president as defined by the organization in which she is the assistant vice president. In order to be a manager, Mary, of our rightsizing scenario, must *act* as a manager according to her company's expectations. In order to be a finder-of-a-five-dollar-bill, Joan must *act* as the finder in ways that are recognizable to her and others. Elaine, Mary, and Joan will enact their presence as AVP, manager, and finder respectively in the freeplay space left by the cultural, organizational, and relational boundaries that surround any named, person-in-performance (a term we also know as a cultural **paradigm**).

The freeplay space of performance means that the cultural, organizational, and relational instructions for the paradigmatic performance are incomplete. Elaine, Mary, and Joan have to complete the enactment out of their own performance stock. They will improvise the final presentation, but it will not be invented anew each time. Michael Jordan's flight to the iron was a trademark move because it had been practiced and performed thousands of times. It was a naturalized performance that was part of his identity as a basketball player.

One of the terms that sometimes gets associated with naturalized practices is "habit." Habit seems to contain the idea of a repeated happenstance. This idea is too simple. Naturalized performances are much more complex. Michael Jordan's playing style was the result of deliberate study and intense practice. The result can be performed with automatic smoothness all the while accounting for the contingencies of the moment. Naturalized practices are the way we tell the beginner from the pro; the newcomer from the established. Note, also, how we speak of MJ the basketball player in the past tense. *That* Michael Jordan is no longer with us.

Here's a possible example: One of the most predictable things in a classroom is seating arrangements. We typically routinize the solution as to where to sit by sitting in the same place each time. The routine is secure enough that teachers can recognize students by where they sit. It is not a perfect identification system—actions are naturalized in repeated improvisations not determined by conditions, but it works well enough that we are surprised when someone "acts out of character."

Let's work a simple scenario to put these ideas together. Jack is picking up a few things from the green grocery after his tennis game. He is making chiles rellenos tonight and he needs some fresh peppers, maybe some Southwestern Hots. It is still early in the afternoon, and only Jack and the cashier are on the shop floor. The cash register rings up a bill of $4.63. Jack hands the cashier a ten dollar bill. She gives him change of $15.37. Jack recognizes the error instantly.

Let's first of all focus on the notion of an "error." The issue that something is not right is factual in this case—meaning that none of us, competent as we are, would say otherwise. Our expectations are governed by the cultural rules of the transaction, rules that include that one charges what the register shows and that change and charge are supposed to add up to what is tendered. None of these actions in an authentic transaction is free to vary. That does not mean that a person cannot violate the transaction. It means that one cannot both produce an authentic transaction and violate those rules.

If the rules had been followed, Jack would know exactly what has happened by virtue of the social practices that define that action. Up until Jack recognizes the extra change, we are witnessing the paradigm of the cashier and the paradigm of the customer in the **syntagm** (a culturally recognizable action line) of the transaction interaction.

In an authentic transaction, the cashier, who does this dozens of time per day, will accomplish her end of the transaction with well-practiced competence (or so we would expect). Jack, who does this dozens of times per month, should enact his performance equally well, although the customer has more freeplay space because there are fewer rules (but there are rules) and less supervision in place. These are two socially defined individuals— paradigms of the cashier and the customer. We need to know nothing more about them to recognize both their subject positions and the action they are in. Jack and the yet unnamed cashier are *framed* in the organization of the transaction. The ethical character of their conduct—what is right and wrong for those two people to do—is contained within that frame also.

In our scenario, of course, the rules have not been followed. The action has been cut loose or (at least loosened) from its cultural understandings. It has to be made sensible; the action is yet to be defined. Something else has happened—an error has been made or, perhaps, a gift has been given or an opportunity to cheat or to steal has been created or a message has been sent. With the action in doubt, the identities of our two characters are also in flux.

The first task for the enactors is to resolve for themselves and perhaps for each other what the action is. If Jack silently defines the situation as an error, he has the opportunity to become *honest* or *opportunistic*—the opportunity is provided by the action as defined as an error, but the identity terms are provided by the cultural and societal discourse that illuminates that opportunity.

If the cashier does not recognize the error, she can continue her belief in her competence and would attach no additional qualities to Jack's paradigmatic identity. If Jack announces, "Oh, you gave me too much change" (i.e., makes a bid to define the action as an "error"), he can be publicly acknowledged as "honest" and the cashier as "making the error." But the cashier could also make her own bid. She could deny the error (make a bid to define the action as "no error"). In which case, Jack might be publicly accused of trying to embarrass the cashier. His and her identities are at risk because the action is yet undefined. We pick up the scenario again:

Jack feels the flush of recognition that something new is happening rise up in his face. The woman has been friendly almost flirting whenever he stops at the store. (It is one of the reason he pays the higher prices of this specialty shop.) Did she just make a mistake or is she testing him or setting him up for some other reason?

In evaluating this case for its use here, Elaine was skeptical of the authenticity of the cashier's gambit until she saw it enacted with her husband as the target in a bookstore transaction. She reported that her husband replied with forthright good humor. (Of course Elaine was standing less than 10 feet away.)

What we have done in those few lines is to add another syntagmatic layer of meaning to the relationship. No longer is it simply a business transaction in which both sides are presumed to be competent and charged with minding their own part of the bargain. We've introduced man/woman, a hint of romance or friendship. This changes the reading. The transaction is still not authentic, but it may not be an error.

If it is an error, Jack has cultural support for either the taking or the returning of the extra change. In the taking, Jack is supported by lines of thought concerning the impersonal nature of business transactions or that the cashier will benefit from her mistakes. In the returning, he is supported by lines of thought concerning his obligation not to benefit from another's mistake or that harm may accrue to the cashier. If it is not an error but a test, the ethical question of taking or returning disappears for Jack (although a different one appears for the cashier). If we move the action from the frame or syntagm of a transaction to the frame of a relational test, we change the meaning and the ethical consequences of what is to be done. In the frame or syntagm of the test, we are in a fairly simple, communicatively consequential action. Jack takes the money and loses a friend; Jack returns the money and passes the test.

Jack puts his elbows on the counter, reads Julie's name off her tag, snaps the ten spot from the change and in his best singles bar voice oils, "Julie, I know I'm the handsomest one here, but I really don't deserve this."

Well, now, Jack has made his decision. Whatever the cashier performed—error or test, Jack makes his play using a performance stock clearly out of place to firmly establish the action as a request for a new level of relationship. Julie now has her own opportunity to further her identity. The opportunity is provided by Jack's enactment of cultural texts she knows as well as Jack does. She knows that he is attempting to establish the meaning of the situation as a bid for a new relationship, even if she initially made an error. She can extend, ignore, or reject the definitional bid that Jack has attempted, but she cannot avoid the differential changes in her identity that will occur by her choice.

"Oh," the cashier replied in a flat but pleasant voice, "Did I make a mistake? Well, I certainly thank you for your honesty. Have a nice day." "What a jerk!" thought both the cashier and Jack as he picked up his package to leave. Both were referring to Jack but neither to the money.

Jack read the situation correctly but failed to enact an appropriate response. By invoking the singles bar line in the well-practiced competence of a naturalized, toxic bachelor performance without hesitation, embarrassment, or irony, he shifted his identity from nice guy in the kitchen to the more-predatory lounge lizard. Note that we are making no argument about who Jack really is. Jack really is what he can competently enact; both nice guy in the kitchen and lounge lizard. He could also be a tyrant in the kitchen and a nice guy at a singles bar. It is in their repeated performance, however, that any of these enactments become the naturalized practices emblematic of an identity.

We use four different terms to distinguish gender and gender practice: Female and male refer to biological differences; feminine and masculine refer to cultural ideal types; feminist and masculinist refer to social theory or political action cosmologies; and men and women refer to practical, situationally enacted individuals.

PRINCIPAL CONCEPTS

The second component of identity is naturalized practice. Naturalized practices are part of the cultural and societal processes that provide us with a rich system of performance in which the self materializes. As part of our naturalized practices, each of us is an agent of culture and society as well as sets of organizational memberships and interpersonal relationships.

It is true that although the practices are Jack's performances, they are not his to define. In choosing between "nice guy in the kitchen" and "lounge lizard," Jack chooses between the cultural extremes of the masculine—hero or rapist. In choosing to resist his bid, Julie chose between the cultural extremes of the feminine—virgin or whore. Jack may have intended the respect of friendship, but he chose his action text unwisely, given that he was going to perform it unself-consciously. He should have picked one of his naturalized performances from the hero side. Of course, he could have failed in his definitional bid there as well, because he does not control the outcome. He may control aspects of his identity in his naturalized practices, but the outcome—and who Jack is in that moment—is a joint enactment. In this case both agree: he is a jerk.

Identity: Images in Discourse and Action

Through word and action we regularly practice who we are. These performances are the texts of our selves. These texts are our personality, our aptitudes, value structures, and other cognitive configurations. Others read them and we read them, too, in our hearing, seeing, and kinesthetic perceptions. This section concerns our own reading of our textual selves and the persistent images that those readings provide. A friend writes:

> I am disciplining my children and I hear my mother's voice. It is an out-of-place, out-of-time experience. I am the one speaking my mother's words, but I stand in the middle. My mother towers over me as I tower over my children. I cringe in the presence of her power as my children cringe in mine. I cannot sustain this posture. This is not who I want to be. Suddenly I am on my knees, hugging my two small children asking their forgiveness.

A fellow referee remarked to Jim while both were changing in the officials' locker room:

You know, until a couple of years ago I never thought much about my body. I mean I kept in shape, did my work-outs and all that. I'd go out on the field and everything worked just fine. Now I run and work out even more, but I still don't know who is going to show up. Will it be that 30-year-old who can run all day or will it be that old guy who can barely make it from box to box? Damn, I hope it's not the old guy today.

A young woman recounted this story:

I *had* to get those jeans on. They were the proof of my desirability, my power. They told me what kind of person I was: If I got them on, I had been good; if I couldn't get them on, I was bad. I had to lay on the bed to pull them on. It embarrasses me to even think about it now. But my mother would help me.

And one more:

The delivery man came today, bringing my new desk chair. I am some-what uncomfortable meeting him at the door in bare feet, sweat pants, and baseball shirt. He talks to me in a down-home accent: "Gotchur chair. This here one gots all yer bells and whistles." I wish I could talk like that. Somebody who can talk like that belongs somewhere. I respond in my broadcast news voice. I could be from anywhere. Who would care? He tries to help me carry the chair upstairs, but I defer, "I think it's a one-man job." I know the chair is heavy. I saw him struggle with it up the porch steps, and weeks earlier I carried in the loaner from the store. He follows me up the stairs to retrieve the loaner. I sense we're better connected now. I think I showed him something more than a man being home in the middle of the day. "OK," he says, "Let me fix it up fer ya." He goes through the levers and knobs until it fits right. There are seven different controls on this chair. "I need a license," I joke. "You got that right," he answers. I offer to help with the loaner, but he says no and carries it down—with effort, I am pleased to see. Taking the loaner through the hall to the foyer, he makes some comments about how nice the house is and then looks at me directly. "What do you do?" Nonplused, I start to answer "professor" but stop in mid-breath because people might question a "professor" working at home. "I'm a writer," I say. "Oh," he says and I can see that now it all makes sense. "That's why I need a good chair," I add, appealing for understanding and simultaneously justifying the extravagance. "Yes sir, you do," he confirms and rolls the loaner to the truck.

These examples serve to show that we interpret ourselves as much as and probably more than we interpret others. We answer the question of what kind of mother, athlete, woman, or man am I in the reading of our performances.

> ## PRINCIPAL CONCEPTS
>
> The third component of identity is composed of one's self-images. These identity images are found in performance of discourse and action. We constitute or seek out the performances that confirm our identity and avoid those that don't. The performances are the texts of our selves.

There is once more an organizing or framing principle at work here, because to the extent that we can, we constitute or seek out the occasions of those performances that confirm our identity and avoid those that don't. The young woman doesn't prove herself by buying a larger pair of jeans. That would be proof of her failure. The mother denies the replication of her mother's identity by disrupting that performance and guarding against its reappearance. Jim's fellow official is coming to grips with the necessity of retirement, and the professor seeks his manhood in action that will make his masculine self sensible to another as well as to himself.

We see ourselves as too fat, too short, too tall, too smart, too ignorant, too fast, too slow, really quick, so smooth, gorgeous, with beautiful hair, very smart, so very kind, insightful even, in the performances we give. And we look to give those performances that confirm the images they present.

There is a ski resort in Utah where the runs are wide and the grooming impeccable. People go there not simply to ski but because they can be skiers. They can edge, carve, and link those tight parallel turns, feeling in the body the image of their identity. We gain an understanding of ourselves in our own action and discourse. The action or discourse that is enabled or permitted by the circumstances in which we act or speak provides the text of our identity. Such is the significance of the constraints on action and discourse that arise from position, ethnicity, gender, and other organizational and cultural controls. In limiting what we can say or do, they limit our ability to be; they limit our identity. It is also the significance of the constraints we place on ourselves. We do work to select and modify the environments of our action and discourse. That work participates in our identity.

IDENTITY: RELATIONSHIPS AND MEMBERSHIPS

Father to son: "What are you? You're not married—don't even have a girlfriend. You don't have a job. You're not in school. You haven't been to church in years. Twenty-five and you're still living at home. What's the matter with you? When are you ever going to be something?" [Heard across a Utah fence.]

The distinction between relationships and memberships has to do with the different practices of each. Generally a membership is an identity managed by boundary practices between an individual and a group; a relationship is an identity managed by the terms of obligation between individuals or subject positions. (And, clearly there are dyadic relationships that can be considered memberships.) Memberships and relationships provide for one another. Relationships occur inside memberships: Elaine is a member of a specific academic institution. She has a workplace relationship with her administrative assistant who is her assistant because he also is a member of the same institution. And relationships are the source of membership: Jim is a member of his wife's family because of his relationship with his wife.

The last in this list of the persistent characteristics of the self we call identity are the **relationships and memberships** we maintain and are recognized by others. Now by relationships and memberships, we are not talking about that aunt you last saw 15 years ago and wouldn't recognize if you saw again or that AAA card you carry in your billfold. We are talking about the relationships and memberships that are regularly exercised, that have naturalized practices that define them. These relationships and memberships are emblematic; they establish long standing debts of obligation, show our connectedness, set our social location, assign relational closure. Elaine and Jim have been parents most of their adult lives. It is, of course, not simple biology that makes that so. It is the fact that each maintains that status through regular, specific, and recognizable action and that others—including our children—enact our parenthood by demanding those actions and performing reciprocal action in response.

The relationships and memberships of marriage, career, religion, social groups, and even sports and recreation provide continuous reference points in the on-going activity of the presentation of the self. The more of those points in sight the clearer the answer to the question of "Who am I?" Performance of the obligations and demands on action and discourse entailed by essence-fixing relationships and membership provides ample evidence of one's identity. I—the keyboardist—may claim to be your friend, dear reader, but to fulfill that claim, I have to act in recognizable ways as a friend. That recognition is a joint recognition. I cannot be your friend—enter into a friendship relationship—unless you let me and together we recognize what we do in the name of the friendship as acts of friendship. It is

---

PRINCIPAL CONCEPTS

The fourth component of identity is found in the relationships and memberships that are regularly exercised and that have naturalized practices that define them. The nature of obligation in relationships and memberships acts as a basis for evaluating the moral character of our action. Others also recognize our entity through our relationships and memberships.

---

in this conjoint character of relationships and memberships that other people come to populate our identity. I don't own our friendship, I share it. If I don't own our friendship, I also don't own the identity it provides. We each have a controlling interest in that identity. So, I don't have absolute control of my identity. It is daily at risk in the relationships and memberships that provide no small part of its resources.

The relationships and memberships that are identity resources have six characteristics: (a) they carry the naturalized performances of their enactment; (b) they are regularly exercised; (c) the regular exercise of the specific actions of naturalized performances entails obligations-to-do with a resultant appearance of have-to-be; (d) they are jointly constituted and in that constitution create a closure of the self; (e) to the extent that they are the resources for identity, they put that identity at risk. And (f), relationships and memberships are also powerful systems of organization. They connect moments of time and elemental acts into doing and being. They constrain act into action and existence into identity at the same time they enable the action to be performed and the identity to appear. To be a member I must act in certain ways, but I cannot be a member unless I act in those ways.

Consider Bill Rodriguez of the rightsizing scenario of Chapter 1. As a purchasing agent for ELCO, Bill got up at 6 A.M., 5 days a week, commuted to the office, performed a prescribed set of activities for 8 to 10 hours, and commuted home to sometimes do work there. In order to be a purchasing agent for ELCO, he had to do those things and submit to the authority of others. When he is fired, he no longer has to do those things and at the same time he is no longer allowed to do those things. He has gained and lost freedom as he has gained and lost opportunity. His time and action once sensible as a purchasing agent are now without that meaningful organizing identity. He recognizes this deeply felt loss of identity. The road back is to re-organize—find another place to be a purchasing agent or redefine his self in terms of other reference points, perhaps, even a man who has been fired.

TABLE 4.1   **Systems of Identity**

TYPE	SOURCES	PERSISTENCES	CONTRIBUTION
The Instrument	Materiality of the body; physical structure, mechanical and biological operations and functions	Material properties, size, shape, color, physiognomy, voice, physical capabilities	The unity of the material object in a material world
Naturalized Practices	Socialization into cultural and societal action forms, family memberships, muscle memories, regular performance	Discourses and action routines, vocabularies, skills, abilities	Characteristic ways of being in the world
Images	Practical texts of personality formation, aptitudes, cognitive configurations	Sense of self	Coherence of the self
Durable Relationships and Memberships	Terms of obligation, membership practice, recognition of and by the other	Social location, social closure, connectedness, emblematic memberships	Place in social worlds

One's identity therefore is in no small part dependent upon relationships and memberships to provide the resources for being this or that person. Those relationships and memberships do more than just give us a title; they also provide a basis for evaluating the moral character of our action. Taking risks on a rock face may be appropriate for a single person, but if a fall leaves two small children bereft of a parent, the terms of what is appropriate risk taking change. The activity has not changed, but the consequences have because of the identity of the person involved.

IDENTITY: SUMMARY

Table 4.1 presents a summary of the four systems of identity that we have discussed, giving the type of system, the sources that contribute to it, the persistences that it produces and the contribution these persistences make to one's identity.

We began our discussion of identity by acknowledging this difficulty: We theorists insist on denying the existence of some central, enduring principle of the self and look instead to some enacted composite. At the same time, our own experience tells us that what we were yesterday is pretty much what we are going to be today (even though you may change quite a bit). A resolution to this difficulty has been sought in the persistences that contribute to our identity: the corporeal stability of the body, the constancy of desire, the universality of language, the inertia of practiced discourse and action, the management of the texts of ourselves, and our durable relationships and memberships all make this contribution. And, necessarily, bodily changes—puberty, menopause, conditioning, aging, illness or injury, the shifting objects of desire, the changing manner in which we are positioned by language, the rise or fall of opportunity to say or do, the commitment or collapse of relationships, all constitute peril or promise to identity. Our identity is never fixed and it is always at risk, but it does persist.

We pass now to the next chapter that continues our discussion of the organizational agent under the terms of its subjectivity.

CASE STUDY

Gwen and a co-worker are on an airline to hand-deliver a bid for a major government contract. Gwen strikes up a conversation with the individual on her left. The two immediately like one another and share some stories and experiences that show their commonalities. It turns out that Gwen and her "seat mate" are in identical professions with similar educational backgrounds. Two hours into the flight, Gwen's seat mate confesses that he despises the firm which employs him and wonders if there are any openings at Gwen's place of employment. She explains to him that she works for a small, fledgling company, and that she is hand-delivering a bid that could make or break the future of the company. In fact if the bid were awarded, there would most likely be two job openings. Shocked, the seat mate explains that he too is delivering a bid for this contract, and that his firm is most likely Gwen's strongest competition. He opens his travel case and takes out what is obviously his company's bid, and begins to read over it. A few moments later, he excuses himself to go to the lavatory and stretch for "15 minutes or so." He leaves the bid on his seat and goes to the back of the plane.

1. Gwen reads the bid. Now does she make changes in her own company's bid? Justify her actions. How would we frame the ethical implications of her reading the bid and changing her company's proposal?
2. Gwen does not read the bid. Justify her actions. What are the ethical implications of not reading the bid?
3. Gwen reads the bid, makes changes and her company gets the contract. Now does her company owe the seat mate a job? Explain the ethical features of this complication.
4. Gwen does not read the bid, but her company gets the contract. Should she contact her seat mate and offer him a job?

5

THE ORGANIZATIONAL AGENT
Part II: Subjectivity

PREVIEW

This chapter continues our discussion of the self, taking up subjectivity—the complicity of the other in the formulation of the self. In subjectivity we consider the cultural marks by which we distinguish and position the acting agent and establish a good number of the terms of its ethical conduct. We look at race, age, ethnicity, caste, and gender for examples. Finally we see how organizations as cultural modifiers deepen the laminations of identity and subjectivity as the self is materialized situationally.

This chapter continues our discussion of the organizational agent, that contingent self that enacts, represents, and makes a difference in the organization—in short any and every member. In Chapter 4 we considered identity as the elements of the self that are both durable and create a sense of individuality. In this chapter we consider subjectivity as the elements of the self that are collectively contingent from the deep layers of cultural institutions to the very present layer of self and other.[1]

---

[1] The work of this chapter is informed by Bakhtin, 1981, 1986, 1990; Benhabib, 1992; Bourdieu, 1984; Bourdieu & Wacquant, 1992; Brockelman, 1985; Butler, 1993; Chafe, 1994; Clark & Holquist, 1984; Coupland, Coupland, & Giles, 1991; Csordias, 1994; Dunne, 1996; Edwards & Potter, 1992; Farchild, 1985; Foucault, 1986; Gergen, 1991, 1994; Giddens, 1990, 1991; Katz, 1978; Knights & Willmott, 1989; Martin, Gutman, & Hutton, 1988; Mills, 1993; Potter & Wetherell, 1987; Rasmussen, 1996; Rawlins, 1992; Ricoeur, 1992; Sartre, 1956; Shotter, 1993a, 1993b; Taylor, 1980; Volosinov, 1973, 1976; Vygotsky, 1978; Wade, 1996; West, 1982; Wilber, 1993.

SUBJECTIVITY

In our examination of the self as organizational agent through the concepts of identity and subjectivity, we find subjectivity to be the more important. In fact, throughout our discussion of identity, we kept discovering the intrusion of the other in the form of cultural understandings, societal norms, and relational obligations into even the most secure locations of our identity. We are continually the subject of the other. We are employee, parent, student, boss, lover, winner, loser, rich, poor, tall, short, or whatever subject position, only with the complicity of the other. The complicity of the other in the formulation of the self is called **subjectivity.** We remarked earlier that Jim carries the marks of ancestry and gender in his body but the significance of those marks was under social control. Jim cannot avoid being a man or avoid the pressures to act like a man or the judgments of his manly character. But none of this is a matter of simple biology. It is mostly a function of the cultural and social attributions that craft this subject position given the biological difference.

In U.S. writings at least, "subjectivity" has had a devastating relationship with the term "**objectivity**." Something that was subjective was biased, opinionated, and certainly not to be trusted. Something that was objective was true, factual, and credible. Postmodernists have attempted to show that objectivity is a rhetorical stance—a way of masking the social effort by which the factual is created. Objectivity is a remnant of a particular empiricism that held that reality could be addressed directly. Subjectivity, in its contemporary form, is an acknowledgment that reality has to be addressed from some method of understanding.

For example, the evidence is quite strong that if Jim and Elaine were to argue contrary positions with roughly equivalent evidence before a jury of their peers, Jim would have somewhat better odds of winning—with even better odds before a jury of women—simply because of the cultural positioning of men and women. In this simple comparison, Jim benefits from and Elaine is hindered by their respective subjectivities.

Subjectivity, then, is the prior conditions of self-actualization. These conditions are the cultural resources that allow us to be recognized as someone.

These resources both constrain who we can be and enable who we are. Our discussion of subjectivity considers its constituting marks, subject positions, and action routine and then turns to an extended examination of its ethical implications.

PRINCIPAL CONCEPTS ────────────────

We are continually the subject of the other. We necessarily appear in the subject positions that are the cultural resources of the self. These subject positions exist through the complicity of the other and implicate our action in the subjectivity they invoke.

CULTURAL MARKS OF SUBJECTIVITY

Subjectivity is one's cultural and social identity located across the dimensions of difference. These are the dimensions that have been nominated as the organizing principles of the sociocultural structures we enact. Eurobased cultures, for example, are organized in particular ways across color, ethnicity, gender, caste, age, families, and memberships. Whether we approve of it or not, the color of one's skin; one's ethnicity; one's gender; one's socioeconomic position; age; family of birth or marriage; and conferred political, religious, and social memberships play a part in who we can be.

Contrary to the words of the Declaration of Independence, we do not all start equally, and in every opportunity advantage accrues to those culturally favored types. In the United States, for example, top management has been typically occupied by white, Protestant, Republican males of northern European ancestry. Despite the feminist revolution, affirmative action, and the erosion of church membership, this characteristic is still principally true. Not every segment of U.S. society is organized in the manner of *Fortune 500* corporations, but every segment makes use of some hierarchy of subjectivity. There is always an "us" that is somehow privileged.

ENACTING SUBJECTIVITY: MATERIALIZING THE SUBJECT POSITION

One's subjectivity is an assimilated position. By that we mean not only is our subjectivity imposed on us, but also we are socialized into it. Jim is not only male, but he knows how to enact the masculine. (Moral issues arise if he expects the rights and privileges of the masculine or considers it to be the norm.) He writes of a classroom incident:

> I am the instructor in a class called "Teaching the Communication Curriculum." It is aimed at improving the teaching skills of our graduate

students. This afternoon we were sitting around just before class was to start, waiting for the others to arrive. One of the women was talking about the success of the intramural softball team the department plays in. I mentioned that I had signed up to play. "Oh," the woman replied, "can you play?" Her voice didn't rise as a question but stayed level as if a challenge. I said nothing, but my eyes snapped immediately to hers. "No, no," she said, "I meant can you play tomorrow." She flushed, flipped her hair, and put her hand to her neck, "I wasn't asking if you were good or not."

In the instant of her production of the word "play" and my visual response, we put hierarchy and gender on the table. Her vocalization, heard as a challenge by both of us, evoked my reply. My masculine move feminized her. There was no more intentionality than a knee jerk. Our subjectivity is always already there.

The self is of color, or not, young, old, working class, elite, masculine, feminine or of whatever subjectivity by virtue of the typology we culturally enact. Subjectivity is the enactment of culturally produced subject positions, those intersections of the hegemonic, institutionalized, paradigmatic, relational, and practical signs of the self. It is evoked in the self by the way the other acts toward it, and it is invoked by the self in the enactment of self toward other.

In this text, we consistently use race as a cultural boundary marker rather than a genetic state or culture. We reject notions of an essential white or black culture or that skin color is somehow associated with unique human qualities. At the same time, however, we recognize that there are social and cultural practices associated with those boundaries that create the subjectivity of race and cultural memberships by color. Nonetheless, race would disappear if we did not daily enact the practices of race and racism over the marker of color.

Gender, race, ethnicity, age, caste, and the rest, therefore, are not objective facts but practices of subjectivity. In each case we take some condition and essentialize typifying differences through cultural practices. In other words, we take the biological differences of males and females and essentialize (create the essence of) the masculine and feminine subject positions through the means we use to mark and perform these subjectivities. The "we" in these sentences is instructive, because we all do it together. We as members of the cultural community are complicit in the understandings that create our subjectivity in that community. The doctrine of complicity holds that we are all implicated in the accomplishment of this typology. No type is simply a victim; none simply a victimizer. The relationship is a hegemonic one in which these subjectivities participate in their own conditions. Women, for example, will not overcome the dominance of the masculine because they practice the feminine. And men will not end their subjugation to their desire of the feminine because they practice the masculine.

We are unflinchingly advancing a single line of argument in a very contentious area. The reader needs to know that there are many who believe that what we call "cultural practices" are natural or in scientific terms materially real. There are those who believe the relationship between men and women and even between people of different color has been handed down by God. There are those who reject complicity, casting women, for example, solely as victims. There are even those who believe in Utopian solutions to the struggle of subjectivity—sometimes as ravagingly *final* solutions.

Hegemonic complicity supports the postmodern notion that control is not only institutionalized but also fully distributed across cultural members—the celebrated and the muted. We can change leaders, restructure institutions, rewrite laws, but it is our own common practice that enacts the conditions we seek to change. To effect the change we have to change ourselves, meaning to change who we are.

THE SUBJECTIVITY OF ACTION AND DISCOURSE

Action itself concatenates with subjectivity. We have noted that human action is not the result of trial and error. It is not an assemblage of separate acts. It is not a process of accretion. Action is a meaningful unity, a recognizable performance, what Anderson & Meyer (1988) have called the routine. **Action routines** make sensible the acts that compose them, and they put into place the discipline of their performance. Acts are under the governance of the overarching understanding that allows them to be recognized as a component of a routine in the same way the words of this sentence are recognizable as parts of the sentence. Human behavior, then, is understandable within a semiotics of action just as phonemes are understandable within a semiotics of language.

If you want to test the power of subjectivity, try being a "person-out-of-place"—a man wandering the halls of an elementary school, a woman customer in a plumbing contractors supply shop, a young person in a senior residence, a faculty member at a fraternity party. The first response—positive or negative—will be to your cultural identity, your "out-of-place-ness." The merit of your presence will have to be explained.

The action routine is the sign of what is being done. It carries rules of performance and implicates the character of the enactor within those rules. The enactor is necessarily an agent of the routine. Fixing the car, doing the dishes, watching television, writing a paper, having a beer, and so on through the lexicon of action routines all implicate the enactor in the value and qualities of the routine. The person watching television (enacting that routine) has different rights and duties from the person enacting the routine of writing a paper. Easily a parent could be surprised by the claim "I have to do this for school" offered by a child watching television.

We can hear the subjectivity of the routine in the following phrases:

Subordinated: "Too bad you have to do that."

Unauthorized agent: "Why are you doing that?"

Unjustly subordinated: "You shouldn't have to do that."

Gender violation: "That's a man's job."

Incompetent: "You're doing that all wrong."

Character violation: "You actually did that?"

We also experience our subjectivity in our sense of success or failure, closure or collapse, elegance or awkwardness, esteem or shame of the enactment. An action routine has consequences for who we are.

Discourse, similarly, speaks us into place. Here, we can think of discourse as enacted language or language in action. Discourse is always materialized in action, but its intentions are greater than the action can contain (Eco, 1992). One cannot speak like a man in Teamsterville (Philipsen, 1975) unless one can enact a man in Teamsterville. Jim cannot "do" Valley girl speech except in irony, parody, or incompetence. We recognize all too easily the misappropriations of discourse by those not eligible.

We can bring the positioning effects of action and discourse into focus by considering that Elaine is to "give a speech" (enact a recognizable performance of speech-giving). Our first question might be, "What is the character of the agency of her speaking—how is she to be the agent of her speaking?" Elaine cannot just speak. She must speak *as* someone authorized to speak, and she must speak *to* someone (even if only to herself), and she must speak *with* some discursive means. Because of her place in the system of allocation, Elaine has a number of options for *speaking as*. She can speak as wife, mother, assistant vice president, county planner, professor, or book author. She may even manage combinations of these. But each of these speakings will require her to use a particular vocabulary in a particular syntax over particular topics and in specific discourses within some recognizable action. These requirements may be made even more complex by whom she is *speaking to*. It may be impossible, for example, to speak as an assistant vice president to her children.

All of these particulars constitute and reproduce the cultural rules of what one can and cannot do as an agent of action. As an agent she is activated in the framework of her agency. If she is to speak, that is, to produce an action recognizable as giving a speech, she is required to reproduce what is already meaningful in language and action within the venue of the actual speaking. She may be brilliant, engaging, incompetent, inventive, incoherent, or whatever, but always under its terms. She never escapes the cultural framing of her agency, although her action being an improvisation within a particular framework is governed, but not determined by, that framework.

Her agency—her ability to do otherwise—comes from her right to do what is required, the improvisational nature of action, and her participation in the meaningfulness of her action. Jim cannot speak as wife, mother, or assistant vice president. He does not have those choices. Elaine can choose to speak or be silent in each of these.

Once she chooses to speak, she must produce the moment out of the allowed and even the disallowed. She must achieve a voice, a modality of performance. And her performance must be sufficiently competent to enforce the requirement of listening.

Her performance will be one of the many that are recognizable (and every performance is recognizable even if as the unknown), but she must create it out of the resources at hand. Just as the punctuation mark is the only knowable outcome of this sentence just started, so the conclusion of the action is the only known outcome of Elaine's speaking. Her performance, as are all performances, is a locally governed, contingent improvisation that is a partial representation of all that could be done.

Finally, Elaine will participate in the sense-making process that establishes the meaningfulness of her performance. The character and quality of

> **PRINCIPAL CONCEPTS**
>
> One's subjectivity appears in the marks of culturally nominated dif-
> ference, in the enactment of culturally produced subject positions,
> and in the demands of action. Subjectivity is evoked in the way other
> treats self and invoked in the performance of self toward other.

a performance are not inherent. They are interpreted. Elaine participates in
this interpretation. She may do so by providing resources ("Now, you may
be wondering how this is a speech from a vice president . . . "), by supervising ("I'm speaking to you as your mother!"), or even by meeting the expectations of the other. There are no guarantees, but she can readily enlarge the
scope of her agency in her participation in the declaration of what is.

THE ETHICS OF SUBJECTIVITY

The cultural marks, subject positions, and action routines that are the resources of subjectivity are important to us for a number of reasons, but one
of greater moral concern is the fact that subjectivity materializes a differential set of rights, privileges, obligations, enablements, and constraints across
people who would not otherwise be so differentiated. For example, popu-
larly reported U.S. studies (e.g., Faludi, 1991) have indicated that the married man and the unmarried woman are happier than the married woman
and the unmarried man (who is the least happy). They have also shown that
women initiate the majority of divorces. (They initiate this action despite
the fact that one of the largest segments of the working poor is the divorced
woman with children.) The reason for these differences may well be because
marriage, as it is practiced culturally, is a patriarchal institution intended to
advance masculine interests.

Under traditional British and American law, the married woman had
been subjugated to her husband. These laws simply reflected what was and,
according to some, still is culturally practiced. Although the majority of
women work outside the home, they are still responsible for nearly all of the
child care, housework, and nutritional and nurturance needs of the family.
(And in that job outside the home, they get 76 cents on the male dollar.)

Consider this reasonably reliable observation of both rural and suburban
practices: Put a group of men and women in the kitchen at a party and the

division of labor is clear. The women are immediately comfortable to go to work; the men talk (or ask permission to help out and are usually refused). What we see in that division is not some natural law but the subjectivity of gender. Part of the feminine identity is expressed in culturally defined "women's work" and in the control of domestic spaces. The woman who does not help but rather stands with the men, as the Bible story goes, is criticized, and the man who seeks to help is often suspect or unwanted.

Men, of course, are not simply free to be. They are equally as defined culturally as women. Two examples: (a) Men are expected to have an income-producing job and to work at that job for an increasing number of years. Although the majority of women do work outside the home, nearly four times as many women as men choose not to work outside the home. Men typically do not have the same freedom of that choice.[2] (b) There was a tragic story reported locally (*Salt Lake Tribune*, July 23, 1997) of a group out hiking and camping in Utah's red-rock country. The group got caught in rising waters in one of the canyon trails, and a man's daughter was washed away to her death. One of the women of the group commented that he was their leader and had to be strong. "He did not cry. If he had cried we all would have been lost." The man was not permitted to openly grieve his daughter's death. He was culturally prohibited because the safety of the others was seen in his enactment of the masculine.

The following sections offer similar examples of culturally prescribed behavior for race, ethnicity, age, and caste. Each intersection carries with it expectations of the right set of circumstances or the proper thing to do in action implicated by type.

Race

An African-American student writes a paper on the black woman's use of "Uh-huh" as a code to express everything from agreement to derision. She comments that the competent performance of this discourse signals an effective marker of the cultural enactment of race. A nonmember's attempt— even if perfect—can be dismissed as inexpressive, arrogance, or wrongful

---

[2] Nonetheless, choosing not to be in the corporate workforce is becoming an increasingly popular if difficult social position to manage as the rise of support groups for both women and men who choose a domestic life attest (*Salt Lake Tribune*, August 30, 1998, p. E1).

appropriation. It is improper for the nonmember to take what belongs to the membership.

An editor of an international journal reports that he is asked by the journal's governing board to report authorship and reviewers by, among other things, race. He writes that he will not report race because to do so is to participate in the social processes that constitute race. He considers that participation to be unethical in a racially delineated society where one color subjugates another. He argues that there is nothing about the color of one's skin that constitutes the quality of the work. He faces the counterarguments that (a) color does reflect quality because claims about the experiences of color can be authentic or inauthentic by virtue of membership and that (b) those subjugated have a right to document their advancement.

Age

In the parks and playgrounds of our society, a mixed-age game of football carries a different set of sensibilities from an age-cohort game. If a 200-pound, 15-year-old knocks a 120-pound 15-year-old silly, well, it's the latter player's lookout. He shouldn't have been in the game. But if a 200-pound adult flattens a 120-pound boy, the adult has misplayed the game. The boy has a right to be there, and the adult has to account for the difference. No amount of local negotiation will relieve the man of his cultural obligations. The definition of fair play (one's ethical behavior) changes across these situations.

Ethnicity

Ethnicity, or one's cultural heritage, has become reified in the identity politics of higher education's move to cultural diversity. The goal of this move is laudable—greater understanding, respect, and tolerance for one another and a greater sense of self for the culturally different. But the move has the usually unintended consequence of sharpening the tools by which those differences are constituted and maintained. We cannot celebrate an ethnic voice without proclaiming the ethnic difference. That proclamation of difference essentializes an ethnic quality that can become implicated in the processes of subjugation. If we announce the Irish ballad to be superior because of its pathos in adversity, we give comfort to the agents of economic oppression that created that adversity. The Irish (or whatever ethnicity is so distinguished) should suffer so that we can have their culture.

Caste

A friend visiting Kansas writes:

> My cousin looks at me with hard eyes. As boys we used to throw cherry bombs into the water troughs on his father's farm. We fought in the hayloft and rode the old palomino mare bareback together. But that was 40 years ago. Now I'm just some overeducated city type that doesn't understand the political and economic realities of farm life. He is a college graduate who manages a million dollar business, but here he is plain folk and I am not. His wealth is in commodities and land; mine in information and salary. His knowledge is real; mine is from books. We are separated from one another by a sense of social location as powerful as any practiced in India. I'm welcome to visit, of course.

A Return to Gender

Let's end this section by taking up an extended analysis of the masculine and feminine in the gendered venues of the classroom that prepare us for the gendered venues of the workplace.

In our classrooms we enculturate masculine authority by a variety of actual practices, including calling on boys more often and giving them greater access to the tools of technology. On balance, we expect Joe to give the answer, to run the video camera, to be at the computer keyboard. Classrooms become masculine venues (just as domestic service is a feminine venue). As we move up through elementary education, girls are subtly muted, denied, and redirected. By college, men appropriate technology, sometimes taking it right out of the hands of their women colleagues who are often all too happy to give it up. And even at the highest levels of graduate school, women complain that their answers are not as accepted or that they are silenced by masculine voices. In these practices, we establish the masculine right and obligation to *engage* in the classroom—and by extension in the workplace—and the feminine right and obligation to *withdraw*. The masculine reads the situation as "I should speak." The feminine reads the situation as "He should speak and I should listen."

Gendered venues effectively clarify the roles of men and women, but they are also considered unfair because they inappropriately limit an individual's opportunity to act. In the classroom it is more difficult for the feminine to speak, more difficult for the masculine to listen. Men can be considered "sensitive" when they listen, women "tough" when they speak. Each of these somewhat questionable characterizations occurs not because of some individual quality but because of the violation of gender expectations. The woman and the man each becomes something beyond their control in the action.

This inequity is heightened when what each is given to do has differential rewards attached to it. Generally, it is considered more valuable to speak than to listen. To enact the masculine is to deny the feminine equal access to the reward system. When men and women are positioned by masculine and feminine models, men get more of what we consider rewarding—higher grades, better positions, more money. On the other hand, working against type can be punishing as we have seen. The result is that men are rewarded by the masculine in masculine venues and at risk for enacting the feminine. Women are limited by the feminine in masculine venues and at risk for enacting the masculine.

We can readily agree that this inequity is unethical. The solution is more difficult. Perhaps the solution is not for men to put themselves at risk by adopting the feminine, but for men and women together to render the classroom and the workplace gender neutral—a place where neither the masculine nor the feminine has control in and of itself. Yet, that means that the feminine has to give up what control it has in order to attempt a reconstruction of the organizational reality. Pretty scary stuff when one is on the underside of the power equation to begin with. Further, gender neutrality is apparently not easily reached. In one of our consultancies, an organization went from 80 percent male managers to 80 percent female managers in 5 years. It's easy to read this as a payback period, a win for the feminine. The salary totals for the female managers, however, represented a substantial savings for the organization compared to those paid to the male managers. Generally, the increase of women in a corporate sector has meant the reduction of wage costs for the firm. That's pretty scary too, if you're a man looking for advancement.

This analysis is not a license to do nothing. It is a recognition that local solutions to cultural inequities require constant supervision and management. Like a levee in a flood, the pressure against is constant and there is always leakage to be policed.

Equally to the point is that men and women in the classroom and in the workplace are positioned by their gender. Our consultancy notes provide a good example. A woman vice president (VP) in charge of product sales found it necessary to rein in one of her midline managers who was aggressively expanding his territory beyond what she felt the company could serve. The two had come into the company together. He had worked in research and development (R&D) for a number of years before coming back onto the management track. She had entered management early and rose to her present position, which most agreed—and as she was acutely aware—was as high as she could go, given her limited international experience and national exposure, neither of which had been provided for by the company. He, on the other hand, had an international reputation as an R&D man and in that position had regularly taken management to task for their bureaucratic ways with sometimes brilliant and usually biting arguments.

In her planning, the VP decided that this meeting was not to be a discussion. The VP wanted to get her points across—basically a woodshedding—and get him out of her office before he could argue or make appeals to their common history. The meeting started cordially enough with the usual inquiries and coffee service. Then the VP started her statement. Two sentences in the manager interrupted her saying, "I don't understand what you mean." The VP's face turned angry, "You listen to me!" she started and went on for several sentences detailing her displeasure. "I honestly just didn't understand you," he meekly protested after she paused. "Well, you would have had you let me finish," she snapped. After the meeting, the manager's boss who had been there with him asked him, "What did you do? I've never seen her act like that." "I don't know," the manager replied, "it must be something in our history."

From subsequent discussions the following analysis emerged. The VP had read the interruption as a masculine challenge to a woman in a position of control. "He acts like that in meetings all the time," she commented. She felt that she had to respond forcefully to show that she could exercise that control and that she deserved the full respect of her position. The manager for his part had misread the situation thinking that it was two old friends coming together to solve a mutual problem. His question about understanding was not about what was being said but about what was being done. "Why was she talking to me like that?" Each in their way had positioned the other in a particular subjectivity and interpreted the action in the terms of that subjectivity.

One should not discount the VP's concern. A female division manager related the following, "I'm the only female manager in my company. When we meet in the manager meetings, I often feel as if my colleagues just don't understand me. I would like some women colleagues at the table. Earlier today I was making a point I felt was important. When one of the other managers interrupted me and said, 'Chris, you don't really mean that. What you mean is. . . .' He then went on to state his position. I was silenced by him. He didn't try to understand my point, and I lost the political momentum to try to express it again. I felt angry with him but was unable to do anything about it without appearing out of control."

> ## PRINCIPAL CONCEPTS
>
> Subjectivity materializes a differential set of rights, privileges, obliga-
> tions, enablements, and constraints according to the cultural defini-
> tions of a subject position. The acting agent is marked by the cultural
> signs of difference, always occupies some subject position, and carries
> the performance responsibilities of the action in which the self is ma-
> terialized. The self encounters its agency under those marks, from
> that position, and within that action. There is, therefore, no "objec-
> tive" place from which to act morally or to judge moral actions.

The case shows the complexity of relational analysis. The VP and the
manager are superior and subordinate, friends and cohorts. They have a
decade long history of being colleagues. They are now hierarchically framed
by the organizing processes that confer control. They also carry the symbols
of the masculine and the feminine. All of this has to be managed in the interaction. In this case it was not done well. She determined that he was acting like a man because she was a woman. And he discovered that she was
acting like a boss when he expected a collaborator.

Are there ethical responsibilities here? There are, both personal and professional. The vice president has acted toward the manager as if he behaves
toward women in organizational status roles differently from men in those
same roles, subordinating them through masculine practices that include
interrupting and controlling conversations. If, however, he interrupts everybody which may be the case given her comment about his performance in
meetings, then she has no basis to make the charge. He may be rude or just
passionate in discussion, but he does not discriminate. If he is only rude or
passionate, and she acts as if he discriminates, then she does him a great
wrong.

Note that she can get just as angry about his rudeness, but sexual discrimination is an actionable event. It is a far more serious complaint with
career-ending implications. If he discriminates, she has a professional responsibility to determine if he discriminates against women who are his
subordinates because the company is at risk from his actions. If he does not
discriminate, his interruptions being instrumental, she has both a personal
and professional responsibility to revise her image of and her actions toward the manager.

And what of the manager? His ethical issues are of somewhat lesser
standing because his authority to act is less. He did enact what could be

read as the classic masculine interruption. In doing so, he provided the material for the VP's interpretation. He presumably unintentionally misled the VP. There is some reason to hold him responsible for that misdirection and some reason for not. His enactment would not have been an interruption if the action had been between colleagues as those moments of give and take are not considered interruptions in those sorts of conversations. His prior belief about the meeting releases him here. The VP, of course, had determined the action to be a statement and not a conversation. While the manager was neither part of nor introduced to this determination by the VP, he should have been prepared for it because the conferred control relationship provides for it. Here he is trapped in his prior belief about the meeting and becomes responsible for misleading the VP.

Finally, in offenses of this kind, the analyst has to examine both the giving and the taking. The manager was *not* prepared to *give offense* (by enacting a masculine interruption), although ostensibly he did so. The VP, however, *was* prepared to *take offense*. She positioned him "as a man" and herself "as a woman in harm's way." She treats him "as a man" because she will not be treated "as a woman." The rest, as they say, is history.

SUBJECTIVITY: A SUMMARY

In this section we have been looking at the second grand contributor to the self: its subjectivity. Subjectivity is a cultural production. It is the cultural meanings symbolized in the marks of identity. To put it in our own odd language, the female instrument (body) carries the mark of the cultural subjectivity of the feminine. Any subjectivity symbol is as coherent and consistent as the cultural practices that produce it. When those practices are unified and singularly dominant, that quality of the self is equally clear. But when those practices are contested, contradictory, multiple, or dissonant, the symbol is equally uncertain. (We are, for example, changing the subjectivity of age as the number of people over 50 overtakes people under 18.)

As coconspirators in these cultural practices, we both react to and enact these symbols of subjectivity. We react to a person's symbolic values. We enact those values of which we are the mark. And we consider it deceptive when individuals enact symbols of which they are not the mark. (It is illegal in some states to cross-dress, acting outside one's racial boundary is called "passing," and we are all cautioned to "act our age.") That is one of the ways by which we ensure that the symbols retain their value. One's subjectivity, then, is both evoked and invoked. It is evoked by the action of others toward the self and can be invoked by the self in its presentation to others. The VP read the masculine in the manager and considered it inappropriate to the situation. Jim invoked the masculine to respond to the heard challenge. That invocation evoked a feminine reply.

The **evocation/invocation** principle tells us that subjectivities are not essences but actions. Jim is not a man because he is male but because he uses his maleness in "acting like a man." He had no choice in his male birth, but he has choices in enacting his manhood. The evocation/invocation principle also tells us that while identity always carries the signs of the cultural value of the self, those signs are not always all equally in play at any moment. The VP framed the action in the cultural values of gender; the manager framed the action in the cultural values of friends. Each put into play a different set of signs of the subjective.

Finally, cultural meanings, of which the subjective is one set, are the product of durable, pervasive, recurring, social practices. That they are long-lasting, widespread, regularly repeated, and conjointly enacted establishes both their power to state the meaning of a sign and their slowness to change. Cultural signs are distributed institutionally through our media, schools, churches, workplaces, neighborhoods, and homes. If a sign is to have cultural significance, all competent members have to be able to practice that interpretation, according to their membership.

That each is knowledgeable of these texts means that the institutions of distribution (media, schools, churches, etc.) will necessarily use them in their narratives. The examples, scenarios, and stories of this textbook, for example, have to be true to cultural meanings, even while examining or questioning them. If they did not, you, dear reader, would reject them as being false or impossible. The recursive practice of what-cultural-members-know is what-cultural-institutions-distribute creates a flat spiral of meaning moving in time.

That spiral helps explain why each of us is not in control of her or his self. We start with the fact that the self is a composite and there is nowhere a unity that could exercise a singular control of who we are and of what we do. But further, there is a vast effort beyond each of us that sets the terms by which we can be known. We enter those terms in the subjectivity of the self. Those terms carry complex and detailed instructions as to who we are and how we should act. Any moral analysis of action has to take up the invoked and evoked subjectivities of the acting self.

TABLE 5.1   **Systems of Subjectivity**

TYPE	SOURCE	PRODUCTION	VOCATIVES
Enacted Marks of Différance	Physical, biological, societal, identity differences	Cultural location	Calls forth race, gender, age, ethnicity, caste, memberships
Subject Position	Hegemonies, apparatuses, paradigmatic figures— hero, virgin, manager, student, etc	Privileges and prohibitions of discourse and action	Calls forth presumptions of authority, competence, significance, control, rights, and duties
Action Routines and Discourses	Semiotic systems of action and language use, disciplines, syntagms	Intentions and governances of actional and discursive texts	Calls forth the acting agent as a representative of actional and discursive forms

Table 5.1 summarizes the systems of subjectivity that we have discussed, giving the type of system, its sources of influence, the product of its enactment and the vocatives—invocations and evocations—that are possible in its results.

THE SELF AS ORGANIZATIONAL AGENT

We have been looking at the conditions by which the self comes into existence. Far from a central unity, we have argued for a composite of identity and subjectivity. In identity we examined the persistent material, biological, semiotic, and relational condition—the instrument of the body; its material, biological, and semiotic configurations; our naturalized practices of being in the world; our reflexive images; and our durable memberships. In subjectivity we looked at the cultural meanings of the signs of identity—how the instrument, practices, images, and memberships are located in consequential **hierarchies.** We now bring that self into the organization. As the self steps into the frame of the organization, it loses none of its identity or subjectivity but acquires another lamination of each. The instrument will change as the disciplines of the organization write on the body as it adapts to the conditions of its use, adding or losing mass, acquiring new muscle memories, and so on.

PRINCIPAL CONCEPTS

The self is a construction of identity and subjectivity that materializes the acting agent. Our organizational memberships participate in that construction and provide the meaningful frame in which its actions make sense.

We will acquire new practices and methods of sensemaking. We will achieve membership and be organized in relation to others, both of which reflect new images to us. And, the practices of organizational members will generate additional meanings by which our identity will have value.

There being no simple unity to transport from one location to another, the self is always materialized situationally. The keyboardist here is framed by the task of writing. What is good work—proper action—and what is not is set by the task. You, the reader, are framed by the task of reading and, perhaps, more specifically in studying, as in being a student. Your obligations are different from the keyboardist's obligations. Who we are—writer and reader—and what we ought to do—write well and read well—appear in the situation of our writing and reading.

There are, however, no natural laws of good writing or good reading. There are rules for each, of course, enunciated by those authorized to speak and supervised by those to whom we attribute the power. You can trace some of the rules of good student reading by going into the used book section of any college bookstore. There archived in the underlines, marks, and notations left by previous owners are the indicators of how to do that job.

It is the same in each of our situations. We step into the frame of some organizing process and we become worker, parent, child, student, whatever is called for. Our conscience and actions are sensible and justified by that frame. A recent study by the Ethics Officers Association—a group of corporate managers charged with business ethics—reported that almost half of the workers surveyed admitted to violations of common ethics in their work (*USA Today*, April 3, 1997, p. 1). Many of those violations dealt with relations with customers: misleading, lying, overcharging, overselling, and the like. Now how is it possible that I as a salesperson would lie to you as a customer, but would carefully explain to you as a neighbor what you can expect from "those salespeople?" The next chapter takes up the answer to that question by looking at the organization as a domain of agency—an arena of choice and moral standards.

TRANSITIONS

In this chapter we have completed the position of the self as a composite of identity and subjectivity that is situationally materialized. We offered this position in contrast to the traditional view of the self as a fully formed unity of intellect and will that moves unmarked from context to context. In examining the situated self, we took an introductory look at the role organizing processes play in providing a framework for the appearance of the self. We then moved to constitutive forces of identity—those durable and persisting elements that begin with the body and include our naturalized practices, practiced images, and long-term relationships. We discovered that identity carries many of the marks of our subjectivity, including gender, race, ethnicity, age, caste, and so forth, that are the long-standing, pervasive, recurring, and conjoint practices that produce consequential hierarchies of cultural value. Our subjectivity, we argued, was not an essence, but an enactment that often makes use of the material and biological conditions of the body. This enactment is invoked by the self or evoked by others in the situational contingencies of the presentation of self. Our conclusion took up the framing action of organizing as we moved the self as material and practiced identity and potential and enacted subjectivity into the organizational domain of agency—that field of the organizational agent in action.

CASE STUDY

Joe is a student badly in need of money, and he has been complaining to Jenna, a student in one of his classes, about being broke, especially with the holidays coming up. Luckily, Jenna is a supervisor in a local business owned by her father. Jenna offers Joe a temporary job during the holidays. She will pay him $8.50 an hour. Joe quickly agrees.

The job was to last 3 weeks, and after the first week, Jenna paid Joe in cash at the agreed upon $8.50 per hour. This continued the second week as well, but during the third week, Jenna came to Joe and told him, if asked, he should tell everyone he was making $12.00 per hour.

1. Joe wondered about being paid in cash, and wondered about the discrepancy between $12.00 and $8.50 per hour. Is there an ethical problem? What are his options?
2. Joe is asked how much he is making. Is Joe morally obligated to lie for Jenna? Explain in detail the ethical implications.
3. What are the problems caused by a friendship in this case? Does it make Joe's position different from that of working for a stranger? Should Joe talk with Jenna about the pay difference, the request to lie, or the method of cash payment?

6

ORGANIZING AS A DOMAIN OF AGENCY

PREVIEW

Coming off of our investigation of the self as the acting agent, this chapter puts that self into action within organizational domains of agency. We begin by considering the ideas of the will, its agency, and its action in choice. We then return to the study of organizations, investigating the means by which organizing produces a domain of agency and thereby of action. Among those means we find memberships and relationships, hierarchies of action and language, implication and complicity, location, and thematics. In the end we find the self as a standpoint within this domain of agency, positioned and made meaningful with much reduced freedom and autonomy, executing choices that make sense within this domain.

Agency has been defined as the ability to do otherwise. Agency is an absolute requirement for ethics. If we do not have the ability to do otherwise, if we have no choice of action, then there can be no question about the morality of one's action. Consequently if there is to be the study of ethics at all, there has to be genuine choice.

THE PROBLEM OF CHOICE

Although a simple concept, the principle of choice has had a central and contentious role in human theory. But the principle of genuine choice runs contrary to modernist thought, with its emphasis on control and closure and its bias toward determinism. The modernist wants a prior condition for every action, an explanation *for* (not simply an explanation *of*) everything. The orthodox modernist would reject the possibility of agency when defined as an immanent action, an uncaused cause, a nondetermined act of the will. For the modernist, choice is simply a finite set of probabilities with the determining elements falling into place at the moment of action. It only looks like choice, but the action is actually contained in a set of determinants.

THE WILL

Postmodern theorists have reintroduced the will into all forms of scholarship, including science. But it is not the Cartesian faculty of right action—that rational intellect pursuing objective choices—or a religious view of free agency that depends on total freedom and autonomy. We start with the idea of unfocused desire, a continuous longing, the inability of closure, the living sense of incompleteness. Desire continually moves us to action, and action calls the self into existence. Desire achieves focus and the willful act ensues situationally, in the moment, location, and meaningful frame of action. The **will,** then, is the product and enactment of desire. It is the act of the will that answers William James's (1890) question "What must be true in order to act?" thereby establishing the capacity for action.[1] The will answers the prod of desire by constituting what is true out of the resources provided by the situation. The situation is a limiting but indeterminant text. It must be read, and it provides for a variety of interpretations. Both the reading and the interpreting are conducted by the situated self—the thoroughly colonized acting agent discussed in Chapters 4 and 5. To act, an interpretation must be put into belief. That is the function of the will.

Postmodernists are insistent that (a) reality is not self-evident, although it may appear obvious to a particular standpoint, and (b) valid, conflicting interpretations of the same situation can be produced. Both the standpoint and the interpretation collectively held to be true are a function of social processes, not of an independent reality.

---

[1] William James (1842–1910) spoke of the will to believe as the necessity of action. One must choose to believe that something is true before that person can act. He uses the example of a climber being on a cliff, and only the belief that she can reach safety will make the action required to reach safety possible.

| **PRINCIPAL CONCEPTS** —————————————————— |

> Agency depends on an undetermined act of the will. The will is the product and enactment of desire. It is an act of the will that creates a belief in the true. To act we must first believe.

We now have the elements necessary to put together the working concept of agency that will guide this chapter. What we are aiming at is a concept of agency that is well between the poles of Cartesian free agency and modernist determinism. We want an agency that retains immanence (the ability to act as an uncaused cause) because without immanence the possibility of authentic choice disappears. On the other hand, we do not want a concept of agency that depends on an essentialist, self-governing self. We have already rejected this Enlightenment notion of the self in our examination of identity and subjectivity. It is the contingent self, situated and colonized, and not the "Enlightenment I" that wills.

If an act has a prior cause, then it is a consequence, not a choice. If choice exists then at some point in the continuing succession of "Why's?" the answer has to be "Because I could." This requirement does not rule out intentional action. It simply moves the choice back to the point of the formation of the intention. It also does not rule out determined behavior (an act caused by something else). It simply does not call that behavior a choice behavior (see Rasch, 1995). Finally, the fact that we can nearly always produce some sort of reason for our action celebrates our ability to tell stories and does not indicate that we actually have no choices.

THE RELATIONSHIP BETWEEN KNOWLEDGE AND AGENCY

To achieve those goals, we begin by considering knowledge and agency as an interrelated duality rather than as independent faculties. The argument for independence of knowledge and agency was a centered effort of British empiricism. For the British seventeenth century empiricists, knowledge was a function of our experience of a directly accessible and independent material reality and our reflection upon that experience.[2] With proper

---

[2] The list of these empiricist philosophers usually includes Francis Bacon (1561–1626), Thomas Hobbes (1588–1679), John Locke (1632–1704), and David Hume (1711–1776).

training and application, both our experiencing and our reflecting could be made foundationally true. Accurate observation and right thinking would invariably lead us to the truth. Many still hold this proposition to be true, and, indeed, it is the cultural foundation of science.

It has been a project of the last half of the twentieth century to undermine this proposition. The work has been to show that (a) observation is accurate only under the set of terms that provides both for the observation and its accuracy and would be inaccurate from another set of terms; and that (b) right reason depends on some set of prior beliefs to make it right. This work pulls the independent and secure foundation right out from under knowledge and rests it instead on belief. Knowledge is socially constructed in collective action—not revealed in authority or discovered in material objects. There is no set of conditions outside of the knowledge claim itself that foundationally validates that claim. Knowledge is knowledge because of our action as a knowing subject, because of what we do, and is validated in what can be done.[3] Knowledge and agency are fully interlaced.

What this rather arcane argument from epistemology means for us in our work to develop a useful concept of agency is that the acting agent is both a standpoint in knowledge rather than a passive conduit for reality and a representative of the beliefs that make knowledge possible. As a standpoint the agent is positioned by the action frame of sense making to hold certain things to be true—to know certain things—and as a representative, the agent is directed to engage the situation in certain ways—to observe in a particular manner. What the agent knows, what the agent can learn, what the agent can consider as possible are all infiltrated by the situation.

This infiltration establishes the boundaries of our choices by establishing what is true about the situation, what resources and alternatives for action are available, and what criteria of right and wrong should be brought to bear. It does not determine the outcome. The situation provides the domain of agency, the time, place, conditions—but not the performance—of action. The situation must still be read and interpreted, and the will to action taken. The possible remains. As long as the possible remains, there can be a "preferred possible," and that possibility raises once again the moral question.

---

[3] The present argument for the social construction of knowledge (sometimes called the social construction of reality) references the writings of Karl Marx, Wilhelm Dilthey, Friedrich Nietzsche, Max Weber, and Karl Mannheim among others. Its current development is usually marked by the works of Berger and Luckmann (1966) and Kuhn (1972).

PRINCIPAL CONCEPTS

Knowledge and agency are fully interlaced. Knowledge is knowledge because of our action as a knowing subject and is validated in what can be done. What the agent knows, what the agent can learn and accept as true, and what the agent can consider as possible lines of action are all infiltrated by the situation.

What we have done in this very condensed argument is to establish that we do have authentic choices, but the terms of those choices are established by the circumstances in which they appear. We have inscribed the freedom and autonomy necessary for choice—topics discussed in the next section— in the conditions of acting.

THE PREREQUISITES OF CHOICE

We end this analysis of agency by considering the elements of choice—freedom and autonomy—as we put the acting agent into a domain of agency.

Freedom

If we are to choose, we must have something from which to choose. **Freedom,** in its simplest definition, means the availability of authentic alternatives of action.[4] An authentic alternative is one that can be recognized from the standpoint of the self and that can be put into action within the domain of agency in which the self is then operating. Organizing, in its processes of ordered relationships, communication strategies, and coordinated activity, necessarily reduces freedom by limiting the alternatives of action. One cannot be a working woman or man without some, usually substantial, loss of freedom. Once the ontological decision is made to be a working woman—to be that doctor, lawyer, merchant chief—then one's freedom is defined within the terms of that existence. It is a mere trick of argument that allows us to turn this existence on and off, even though there are many practical ways in which such an existence can be actualized.

---

[4] Michel Foucault is quoted as saying, "Freedom is the ontological condition of ethics" (Rabinow, 1994, p. xxv). See also Scott, C., 1990.

Our "working self" is not our only self, of course. We are likely to be partners and possibly parents. We also create enclaves of "alternative existences" through nights out, hobbies, and parallel careers where for the moment we are no longer immediately governed by the rules of one definition of who we are. These alternatives increase some sense of overall freedom, but in any given moment one simply exchanges one set of constraints for another.

On the other hand, organizing also increases freedom by creating alternatives of action. Whatever I must do to maintain organizational membership, nonmembers ordinarily cannot do. That distinction may be trivial or even unwanted, but often organizational membership provides a substantial number of highly valued alternatives, as well as the means (e.g., a good salary) to attain others. Organizing increases alternatives as a product of joint action. (I am free to watch television because I live in a society that has advanced beyond subsistence living.) At the same time the membership (and not the member) retains control over these alternatives and couples access to this greater freedom with obligation. The individual must discipline her or his actions to acquire the rights of greater action. The freedom constituted in a domain of agency, then, is understood through an analysis of rights and obligations. There is no inherently free state of existence. That is, at no time is one free to simply do anything. There are always boundaries on what can be done and costs attached to what is done.

Autonomy

Autonomy is described as self-governance. It is the ability to determine for oneself the rightness or wrongness of an action. In a multiple choice test, a student has the freedom to select any of the answers but has little or no autonomy to determine which is right or wrong. That determination is located in the control of the teacher and/ or in the nomination of what is true. In this case, competence is defined by the standard of the item on the test. The only way that the student can be competent is to select the right answer. To select the wrong answer is to be incompetent or, perhaps, deliberately rebellious. The self is an enactment, the culturally recognized instrument in action. One is what one does. In this case the student has the freedom to choose an alternative but not the autonomy to be.

But that principle does not mean that we will not struggle against the imposition of the standard by which we will be known. Common classroom arguments about "the right answer" attest to this struggle for the control of meaning. Often these arguments attempt to claim student competence by

---

PRINCIPAL CONCEPTS

Freedom derives from the availability of authentic alternatives of action. An authentic alternative is one that can be both recognized from the standpoint of the self and put into action with the domain of agency in which the self is then operating. Autonomy is the ability to determine for oneself the rightness or wrongness of an action. It involves self-governance. Organizing can increase or decrease both freedom and autonomy by changing the alternatives of action and the agent's self-governance.

---

demonstrating teacher incompetence. (In practice what sometimes happens is that the teacher will discover that his or her best students are answering an item differently than he or she would. The teacher then begins to reconsider what is the right answer and will sometimes announce to the class that both the student selection and the teacher's right answer are to be deemed correct. Competence is maintained on all sides.)

Here is another example of the relationship between freedom and autonomy: Abusive relationships often develop around a system that provides freedom (i.e., "You don't have to do anything for my birthday.") but then denies autonomy by punishing the alternative chosen (i.e., "You didn't cook my favorite dinner?"). In ordinary situations, these are called "secret tests." In the often deadly relationships of child and spouse abuse, freedom without autonomy can be life-threatening.

Choice: Agency in Action

Existence requires action; freedom provides alternatives of action; autonomy allows authentic choice. The analysis of autonomy within a domain of agency involves the level and detail of supervision, the intricacy and surety of standards and their application, and the certainty of the consequences. Action for which there is a strict protocol (no freedom), constant supervision, and instant punishment for deviation (no local autonomy) creates an automaton self with little authentic choice. (There is also little opportunity for invention or innovation and heightened likelihoods of inattention, resistance, and sabotage.) Many jobs on assembly lines, retail checkout stations, food lines, and office pools, approach these conditions (as well as, unfortunately, more than one classroom).

One cashier offered this description of her work:

> The job isn't half bad when we're busy. I can do the scanning [checking products out on the optical scanner] without thinking. So, except for the occasional interruption by a bag that won't scan or something that isn't in the computer, I'm free to think of other things, watch the craziness of the people who shop here, or just talk to all the people as they come through. It's only when things are slow that I feel trapped, chained to this register. We aren't allowed to read or do anything useful, but I sneak a book under the shelf here to keep me occupied.

This cashier is more than the machine her labor requires. She has greater resources than those provided by the job. She offers a multilayer expression of the self and, consequently, functions in more than one domain of agency. Outside the boundaries of job requirements, she has a level of freedom and autonomy that allows authentic choice, although still constrained by her location and by the degree of her acceptance of (or overt submission to) work rules. Let's run a short scenario to exemplify this complexity further.

Jean, our cashier, works in a major home improvement store that stocks nearly everything from raw materials to tools for the home owner. From putting on an addition, to building a fence, to hanging a picture, they've got it at Home Improvements. Jean greets her next customer:

> "Hi, welcome to Home Improvements. Did you find everything you needed?"
>
> "Well, no, but I was able to substitute for what I wanted."
>
> "So," as she scans the SKU number off a bundle of shingles and counts the bundles in the stack, "it looks like we'll be doing some roofing today." She picks up a tool and asks, "Now, what is this thing?"
>
> "Huh, oh that's a roofing hammer."
>
> "OK, come on, explain it to me."
>
> "Damn, I didn't know there was going to be a test. Let's see, this knife blade lets you cut the shingle. You adjust these knobs to set the amount of exposure on the face of the shingle. And, drive the nail in with, you know, the hammer itself. You can pretty much do the whole roof with this one tool."
>
> "Hey, thanks. Cash or charge?"

The cashier's opening line is required by the protocol of the position. (*Greet the customer in a friendly manner and ask if they found everything.*) If the customer had not found everything the cashier is supposed to check the computer inventory and send a runner to get the product if it shows up in stock. But there are never enough runners; the ones at work are too busy chasing down prices and SKU numbers that aren't in the computer. Few customers want to hang around once they've made it to the checkout, and it lowers the performance record of the cashier anyway.

What Jean does with the answer is to gauge what else she can do with the customer. A pleasant answer tempts her to engage the person in talk about what they are doing, or their lives, or as we saw, how something works. She says that people are amazing in the things they'll attempt, the intimacy they will share, or how often they buy stuff they don't have a clue about. If management knew of her systematic practices they would likely object, maybe even fire her. But as long as it remains below their attention, everything's ok. The risk for Jean is acceptable because the return makes the job tolerable.

The rather unenlightened management of this store operates from the capitalist "golden rule," the person who owns the gold makes the rules. Cashier work protocols appear to have been set up by those without floor experience and then inadequately tested for effectiveness. Cashiers would actually be punished by performance statistics (average of units scanned over time) if they implemented the rules. Jean makes this poorly designed system work for her in the free play space provided by the threshold of supervision where some freedom emerges and she gains some autonomy.

Are there ethical issues involved here? That depends on what level and from what vantage you engage this scenario. Certainly there are ethical systems that would criticize the *quid pro quo* market economy management that develops stultifying jobs with poverty level pay. There are also ethical systems that would position Jean's failure to follow work rules as being false to her word. Both management and Jean, however, would find these separate arguments as irrelevant, even foolish. Why? Because from their standpoints, their performances are perfectly reasonable. They are the practical and necessary solutions to being a manager and to being a cashier. It is at the much earlier point where there is the choice of being a manager or a cashier inside an oppressive domain that the ethical issues of these practical performances need to be addressed.

We see, then, that ethics comes into play at points when and where there is authentic choice. Authentic choice gains its authentication from what is possible at the point of the action. For the worker caught up in the responsibilities of multiple obligations in an unserving sociopolitical system there may be no choice but to continue as an exploitative manager or opportunistic cashier because the risks of failing one's other obligations are too high. Choice—the freedom to enact it and the autonomy to govern it—is the key to our analysis of ethical behavior.

PRINCIPAL CONCEPTS

An ethical analysis is found within the boundaries of agency in action. These boundaries are set by the available freedom and autonomy of action. Some individuals may have actions limited through strict supervision and punishment for deviation. Individuals with more organizational freedom and autonomy may have the opportunity to think through a protocol and make a choice other than the one developed by the organization. This agency in action could prove harmful for the organization, the individual, both, or neither.

A couple of comments might be helpful here. We recognize that a rejection of objectivity includes our own arguments. We look to their utility to support them. As to objects and actions being declared, to a bottom-line western rancher a tree simply uses resources needed for grazing, so the practice of chaining (pulling an anchor chain between two bulldozers) is justified reclamation. For the conservationist it is the wanton destruction of a natural setting.

We need to also point out that our ethical judgments are equally inscribed in the conditions under which we make them. In doing so, we deny the possibility of an objective, final analysis based on a categorical morality. Any effort to find fault, place blame, or condemn another must necessarily be conducted from some standpoint, that is, some position that holds certain things to be true and declares objects and actions to be of one sort rather than another. Our neighborly salesperson of Chapter 5 gets the sale by any means acceptable to his organization and warns the neighbor of what is acceptable. In doing so, she steps from one standpoint to another. Policy and practice in corporations are nearly always in some conflict. They represent different standpoints. Practice gets the work done. Policy remains to punish those we wish to punish. To declare someone wrong implicates our own set of beliefs as to what is right. Our ethical analysis informs us as much about ourselves as about the other. It is sometimes dangerous knowledge.

Constituting the Domain of Agency

The concept of a domain of agency is based on the premise that action—the meaningful things that we do—attains its meaningfulness within the venues

PRINCIPAL CONCEPTS

The possibility of ethics depends on the possibility of authentic choice, which in turn depends on the conditions of freedom and autonomy that are available when the choices are made. Ethical judgments are themselves an action dependent upon the choice the moral judge makes. Ethical analysis and judgment, therefore, are equally dependent on the conditions of their enactment.

and processes of its performance.[5] There is no categorical definition of an action that is independent of the doing. The meaningfulness of action emerges in the performance. Speaking in a certain way in the classroom is called teaching. Speaking in the same way at a party is called boorish. The behavior has not changed but the action has. The action has changed because of the shift of venue and process. The "same" behavior is made meaningful in action in different ways within the two conditions. We would say that the classroom and the party are different domains of agency.

A domain of agency, then, is an arena of action. It is a social location where objects, acts, and discourses are provided or denied states of meaningfulness. A No. 2 pencil is just a pencil at home, but it is the only proper instrument for taking a machine scored test in the classroom, and it is a poor substitute—a mark of the amateur—on a framer's construction site. It may always be all right to hug your friends at a party, but such an act, even if fully innocent, may constitute part of the basis for a sexual harassment suit at the workplace. And one cannot speak as a leader unless authorized to speak as a leader. (Students, for example, do not ordinarily confer validity on the academic discourse of other students in the classroom. For that speech to be valid, it has to be confirmed by the instructor.)

A domain of agency is a sense-making frame that establishes many of the prior conditions of knowledge and belief and the ongoing conditions of freedom and autonomy under which choice can be practiced. Contained in those conditions are (a) the alternatives we have for enacting, (b) many of the

---

[5] Much of the work in this section has been informed by continental, poststructuralist argument, notably in the works of Bourdieu, de Certeau, Foucault, and Lyotard. It also draws on the principles of discursive psychology (Edwards & Potter, 1992) and **social constructionism** (Harré, 1986). Its central location, however, is in **social action theory** that traces its lineage from Weber to Mead to Schutz and includes Goffman and Giddens.

PRINCIPAL CONCEPTS

The domain of agency is the arena of action. It is a social location where objects, acts, and discourses are provided or denied particular states of meaningfulness. Organizations create domains of action that are always domains of agency.

---

consequences of the enactment, (c) the criteria by which we judge the value of the action, and (d) the means and methods of performing the choice.

When an ethnographer (one who studies cultural domains of action), for example, steps into a new domain, what she sees is people in action. Her line of inquiry often follows this order:

1. "What are you doing?" allows the ethnographer to find out the name of the activity so that she can reference it to its alternatives.
2. "Why are you doing it?" seeks the instrumentality of the action, its consequential outcome.
3. "Is it going well?" and "Will it turn out all right?" are questions about the criteria by which the quality of the action is judged.
4. "How does all this get done?" probes the methods and means of the action.

The good ethnographer never presumes to know the answer to these questions, because the answers are held in the understanding of the competent membership not in some material, absolute, or literal quality inherent in the objects, behavior, or discourse.

One of the principal activities of organizing is the creation of domains of action, and domains of action are always domains of agency because agency appears in action when choice is a necessary part of enactment. Organizing, then, does substantially more than give us a title in a relationship (friend, spouse, parent, child) or in a job. Organizing orders relationships and, therefore, meaningfulness, and in that ordering provides for the action and, therefore, the conditions of agency of organizational members.[6] The

---

[6] This premise parallels Giddens's (1979, 1984) duality of structure in which action generates structure that provides for action. Neither is prior. Here action generates understanding that provides for action. Our language is slightly different because of his sociological and our semiotic leanings, but the idea (presuming that we, your authors, properly understand Giddens's structure) appears to be the same.

ordering processes of organizing provide a number of elements that constitute the domain of agency. The ones we explore here are memberships and relationships, hierarchies of action and discourse, location, and thematics.

Constituting the Domain of Agency: Memberships and Relationships

This is the third time we have taken up memberships and relationships. In Chapters 4 and 5 we considered them as resources in the construction of the self. Here we want to consider how the boundaries that designate *member/ nonmember* or *in a relationship or not* are made visible through attached sets of expectations, enablements, and constraints of discourse and action.

Memberships and relationships are meaningful to the extent that they are consequential—to the extent that they make a difference in what we expect of ourselves and what we actually say and do. Linda may declare herself to be Carla's friend, but if she obligates herself to no more than that declaration, she is not much of a friend.

Organizing processes order us by memberships and relationships. John is or is not a member of a particular work group. Lars stands in relation to Ingrid as subordinate to superior. Pamela is assigned as Ingrid's secretary. Each designation opens up a field of action that in turn is a domain of agency. Take John for example. He belongs to a work group charged with developing the quality control standards for the manufacture of a new line of lawn mowers. Because this product is to have worldwide distribution, various national safety requirements have to be accommodated in a way that still keeps the line profitable—no simple task. To be the perfect member, John would have to have expert knowledge of (a) quality control both on an industry wide and locally enacted basis, (b) the specific product safety requirements as they relate to quality control, and (c) the means and costs of manufacture.

That's a daunting list. It is unlikely that any one person could fulfill it which is exactly why a group is appointed to the task. Each member is expected to bring some part of the expertise that is needed to complete the work.

Group processes routinely involve struggle and negotiation. John has to find his place, establish his presence, ensure that his voice is heard, *make* his contribution. His group membership sets this field of action. John will exercise his agency in the choices he makes within that field. He could, for example, simply opt out, sit shyly silent on the edges of the action. He could achieve success by merely "being a member" of a successful work group. He also runs the risk of being reported as "worthless."

This claim of an ethical requirement assumes a society with a reasonably open opportunity for work. If John's opportunities are unreasonably constrained by a coercive or inequitable social system, then his obligations are less and may in fact be reversed. If the dominant interests in a society establish conditions that allow the subordinated only limited access or deliberately reduced pay, "doing a good job" only supports the inequitable system. There is an obligation to resist, and resistance may include doing no more than opportunity or pay provides.

John's ethical responsibilities are to do the work for which he is being paid. "The work" is defined by his membership, and, as we see, it is much more than writing standards. John has a moral obligation to be a *contributing* member, to both manage the group process and to be competent as a quality control engineer. But suppose John is genuinely suppressed by the competitiveness of other members. Perhaps he comes from a cultural milieu where competitive argument was not practiced. Would his obligation to contribute be discharged by this circumstance? Or would he need to resign his position or find another way to do the job?

John's membership is consequential. It establishes expectations for his performance; it enables certain forms of actions; and it both puts in place and reveals constraints and limitations. In John's case he is expected to contribute to the writing of quality control standards; the membership enables competitive argument as the method and constrains other forms of consensus building. John's means of contributing are, thereby limited. He has to get in there and argue his points or find another way.

Organizations also provide us with what might be called **vested relationships.** They are the relational forms that enact one's title. It is a relationship vested by a conferred status. For example, a deputy sheriff pulls you over for a traffic violation. You notice that she is a deputy of Madison county and you are in Jefferson. The relationship between you and her immediately changes (be careful here, stay respectful, state laws vary, get competent legal advice, etc.). It changes because she no longer fits the category of a law enforcement officer. She is outside the boundary of her conferred status of that membership, and, therefore, the expected relationship changes.

Lars cocreates Ingrid's authority by acting as a subordinate. Ingrid's authority is contained, at that moment, in the manner of Lars's enactment.

Should Lars refuse to follow, Ingrid has some choices. She can fire him, but only if others grant her that authority. She can ignore him and work only with those who do choose to follow, but only if Lars agrees to be ignored and the others accept the strategy. Ingrid's authority is not in her title, but in the enacted relationships that are her entitlement. An organizational chart symbolizes lines of command. The actual meaning of command, however, will be demonstrated in the relational practices among those diagrammed.

An organizational chart is part of an organizing process that provides for and orders the relationship among organizational members. It informs the members of what is appropriate and what is risky in action and discourse toward another. A medical friend writes:

> We have the usual medical hierarchy in our shop with the docs holding the top hand and fighting among themselves over who is better, but I was deeply embarrassed by the action our administrator took against a staffer who is a patient relations specialist. The staffer is a feisty woman who has battled cancer, crippling arthritis, and tragic injuries. She knows firsthand the occasional callous mistreatment we medical types can provide. She gets additional evidence almost daily as she handles the complaints of patients, solving problems, getting things done right that we doctors should have done in the first place. She does her job well, but perhaps because she does and perhaps because she sees all too well our fallibility, she treated the docs as if she and they were equals. Some grumbled about it, but I enjoyed it. She and I would banter together. We called each other by our first names. When the new administrator came on board, she made the staffer write an open letter to the whole shop, apologizing for "correcting" the doctors (who, of course, make no mistakes) and for not calling them by their proper title. It was an insistence on privilege by an already overprivileged class. The administrator was a woman, whose actions repeated the oft said stereotype that women superiors are not supportive of women subordinates. My shame was in my silence.

Our medical friend believes she has behaved unethically in not picking up the cause of the staffer and righting the wrong of the staffer's subjugation. What silenced the doctor? A partial answer lies in the relationships in which the physician participates. She has organizationally defined relationships with the administrator, her fellow physicians, and the staffer. The administrator has power over certain communal resources but is subordinate to the physician on medical issues. It is likely that the physician has personal friends among her colleagues, maybe among even those who complained.

PRINCIPAL CONCEPTS ──────────────────

Memberships and relationships are meaningful to the extent that they make a difference in what we expect of ourselves and what we actually say and do. Organizing processes order us through memberships and relationships. Each position opens up a field of action/agency. The ethical character of our action will occur within that field.

She has a personal connection to the staffer, but it is unlikely that she is her friend, in the sense of doing things together and providing for one another.

If the physician takes up the cause of the staffer—something she feels is right but has not been asked to do—she implicates all these relationships. She takes on the administrator in an arena where the administrator has authority and the physician does not. Her actions would be critical of her colleagues and possibly her friends. The staffer may even ask why she is causing trouble, using the staffer's circumstance to pursue her own "do-gooder" agenda.

The deliberate humiliation of the staffer appears to be wrong, but the corrective actions that could be taken by the physician do not appear to be right. She is positioned by a nexus of relationships that prevent her from having a clear course of action. They define her domain of agency by defining the consequences of her action. In those consequences, the potential damage of her action is greater than the possible benefit. She has good justification in being silent, offering personal support to the staffer, and biding her time for a better opportunity.

Constituting the Domain of Agency: Hierarchies of Action and Language

The central mark of the human condition has been the collective achievement of the semiotic systems of language and action. Our positioning within these systems constitute who we can be, how we are to act, and the moral consequences of both. We take up the system of action first.

Action

Action is the meaningful things we do, like going to work, writing a paper, making love, stealing a dollar. Action integrates behavior into connected skeins of acts that form a complete activity statement just as graphemes are integrated into words that form a sentence. A man lazing in a hammock is challenged by his partner, "I thought you were going to paint the deck!" Despite his protestations that he is in the "building energy phase of painting" no one believes he is painting the deck. His behavior simply does not make sense under the rubric of that action.

The reason we know that he is not actually painting the deck is because we understand the language—or in more precise terms, the semiotics—of action. We do not each invent what we do or build it up through trial and error. Instead, we are each born into a preexisting action system that we model and reproduce. An action, then, is behavior with coherence that conveys the significance of the acts that comprise it.

Action has the same semiotic qualities as language. It depends on a huge collective effort to make possible the actions we enact, just as language depends on a huge collective effort to provide the signs and syntax that allow us to craft sentences and to enter into discourse. Action, then, is not an invention of something new but an improvisation on what is already known.[7]

Just as language distributes itself across discourses, action distributes itself across routines. Consequential memberships—memberships that affect who we are— have distinctive ways of speaking and acting. In action we say that such memberships have emblematic routines. What one does and does not do is part of the mark of membership. (Documenting those marks is part of the analytic responsibility for an organizational scholar.) In these emblematic routines, memberships typically confer differential rights and obligations of action on their members. They create membership fields of action.

A **membership field of action** involves (a) routines (action signs, the meaningful things that can be done) and their improvisational performance; (b) the declarations, bids, calls, acceptances, rejections, denials, deferrals, suppressions, redirections, innovations, and failed and fragmented enactments of and for action (these describe the processes of action); (c) the resources, times, and places of enactment (action is a material performance requiring time, space, and means); (d) the reproduction of significance (it must be maintained as a sign of what is being done); and (e) the management of meaning (it has to be collectively validated.)

---

[7] For a quick review of these social action principles, see the Preface of this text; for a more extensive review, see Schoening and Anderson (1995).

The consequence of action is understood in its competence (the right to action and the quality level of its performance), modality (its paradigmatic value—sincerity, irony, humor), and effectiveness (recognizability, necessity of engagement). Note that the consequence we are talking about here is not its instrumentality—not that people get to work, finish a paper, have sex, or get a dollar richer. The consequence of action as action is that it can be known by what it claims to be. The consequence of your action is that we have to account for it in what it signifies. A colleague offers this episode by way of explanation:

> I was walking downtown in the tourist section by the Square [the enclave of historic buildings in Salt Lake City known as Temple Square] and this disheveled guy is doing "tour guide." He is pointing out the buildings and replicating the tone and character, but none of the facts that the actual tour guides use. Most people hurried on by, but I stood and watched. He was oblivious.

How did our observer know that the man's actions were inauthentic? They failed the first test—competence. The man displayed none of the emblems of authority to enact temple tour guide and the quality of performance, while right-on in some respects, was inappropriate in others. Given the failure of competence, the modality has to be that of imitation. Finally it fails in effectiveness. Although its form is recognizable as "tour guide," it is not engaged as "tour guide." Our observer is not under the governance of that performance. He does not have to treat the man as a tour guide. He can stand and watch without obligation.

Let's review by bringing all of the elements to bear. The man ostensibly attempted to enact the action sign of "tour guide." He made a bid that we would read his action as such by simulating the form in what was a failed performance. The time and place were adequate, but he lacked the resources (proper clothes, grooming, badges, deportment). He reproduced the significance of "tour guide" (we can acknowledge that sign), but that was not the sign of what was being done. And finally, given that he was denied the authority of his performance, he could not manage the meaning others would make of it.

The importance of the concept of action in the study of ethics is twofold. First, no one can do whatever, whenever. Action has requirements of domain, authority, ability, time, place, means, and the concurrence and complicity of others. Second, action is a text, not an empirical fact. It is not literal but must be interpreted and that interpretation must proceed from

> **PRINCIPAL CONCEPTS** ——————————
>
> Action is the sign of what is being done. Action is judged in its competence, modality, and demand to be recognized. Hierarchies of action place us in the authentic practices of everyday life. They do not form moral imperatives but create the conditions in which ethical action can be taken.

some standpoint. What an action is, is a declaration, and our culpability stems from that declaration.

These two consequences of the notion of action take us out of the reach of moral imperatives and plunge us into the authentic practices of everyday life. They do not release us from our ethical responsibilities, but they clarify them: Each of us can do something in every place, and the more powerfully we do what we can do, the more we manage its declaration. Who, what, when, where, and how are all in play in every choice of action.

Discourse

Discourse, as we have said, is any extended language use that is recognizable as its type and does work according to its type. A discursive type has a distinctive vocabulary-in-use; typical phrases; and more importantly, encodes a particular standpoint on reality. For example, legal discourse, up until very recently, coded women as "weaker," as persons "to be protected," not to be exposed to the harsh realities in which men functioned. This language guided court decisions in particular cases and denied equality to women. As another example, the discursive patterns that describe higher education generally encode a retail store model: Students *pick up* a few credits; professors *deliver* information. Education is something you *get* and *have*. It is a *commodity*.

Discourse is used metonymically—a fragment invokes the whole. For example, in a teen talk Sunday magazine column, a 14-year-old boy invoked all of patriarchal discourse by informing girls that "We are guys, we can do whatever we want whenever we want to [in the company of girls]" (*Parade*, May 19, 1997, p. 26). The boy will certainly find his claim tested, but the fact that he can say it as an authentic statement and that we can recognize the conditions of its cultural truth establishes the connection to the underlying social practices that provide for it. It is not just any sentence, but is a

> ## PRINCIPAL CONCEPTS
>
> Discourse is any extended language use. Discourses are particular
> forms of language use that order, represent, or constitute particular
> understanding of reality. A discursive performance is judged in its au-
> thority, voice, and significance.

sentence from a culture that has different rules of speaking and acting for
males and females.

Discursive power is seen in authority (the right to speak and the quality
of the speaking), voice (the cultural location of the speaking), and significance (the necessity to listen).[8] These elements parallel the competence,
modality, and effectiveness of action. The authority of a discursive performance begins with the conferred rights of speaking. Reported as a white
male from Texas, the quoted boy carries nearly all of the cultural marks—
being middle aged and wealthy would complete the set—of authority to enact patriarchal speech. That authority has to be competently performed. A
corporate memo, for example, has to have the appropriate form and be
grammatically correct with proper spelling to execute its full authority.

The voice of discourse is its cultural location in turn defined by its time,
place, and conditions of presentation. Medical discourse in an American
Medical Association journal is authentic (it may be disputed or even condemned but it is still authentic.); medical discourse on a television drama is
mimicry.

Finally, the significance of discourse—as in the significance of action—
is not in its immediate instrumentality, not in what is said, but in its force
as discourse, in requiring us to listen inside its **frame of meaning.** The
Texas boy's quotation has discursive significance, not because of its claims
about what boys can do, but because of its representation of **patriarchy.**

As with action, the rights and obligations of discourse are differentially
distributed across constituted selves, their relationships and memberships.
One cannot say just anything anywhere. Traditionally structured corporations, for example, routinely suppress lower order employees from speaking

---

[8] It is the common convention to use "speech" and its forms as the marker for all forms of discursive communication.

authoritatively on topics reserved for management. Such employees are denied access to the discussions, not given rights to distribute materials, are refused information, and given no decision-making power even in conditions where they have the expert knowledge of actual practice. So clear are these boundaries, that asking them to speak would not even be considered. Speaking up within those conditions is very risky. The usual case of whistleblowers, reviled as trouble makers, castigated as disloyal, and often fired, is instructive.

Hierarchies

In our medical friend's story, the staffer spoke and acted like a doctor in her working relationships with the physicians. In doing so, she crossed a hierarchical boundary of discourse and action. One of the means of organizational ordering is in the conferring and denying of ways of saying and doing. In our staffer's case, the expectation was that she would be deferential and indirect. Given an order that needed to be signed, it would not be expected that she would personally confront the physician with a simple "sign this" command. Rather the form would be sent indirectly to a mail box with a request, "Please sign on the tagged lines and return to Ruthie (note first name, diminutive) as soon as possible."

Part of the way in which we define children is by what they are required and allowed to do. Generally those are age-related gateways. We have school, curfews, bedtimes, and chores according to age. We become "old enough" to stay home alone, to wear make-up, to date, to drive a car, to vote, to buy a beer. As we move through those gateways, we struggle with new privileges, new responsibilities, new forms of relationships, new ethical requirements. In many cultural texts, being of age, having a job, yet living at home and not paying rent, enacts an anachronistic form of a child's privilege and a parent's dominion. Both can be questioned as breaches of ethics.

Age is not the only difference by which we organize families, birth order counts and creates its own relational environment. The eldest is often expected to supervise, protect, and cater to the youngest. In traditionally gendered households, girls contribute meaningfully in household work well before boys, who may never be required to contribute at the same level.

Families offer a good place to examine discursive hierarchies. As parents we have different standards of truth for what we say to our children and different standards of credibility that we attach to what they say. We expect to lie to them and for them to lie to us, although we don't call it lying—a.k.a.

PRINCIPAL CONCEPTS

Hierarchies define practical rights and duties according to such social constructions as age, gender, ethnicity, caste, even birth order. New ethical responsibilities often accompany one moving through the gateway of one hierarchy to another.

holiday magic, protecting their youth, "they don't know the difference," "soon," "maybe," and "Yes, we will go to Disneyland." We even acknowledge that children tell the unvarnished truth ("out of the mouths of babes"), but then we are not supposed to attach the same consequences to that truth, as if it were unfairly gained.[9] Families tightly control who can speak what and where with authority.

Societal practices patrol discursive subjectivities in much the same manner as families do its members. Subjectivities are made meaningful by what the self in that subjectivity is privileged or prohibited from saying and doing. If there is no consequential difference, there is no subjectivity. Ethical questions, of course, abound in this distribution. Consider these deliberately provocative statements: "You guys get to have 40 percent of your inner city males involved in the legal system (under arrest, indictment, incarceration, or parole supervision) while we, who won't live in the inner city unless it has been gentrified, have to be the predominant population of the nation's law schools." "You have to put yourself at risk through diets, eating disorders, body augmentation, while we have to get paid more." "You get to be shot at in ground combat, while we have to be safe." "You get to live under the viaduct, but cannot speak on your own behalf, while we, who mow the grass, have to speak for you."

Implication and Complicity in Discourse and Action

The ethical burden of these statements is that first, they are true; second, they are the result of social practices; and third, those practices implicate all

---

[9] An additional example comes from Art Linkletter of *Kids Say the Darndest Things* fame. He reports that network censors never cut any language spoken by a child even though the same language spoken by an adult would have been censored (*Oprah*, May 15, 1997).

PRINCIPAL CONCEPTS

The structures of action and discourse are the means by which power and resources are distributed in a society. We are each implicated in those structures and to the extent that we do not actively resist them, we are complicit in their effectivity. Implication and complicity requires us to examine how our actions participate in the inequities of those structures. Ethically we are required to consider what is possible—to say and do what we can when it can be said and done.

of us and are possible by the complicity of each of us. The ethical relief comes from an analysis of our domain of agency. In the face of immorality, ethics requires no more of us than to do what we can where we are ordinarily able. It does not require heroics. Here's an example. A recent newspaper account reported that minority admissions to the University of California Berkeley law school were down an incredible 81 percent following the adoption of a so-called race neutral admissions policy (*Salt Lake Tribune*, May 15, 1997, p. A14).

It is our judgment that such policies are not neutral at all but simply pass through the inequities constituted by the racial practices of our society—those practices that ensure that the first sentence in our dramatic list will be true. Here is a case where the University of California regents have chosen the less ethical path because they could be a positive force and chose not to. We, on the other hand, cannot make that choice, but we can write about it.

The ethical principles being illustrated here are called *implication and complicity*. Implication derives from the postmodern notions of the distribution of cultural power across the practices of cultural members. We are each implicated in these power distributions. There are no bystanders. Further these distributions owe their existence to the complicity of all members as we knowingly or unknowingly reproduce these distributions in our everyday practices. These two notions establish the claim that among competent members there are certainly inequalities, but there is no innocence. Perpetrator and victim alike participate knowingly in their relationship. (An example often used is that there can be no thieves without a doctrine of private property. Or in college sports, there can be no recruiting violations without NCAA rules.) Complicity and implication require us to examine how our actions, even as victim, but particularly as beneficiary, participate in these inequalities. They require us to consider what is possible—to say and do what we can, when it can be said and done.

CONSTITUTING THE DOMAIN OF AGENCY: LOCATION

We began this chapter with an example of how lecturing in a classroom is called teaching, but the same sort of lecturing at a party is considered boorish. The difference in the activities is in their location. These different locations may or may not also be different physical places. The party may be in the same room as the class but the place has been reframed as the location of the party. Location, then, is the stage for action. It becomes that stage through some nomination that may be as explicit as a party invitation or as implicit as the happenstance of an impromptu enactment. As a stage location, it is defined by material and semiotic boundaries and contains material and semiotic resources for the performances to be enacted. Again those boundaries and resources may clearly be put in place or established by just what is at hand.

Part of the organizing process is the creation of environments that support the activities of the organization. Schools create classrooms, libraries, cafeterias, gymnasiums, etc., in order to more efficiently accomplish the tasks associated with schooling. Or consider the office pool where clerical and other staff service personnel are located in a common office in rows of desks. The environment of such pools clearly states what is expected from those who work there. The open environment offers constant surveillance and instant access to any individual. Workers are unlikely to be considered reliably self-governing according to terms most favorable to the corporation. No worker has special status and no work to be done has to be specially protected. Those conditions still have to be enacted, and they can be counteracted, but the location provides more for such impersonal connections than for any other.

Locations, then, carry instructions concerning the action they support. Walk into most any manager's office and the manager sits behind a desk, positioned to block the visitor's access to the person behind it. The visitor, however, sits in front of the desk, open, vulnerable. A particular relationship and practice of control are archived in the environment. If Katherine is the manager and John is the visitor, Katherine can invoke that control by simply motioning for John to sit down. She can speak against that relationship by rising, stepping from behind the desk and sitting next to John in one of the side chairs. John is immediately positioned by the environment and

Katherine's use of it. That positioning sets the conditions for what is appropriate for John to say and do.

On the other hand, if John is the president and Katherine a subordinate, Katherine is constrained by the location. She would be foolish to remain behind the desk as such action would invoke an inappropriate signal. In this case, John puts Katherine at some risk because she cannot make ordinary use of her location. He needs to provide clear direction as to what is to be done.

These issues move from questions of good manners to questions of ethics according to the consequential use of the meanings or resources locations provide. If Katherine is a mediator and John one of the clients in mediation, his separate and unexpected visit to Katherine's office is an ethical breach. He cannot be there because it creates an appearance of impropriety. It creates the vision of a relationship beyond that of mediator and client even if none other exists.

One of the rules for ethical communicative practices in the pursuit of what is true is that all members of the communicative process must have equal access to the authority, means, and significance of communication. Each person must be considered equally legitimate, authentic, and competent before any speaking is done (Apel, 1980; Habermas, 1990). Quite often location precludes this possibility and is deliberately used to do so. Ordinarily a teacher in a classroom has higher standing on academic topics than does a student; a physician in a clinic, higher standing on medical issues. This higher standing places a greater ethical burden on the teacher, physician, or whomever benefits from the site to be true in their topics when speaking from location, from the stage of their power.

A change of location changes both expertise and its ethical responsibility. The same question asked on the street rather than in the classroom or clinic does not impose the same burden. For example, Abraham Verghese, a physician writing in *The New Yorker* (September 22, 1997; pp. 76–89) reports his own distrust of an emergency diagnosis. He made this diagnosis while attending to a young woman who collapsed while he was talking to her outside a mall. He noted his reaction "as if the knowledge I possessed within the hospital were suspect when it had to be applied on the street" (p. 78). The location had disempowered him.

Location, as we see, can change the character of relationships and both close down and open up possibilities for action. A teacher can't lecture at a party, appropriately. If one person invites the other into her apartment after a dinner engagement, it offers possibilities that did not exist before the

PRINCIPAL CONCEPTS

As a cultural, social, situational, and physical space, location creates boundaries of thinking, acting, and being. Location can influence the conditions of ethical communication and is one of the means by which organizing practices distribute resources of action and discourse. One's ethical analysis must account for location.

invitation. The other has been invited into a location where more intimate actions can be appropriate. The location provides these possibilities. Control of location gives one a form of control of the other in terms of identity in memberships, the rights and obligations of relationships, and the possibilities of action. We have talked about location as a physical space, but it is equally a cultural, social, and situational space as well. Location is a boundary that enables and disables ways of thinking, acting, and being. Its force of division, its power of separation, allows contradiction in those ways of thinking, acting, and being to flourish.

CONSTITUTING THE DOMAIN OF AGENCY: THEMATICS

Thematics are the organizational descriptions and stories members tell themselves in order to help make sense of what they do. In the telling of the stories, they create the conditions that make them true. The themes are not passive reflections of what is, but active elements in creating the organizational culture (Bormann, 1982; Brown, 1990; Emmott, 1997; Mumby, 1987). If the stories in an organization are mostly about sales coups and rarely about service, one can expect the customer to be positioned in a particular way and the acceptable sales strategies to be considerably aggressive. If the family stories are about successful Arthur and Robert the failure, then Arthur and Robert are likely to be treated differently by the family members. If members of the board of a volunteer organization tell stories of the "crazy volunteers" they work with, they move to separate themselves (as "better" typically) from the very individuals they claim to be. These stories are the coproduction of organizational members (Anderson, R., 1997; Beach, 1998). Tellers and listeners both know the broad lines of development. They each have a history with the "facts of the case." How the story is told—who becomes the hero, the villain, the goat—does specific work that is recognizable in the micromanagement of the recounting. Stories do both institutional and personal work.

In his book, *Images of the Organization*, Gareth Morgan discusses some 27 different metaphors used to describe corporate organizations from "all bottom line" to "just like a family." Again, metaphors such as these are more than simple images. They contain the truths by which we enact the very organization that is described. As Lakoff and Johnson (1988) say, they are metaphors we live by. Consider being hired into a company where the personnel officer tells each hire, "This is a very competitive industry. People who work for us have to work harder, longer, and smarter. In return you'll make more money and go further, faster." Presuming that this discourse is enacted throughout the company, the terms of what are positive and negative, right and wrong, reward and punishment are pretty clear. You're not going to be home at 5:15 working for this company.

In the scholarship of corporate studies, we have a well-rehearsed catalogue of organizational metaphors. Pick up almost any introductory organizational communication or management book, and you will find some combination of frameworks that might include Weberian bureaucracy (Weber, 1909/1947); scientific management (Taylor, 1911); human relations movement (Mayo 1945); systems theory (von Bertalanffy, 1968); contingency management (Mintzberg, 1973); and in the most recent texts, organizational culture (Deal & Kennedy, 1982); feminism (Hegelsen, 1990); autopoiesis (Luhmann, 1990); and strategic empowerment (Conrad, 1994).[10] Each of these frameworks provides a particular way of thinking about organizing and organizational elements. They have their own vocabularies and critical issues.

The thematic of scientific management, for example, is concerned about division of labor, precise job definitions, and clear standards of work. It presumes that what has to be done can be rationally mapped out and that contingencies will be few and manageable within the defined structure. Structure, in fact, is the critical issue. Lines of authority and responsibility are defined by where you are in the structure. Many large organizations make an elaborate display of this rational-bureaucracy form (Perrow, 1986).

This bureaucratic thematic can be contrasted with the empowerment movement with its emphasis on team management and very local decision making. Here, instead of narrow specialization, managers and workers are

---

[10] Generally, a litany of several of these frameworks is repeated in the first or second chapter as a ramp-up to whatever is the focus of the particular text (see for example, Kreps, 1986).

supposed to have broad knowledge of the whole process with special interests and skills within it. Everybody can do everything although each is better at something. No one has exclusive authority over any part of the work. Or so the story goes.

What makes it interesting for an organizational communication scholar is that in actual organizations all of these frameworks may be in play simultaneously. We see, for example, Total Quality Management (TQM) introducing work teams, called **Quality Circles,** with an emphasis on cooperative effort and power sharing into a fully bureaucratized corporation. What often results is separate laminations of empowerment and hierarchical authority. On one level employees might do the TQM hustle recognizing full well that no authentic control has been transferred.

A national do-it-yourself firm, which has since gone bankrupt, used a central inventory control policy that was designed, in principle, to have the last item of a particular stock being sold as the new supply was being brought in. What actually happened was that an "average restocking cycle" developed that had most stores completely sold out of what was in demand most of the time. Customer complaints reflected this condition. A form of TQM was brought in to deal, not with the inventory problem, but with the complaints. What was needed was a reallocation of authority; what was given was public relations training. Customer dissatisfaction was so high that at the bankruptcy sale, people reported their pleasure at seeing the firm go out of business.

So, are the workers who attend their Quality Circles (QCs) knowing that—in this example—such groups are simply another bureaucratic device to discipline and control rather than authentic power sharing living a lie? One analysis might conclude that no, they are being paid to enact a performance whose functional meaning is under the control of a separate layer of authority. It is just another activity required by the corporation like taking lunch at noon. The bureaucratic thematic of hierarchical authority is the "truth" of the matter. The employees are under no ethical compulsion to do real work in their QCs.

Thematic structures in organizations, from families, to firms, to social groups and on, are usually multiple, complex, containing both complementary and competing themes. Flying back from some venue, your keyboardist was sitting next to a fellow who was editing his company's mission statement. The draft read in part:

> [X Company] will never break the trust of a customer in pursuit of business. Truthfulness, honesty, fairness, and integrity are the four cornerstones of the company. No exceptions will be tolerated.

Someone on the distribution list had circled the word "never" and put a big question mark by it.

These complex thematic structures mean that the grounds for action can radically shift. One may hear in one corporate meeting about the need for customer service and in another meeting of the same corporation about the need to bring a product with known defects immediately to market. The two themes of long-term service and short-term profit make sense in their separate locations and may actually provide for one another, as long as nothing goes wrong. But if something goes wrong—buggy products result in lowered sales or service costs threaten profits—the themes are clearly brought into contrast.

It is also common that action one takes under one thematic governance gets evaluated under another. What may be ordinary business practices in one domain of sense making may be indictable offenses in another. We have all experienced the circumstances of a relational partner "misinterpreting" something we did or said as being of one sort of thing while we intended another. The practical fact is that the performance of any sign, whether in action or discourse, always entails risk because the action or discourse has to be interpreted from some standpoint. It does not read itself. Anything you say or do can be held against you. All it takes is the interpretive grounds—the themes of what is true—to do it. What becomes paramount, then, is who gets to tell the story of what was done. Thematics intersect with the practices of the action and discursive sign. Those who have the authority to competently speak and act control the conditions by which discourse and action are evaluated. Ethicists who declare some standard to be true are attempting that control.

In the strategies of action, we are both opportunist and victim of the potential shifting grounds of interpretation. We are equally ready to take advantage of some happy reading of what we are about as we are to defend ourselves against an unhappy one. Thematic diversity allows for a greater diversity of supported action. But it also heightens the likelihood of value conflict and a clash over who is doing right and who is not. Organizationally thematic diversity has to be managed to reduce uncertainty and risk through either member or issue consensus (Martin, 1993). People seek safety by "getting on the same page."

In this manner, organizing thematics represent local, "virtues of the mind" (Zagzebski, 1996)—right ways of thinking in a particular arena of action. They are, therefore, not just interesting stories, but stories that have consequences, that tell us right from wrong. They tell us what is and what is not, what can and cannot be, what can be spoken and what cannot be said.

As with all "right ways of thinking" thematics both reveal and conceal. While they nominate what is true, they exnominate—conceal, disguise, gloss over—the means by which the true is made true as well as suppress what could also be true. They create the familiar, the "of course it's true," by settling matters before they are brought up.

We have an ethnographic site in a "Mobile Watch" district. Mobile Watch is part of community policing practices and has "civilians," certified through police training programs, patrolling their neighborhoods serving the surveillance and intelligence needs of the police. An expoliceman described the police business as one in which "the customer was always wrong." Mobile Watch members, as they become more experienced—better schooled actually—most often reflect that theme, but some newer members take a more cautious view. What becomes contentious, then, among Mobile Watch members are the reportable signs of wrong doing. Are kids hanging around a convenience store something to be noted? Is a person of color ever out of place? What about men in cars in a park at night? Is that van moving slowly late at night, looking for an address or cruising for an unattended house or automobile? The discussions in the Mobile Watch car reflect the struggle for understanding what is going on. They show that people have different stories to explain why those kids, that person of color, those men, that van are where they are. When a call is made after one of these discussions, everyone on the watch listens to the nuances of the dispatcher's response for vindication of their interpretation.

What makes reality construction processes even more complex is that we know each other's stories. A Mobile Watch car, with its big, light-reflecting signs on each side of the car, parked across from a group of kids at a convenience store becomes the basis of delinquent action by kids who wouldn't have thought of doing so until "challenged" by the car's presence and the clear signal of distrust. We see a similar response to corporate policy statements intended to control a workforce in the name of what is right.

We hear the thematics of right and wrong action from our earliest moments to our last: From kindergarten rules of sharing, cleaning up, and fair play; to the playing field's exhortations of effort, courage, and sacrifice; to the classroom's call for concentration and commitment; to workplace mottoes of a day's work for a day's pay, work smarter, and ask for the close; to the wish of old age of a long life but a quick death. At the same time the countertexts are equally in play: Get there first for the best snack; learn how to take out the better player; buy a term paper from any number of companies; take what you can before the company takes you; "I hope I have a stroke and you

> ## PRINCIPAL CONCEPTS
>
> Thematics are the descriptions and stories that organizing practices develop, rehearse, and reproduce. The themes are not passive reflections of what is, but active elements in creating the organization. Thematic performance has a recognizable method and history and do both institutional and personal work.

have to take care of me for 20 years." All these themes and counterthemes are there to justify or condemn whatever we do.[11]

Constituting the Domain of Agency: Summary

Table 6.1 collects the four constituting elements that we have considered, indicating the constitution action of the element and the effect of that constitution on domain of agency. Although Table 6.1 is neatly partitioned, it is important to remember that no element is independent. A relationship, for example, has a priority of discourse and action, requires a location for enactment, and is governed by cultural and local themes. It is the combined influences that erase doubt within a domain of agency to create the conditions of certainty and moral probity.

The Standpoint: Analyzing the Acting Agent

The boundary-setting devices explored here establish the domain of agency, which itself is a bounded space of action in which the acting agent can appear. That acting agent in that space is called a standpoint. The standpoint is the point of departure in any ethics analysis and is the topic we take up next.

At the end of Chapter 5, we brought our analysis of the self as the product of identity and subjectivity down to the concept of an agent—both in the sense of one who initiates and in the sense of one who represents—that is materialized situationally. We now have the tools to understand what it

---

[11] One can see these texts in action in nightly television newscasts and daily papers where contending interests try to put into place one interpretation of events over an alternate.

TABLE 6.1 **Domain of Agency**

ELEMENT	ACTION	EFFECT
Memberships and Relationships	Establish terms of obligation, membership boundaries	Reveals identity of place, expectations (terms of moral action and judgment), enablements, and constraints of action
Hierarchies of Discourse and Action	Priorities of the intentions and governances of discourse and action	Sets the competence, modality, and effectiveness of action and the authority, voice, and significance of discourse
Locations	Creation of the environments of action and discourse in semiotic boundaries and resources	Offers the potential of place for the appearance of paradigmatic subjects and syntagmatic lines of action
Thematics	Invocation of narratives of the true and the moral	Assigns the operating domains of knowledge and moral judgment for proposed and completed action

means to be "materialized situationally." The self cannot be an agent except in some domain of agency. The particular memberships, relationships, hierarchical positioning, location, and operational thematics of that domain represent the most proximate conditions under which the self will appear. Each of us is potentially an agent of many different sorts—parent, child, student, teacher. Who we are and what is legitimate action depends on the domain of agency in which lies our arena of performance.

There are a number of choices to be made to locate oneself along these issues (Chapter 2 of this text; Anderson, 1996). One can start with a consideration of the nature of reality, our observation of it, and our claims about it. The Cartesian self is a transcendental, functionally equivalent form that chooses an objective reality, referentially addressable and directly representable in claim and that disallows individual differences and local conditions to enter into the analysis except as conditional defects. We the authors do not require you the readers to take any particular position but do hope that you will articulate one for yourself and do attempt to hold ourselves to the difficult standard that all of it is in doubt.

PRINCIPAL CONCEPTS

Each of us is an acting agent who materializes an ontological, epistemological, praxeological, and axiological position. This is the standpoint of the action agent. Our standpoint establishes who we are. What is legitimate action for this standpoint depends on its domain of agency in its arena of performance.

In epistemology and ethics, this contingent materialization of the agent is called a standpoint. The concept of the standpoint is one of two alternatives we can take to position the person as the accountable agent of action. As we saw in Chapter 4, the other appears in most traditional analysis where some form of the Cartesian self is used to position the person within the analysis. There is a single standard of a "good person thinking well." That good person thinking well will always reach the same conclusion given the same facts of the case except when some temporary defect prevents the right operation of the mind and the will. This standard cannot fail; only individuals can fail.

It is clear to postmodern analysis that such a standard is fully under the control of those who argue for it. It has but a formal and no actual expression. For our part, we have argued that the self is a multilayered, ongoing construction. As such, it represents a reference point—a standpoint—from which what is known and unknown, sound and unsound can be recognized. The concept of the standpoint allows us to consider justification, what is legitimate in the true and the good, from actual rather than transcendental agents.

A standpoint (Figure 6.1), then, is the position occupied by the acting agent—the person—in ontological (the nature of being, answers the question of who), epistemological (the nature of knowledge, addresses what is known), praxeological (the character of action, answers the question of how it is done), and axiological (the nature of value, addresses the qualities of right and wrong) space. A standpoint analysis of some acting agent requires us, the analysts, to find the answers to *who knowing what acted in what manner according to what set of values.* Further, the application of standpoint analysis entails a reflexive turn to conduct a standpoint analysis on ourselves as the acting agent as we render judgment on the actions of others. Who is the judging self, what is known and of what quality is the

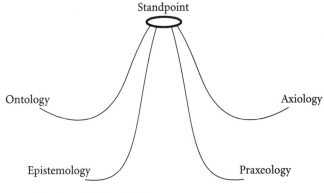

FIGURE 6.1   **Topology of a Standpoint.**

knowledge, what is the action of judging, and from what set of values is that action taken. Each analysis should teach us more about ourselves than about the other. Chapter 7 provides a scenario to demonstrate this sort of standpoint analysis.

SUMMARY

In this chapter we looked at the role of agency in the study of ethics. We found that agency is the counter of determinant behavior. It is the ability to do otherwise. At the beginning of the chapter we discovered that ethics involves the presence of genuine choice. A genuine choice is an act of choosing that has immanence, that has its explanation for doing in the act itself. That choice for the postmodernist begins in the continuous desire of existence that moves us to action. At the end of this section, we discovered that the analysis of ethical behavior involves the point of authentic choice—that point where the agent has the freedom and autonomy to choose. We considered the requirements of freedom and autonomy to produce authentic choice. Authentic choice, we found, is what was possible at the point of action based on the freedom to enact and the autonomy to govern.

But along the way, we examined the formation of the domain of agency, that formation that produces the moment, location, and meaningful frame of action and the alternatives, consequences, criteria, and means from which authentic choosing points may emerge. The process of organizing plays a substantial role in setting the domain of agency. It does so through the memberships and relationships that arise, the hierarchies of action and discourse that it orders, the thematics of right thinking that it produces and the locations of action that it provides.

In memberships and relationships, we looked at the rights and obligations that entail from being a member or not, in a given relationship or not. Memberships and relationships justify actions and provide the means of performance.

In our study of action, we found that action itself has a coherence. "Going to work," for example, is not a set of disconnected acts but an integrated effort whose separate elements (setting the alarm, catching a certain bus, etc.) make sense because one is "going to work." Action was analyzed in its competence, modality, and effectiveness.

Discourse was defined as any extended language use that is recognizable as its type and does work according to its type. To "speak like a man in Teamsterville" (Philipsen, 1975) is to engage in a discursive form. One must have the authority to appropriate a discursive form. Its performance is marked by its voice or cultural location and by its significance.

Organizing orders action and discourse in hierarchies of power. We recognize superior from subordinate according to characteristic ways of acting and speaking, and there is power in both. We examined this distribution of power in the concepts of complicity and implication.

The next boundary process of the formation of the domain of agency we looked at was location. We found location to be a physical, cultural, social, and situational space that enables and disables ways of thinking, acting, and being, thereby allowing contradiction as a commonplace. We saw that organizing often ties justified action to a particular physical/semiotic location. Further, it works to provide those locations as the resources of this appropriate action. The location justifies what is done, and what is done justifies the location.

Thematics led us to the descriptions and narratives by which events and people are made sensible, by which they become organizational history and part of the truths from which we act. Thematics illuminate the criteria of right and wrong, justified and unjustified, from which we might be judged.

The concept of the domain of agency creates the space in which we can consider the acting agent as a standpoint. In ethics, the standpoint is the choosing person located across the dimensions of the self (**ontology**), its knowledge (**epistemology**), abilities (**praxeology**), and values (**axiology**). We began to develop the method of standpoint analysis and its requirements of reflexivity as a prelude to Chapter 7.

Transitions

In Chapter 7, we put the last of the issues concerning the agency of the organizational self on the table by taking up an analysis of power. We look at power as the product of relationship and consider its role in ethical conduct and its analysis.

Case Study

The Alta Club had long been an all-male dining bastion. Its members were movers and shakers in government and industry and all men. A large sign on the front door stated, "Members only. Deliveries and nonmembers must use the side entrance." A group of members wanted to a invite a successful business woman (of course, a nonmember) to the club for a meeting. She is actually honored by the invitation and interested in being a guest at the club. She uses the delivery entrance.

1. Is there genuine choice in this action?
2. What is her domain of agency?
3. What does membership signify?
4. Is the woman complicit in this gender discrimination?

7

ETHICAL ISSUES IN POWER AND RESISTANCE

It's not where you work; it's where *you work.*

Slowly the group of environmental protesters began to break up. Their signs and placards declaring their intent to "save the wetlands" hung loosely from their hands as they moved toward their cars. Todd Hutchins, human resource manager for Intraxs Incorporated watched as they left, feeling good about his efforts to defend the company's decision to build the plant and to build it here. He had forcefully explained the benefits the plant would bring and the efforts Intraxs was expending to safeguard the environmental values of the area. He couldn't understand how people could get the issues so mixed up.

He allowed himself a smile. Even with the protesters the ground-breaking ceremony had been a success. A good mix of government officials and representative press had shown up. The company had sent busloads of employees to fill out the crowd. They seemed to be enjoying the success of the company as much as the dignitaries. Now Todd hurried away from the construction site. The last company bus was leaving. He was looking forward to getting back to the office and finishing off what was looking like a pretty good day.

Todd entered the bus. He was the only suit in sight. The bus was loaded with line mechanics intent on extending their afternoon furlough. Union men all, they knew Todd as the company negotiator, respected for his fairness, and friendly enough.

"Hey, Todd." somebody yelled from the back. "Shut that door so the driver can't get in. We're playing some cards back here."

"Shut that thing and come on back here. We need some of your big money in the game."

"What makes you think I'd lose."

"Oh you'd lose all right. This time it's our deck."

Todd left the door open, but eased his way back to where the men were dealing another hand.

Todd acknowledged the men he knew by name, "Hey Don, Chuck, Brian. What's up, guys?" Then shook his head negatively to a proffered card. He knew as did the men that it wouldn't be a good idea to join in. Win or lose, there was too much risk in how it might be read and reported.

"Ah, we're just trying to get the most of this grand day the company has given us." Todd couldn't tell if the lilt in the answer was Irish or sarcasm. He watched and kibitzed on the play for a few minutes, but then began to look around for the driver. The day was moving on, and he had stuff to do.

"What's the matter, Todd, can't wait to get back to the office?" Don held his cards in hands thickened and scarred by years of hard work. The indelible stains of machines formed an intaglio of lines around his fingernails and knuckles. Todd glanced compulsively at his own hands that seemed almost delicate in comparison.

"Well, yes, I've got some things I'm kinda anxious to get done. This was an interesting break here, but time's a wasting. Don't you have stuff to do?"

"Sure, but it'll all be there tomorrow and right now is 1 less hour of old Frogbutt breathing down my neck." The others chuckled at the local name for John Frogley, the line supervisor. "John, gotta take a leak, boss. John, verify this parts request. John, need a 15-millimeter ream," he then played to the group, "and that's not half as big as I'd like to use on you." The man stood up amidst the laughter and swaggered in the aisle, "And then Mr. High and Mighty comes over, 'Piss in your pants. Your next break is in an hour.' That's how it is over in your office isn't it, Todd? Or is it just fun times with the secretaries?"

Todd was stunned, "Don, come on, you mean you have to get permission to do any of those things?"[1]

"You have to get permission to fart on that line," Brian chimed in. Don continued, now focused on the story, "Look, I'm a certified mechanic with 15 years of experience on these machines. I know everything about them

---

[1] The issue of workers having access to toilet facilities when they need them is a significant enough issue for OSHA to propose regulations guaranteeing that access (*Salt Lake Tribune*, March 15, 1998, p. E1).

PREVIEW

Starting with a story about the distribution of privilege and means of control within an organization that demonstrates the importance of organizational location, this chapter develops a reconceptualization of the notion of power. Power is seen as a function of the terms of obligation; it is a quality of the relationship and not a trait of an individual or an expression of control. As power derives from relationship and as relationship is a joint production, no member is without power. What is differentiated is access to control. Control is separated from power to allow us to explore its material practices and the inequities that such practices can produce. The principal engine of differentiation is the twin processes of illumination and concealment where the rights and privileges of the dominate and the duties and obligations of the subordinate are illuminated but the obverse set is in shadow. Control or any other form of discipline invokes resistance. This chapter ends with an examination of resistance; its qualities and forms of expression; and, surprisingly, finds a redemptive force.

---

and I've got to ask this dork who doesn't know diddly if I can replace a part that's obviously worn out."

"So, what do you do when you have to take a break and he won't let you go?"

"Easy, you overtighten a bolt or crack a line and then it's off to the parts window. Funny how long it takes to get over there and back."

"Well, you can't do the bolt thing any more," Chuck corrected. "They've moved those parts out on the floor."

"So, you just break something else, something really expensive."

An Introduction to Power:
The Ethical Implications

This story is a fictionalization of an episode recounted by a manager in the transportation field. He was telling the story to reveal his understanding of the principle that an organization is not a singular experience—that one's location within organizing practices makes a substantive difference in terms of one's domain of agency and the possible expressions of the self. We are retelling the story to introduce a discussion on power.[2]

Power as Relationship

Power is often mistakenly thought of as an attribute—something that one has and exercises. But **power** is better understood as part of the practical resolutions of the demands of a relationship. A relationship has two components: a rehearsed understanding of its obligations and a set of recognizable practices. If one and other are walking in opposite directions on a narrow sidewalk, they each enter into an imposed relationship (of short duration) that can be played out in a number of ways. What ought to be done is easily given—a mutual giving way. But other could just shoulder one aside as well. Any relationship, whether happenstance, sought after, or imposed, is an accounting of the other. This accounting requires a disciplining of the self in relation to the other. This disciplining is a reconfiguration of the self that admits to the presence of the other. This disciplining, however minor and marginal or significant and centered, is the grant of power that constitutes a mark of the relationship.

Power as Contingent

No relationship is equally everywhere present or invoked in the same manner in every circumstance. Power, therefore, is not continuous, but rather comes into play in contingent moments at points of authorization. That authorization is a condition—negotiated or not—of the relationship, a surrendered right, a granted bid, an unmarked assumption, an acquiesced demand, an answered request, an unregistered assignment. The relationship grants an authority to be, speak, act in particular ways given the conditions of the enactment of that relationship.

---

[2] This discussion of power is informed by the works of Alvesson 1996; Alvesson & Deetz, 1996; Alvesson & Wilmott, 1996; Butler, 1997; Calas & Smircich, 1996; Clegg, 1975, 1979, 1987, 1989; Clegg & Dunkerley, 1980; Daudi, 1986; Deetz, 1992, 1995; Foucault, 1977, 1980; Giddens, 1979, 1984; Hawes, 1999; Hardy & Clegg, 1996; Jermier, Knights, & Nord, 1994; Knights & Vurdubakis, 1994; Knights & Willmott, 1985; Lazega, 1992; Lukes, 1974; Martin, 1977; Mumby, 1988, 1996, 1997b; Nicolson, 1996; Scott, J., 1990; Sheets-Johnstone, 1994; Wrong, 1979.

For example, as consultants we are given the right to speak the right and wrong of an organization in a way that would not be available to us were we members of that organization. That empowerment is a function of the consultant relationship. Our authorization to speak, however, comes only after displays of careful study and whatever demonstration of expertise required. We can ostensibly say what we want whenever we want, but the power to speak right and wrong is granted only under the conditions in which both our credibility and our listeners will appear.

Here's another example: The extent that I, the keyboardist, account for you, the reader, by adjusting the course of an argument, the examples drawn, the vocabulary-in-use describes the relationship that I am enacting and the control that you exert over me in the writing. If I want you to accept the principle that power is not an attribute of an individual but rather a quality of a relationship, I have to do considerably more work than I might want. So in your struggle to read, you may find some small comfort in knowing that you have evoked a struggle to write.

THE RECIPROCAL CHARACTER OF POWER

Power, then, is effectively understood as a reciprocal. One does not have power *over* someone; one has power *with* someone. It is a quality of the relationship and not an attribute of an individual. The reciprocal nature of power does not imply that the expression of power or the experience of power will be the same for every member of the relationship. Reciprocity does not mean equity. Clearly there can, and will be, different conditions of entrance (one may seek to impose the relationship on another), different motives for sustaining the relationship, different costs of disengagement, different consequences for the members that include separate domains of agency, and resources for the expression of self. Organizing and cultural practices are themselves means by which we ensure that the expressions and consequences of power will be different across the different terms of organizational and cultural membership. So, superiors do get to issue directives to which subordinates will be accountable, and in the average household, women still "get to do" 85 percent of the household chores.

All of these possible and actual differences tend to deflect our analysis from the mutual dependence—that equivalent basis—from which power appears. That mutual dependence affirms there is no position of "powerlessness" in any relationship, though the power obtained may not be entirely wanted. Superiors must issue directives, subordinates need not do what they

PRINCIPAL CONCEPTS

Power is not the attribute of an individual or a hierarchical position. It is a quality of a relationship that comes into play at points of authorization. Power is reciprocal but its expression is not necessarily equitable. It is power *with* but it can be control *over* as well. The reciprocal nature of power does not imply that the expression or experience of power will be the same for every member of the relationship.

haven't been told to do, and women often control the character of household space. Members, therefore, are complicit in each other's expressions of power and consequently share, in some part, in the responsibility for their outcomes.

Consider the Intraxs mechanics working under the supervision of John Frogley. They enter into an organizational relationship that gives them a job—a cultural emblem of success, the right to practice their craft—a constitution of the self, and a salary—the means of increased agency. To get these things they subjugate themselves to organizational definitions of relationships, duties, rights, virtues, and utilities—in short, what is right, what is wrong, and who gets to speak the difference. What they retain is the work itself. They must do the work, *but no one else can*. As a result, their point of control in the power relationship with Frogley is in the execution of the work. The organization might well declare some of their expressions to be sabotage, but the workers' actions are the means that they have to redress the wrongs inflicted by a petty tyrant and permitted by the failure of upper management to properly supervise John Frogley and to provide adequate working conditions.

Are their actions of deliberate damage justified? They are justified in exactly the same way that Frogley's overheated supervision is justified. Both sides accuse the other of unethical behavior worthy of punishment. The ethical solution is not to declare one right and the other wrong. The solution is to change the character of the relationship. The mechanics need to take responsibility for a good day's work so that the coercive supervision is not justified. Frogley needs to stop being coercive so that the acts of damage are not justified. The solution seems obvious, but these actual people may not be able to enact it because they may not know how, lacking the personal skills or organizational/cultural resources needed; they may have to give up too much of themselves to do it, enacting a performance that denies who they are; they may be unable to trust one another, rehearsing the stories and thematics of the previous relationship; they may be prevented by organizational others who need their dysfunction to enact their own relationships or self-constitutions. Whatever resolution occurs will have to occur on the shop floor in real time and local performances.

CULTURAL STRUCTURATIONS OF POWER

Any relationship is a constitution of power between its members. That dictum declares that if we want to understand power, we better start looking at relationships. Our first efforts have been to look at relationships with recognizable members, members embodied in a person perhaps before us. But in Chapter 4 where we considered the constitution of the *self* in relation to the *other*, we discovered that we are in many relationships over which we have no choice and no particular person to point to. You remember Jim, that certain-aged, white, heterosexual, middle-classed, U.S. national, native-English-speaking male, who can be so described because the instruments of his identity are entered into a cultural system of relationships that provides those descriptive terms. He is not white because of the color of his skin. He is white because we have nominated particular genetic constellations into an institutionalized system of "race" relationships. His pink-beige hue has very different consequences for him, whether he wants them or not, in Salt Lake City than in Nairobi. He cannot step out of that relationship, but he can commit acts of sabotage within it.

Whether ethical or not, we are positioned in a great number of cultural relationships, nearly all without our assent. Gender, age, ethnicity, language, sexual orientation all enable and disable according to the circumstances of their local enactment. Gender is not our sexual attributes but the relationship coded in sexual difference. Much of what we claim for women and men is not the product of being female and male, but rather is the product of the performance of the feminine and the masculine. We each carry the symbols of our gender, but gender has to be enacted or read into the action. That entrance can be inert or activated, and if activated it can be invoked or evoked, but whether invoked or evoked it will be improvised locally in the circumstances at hand. Gender, as with most cultural relationships, is a repertoire of naturalized performances that often lies below the horizon of consciousness. These repertoires have to be excavated, broken into; their codes captured and pinned for observation.

When a woman takes the unquestioned responsibility for doing the laundry for otherwise able-bodied family members, she enacts one performance of the repertoire of gender. She is subjugated to the task but holds power in the relationship that no one else can properly do it. She is the woman of the house. Her enactment reproduces the cultural understanding of what is women's work and what is a good woman. It reproduces the truth of what is right and good. In that reproduction, she is complicit in her own subjugation. Certainly she may not be participating in any informed way, or if informed, she may not have the apparent means of changing the terms of her gender. But in any case she is implicated.

On the other hand, the laundry has to be done, and while not rocket science, it is more than just pushing a button. Not everyone does it well enough to maximize the appearance and longevity of the clothes. Elaine may determine that she will do the laundry because she wants it done according to her criteria and the costs to her of doing the laundry are lower than the costs of the supervision needed to ensure that it is done right. Elaine is no longer reproducing the gendered terms of her own subjugation but she is sustaining the subjugation of others in her reproduction of ostensible gendered action. She is complicit in maintaining gendered performances even though it is only the appearance of that reproduction. "You do the laundry!?" her friends may challenge, "We would never do the laundry."[3] The challenge feminizes Elaine's actions, coding them in gender. She may protest, but her insertion into gender has been evoked by her friends.

The symbols of our cultural memberships are always at the ready, though the relationships they signal must be activated in enactments or readings that are required to put them in play. The greater the cultural complexity, the greater the diversity that will be understandable as a performance of the relationship. At the close of the twentieth century, Jim can be the sensitive male and Elaine the liberated woman yet still sustain gender. The sensitive male is a different kind of man and the liberated woman a different kind of woman, but man and woman nonetheless. There are thoughtful ethical

---

[3] The challenge can be read as an expression of gender politics. It is not a point of liberation. It simply exchanges one imperative (must do) for another (must never do). It also does not transcend gender but simply expresses it in a different voice.

choices to be made in being a woman or a man, though one is never released from the relationship.

A friend writes:

I had traveled across France by train from the German border to Calais. A night in Paris had pretty well depleted my supply of French francs, so I was glad that I already had my Hovercraft ticket for the trip across the channel. It was a cold, blustery spring day, something more like I would expect in Chicago. I had hauled my luggage from the train station to the stop for the free bus to the pier. A few minutes later a woman came down the steeply sloped street and joined me at the bus stop. We exchanged nods of greeting. Another taxicab circled round. They had been like vultures since my arrival, waiting for me, and now us, to tire of the cold and to pop for the fare. The driver stopped and said something to us in French. The woman replied and a short conversation ensued. She dismissed the driver who drove off.

She turned to me and reported that driver had told her that the Hovercraft was not operating today, there would be no bus, and that we would have to take the ferry across. I was skeptical and so was she, but after 10 more minutes we were both looking for that cab. I told her that I had no Francs. She said not to worry about it. Finally the cab came round again. We were thankful to be out of the cold and on our way. When we got to the pier she handed the cabbie a 10-dollar bill—American dollars—and told him to keep the change. He was pleased. I was puzzled. There had been no negotiation about money. She simply knew what would work and that American funds would be acceptable. Not at all my experience in Paris.

We purchased our ferry tickets; she from a money pouch thick with 50-dollar bills; I with plastic. I paid her back for the cab ride from my own meager stash of dollars. As we walked up the gangplank together I could feel my worries rise about who this woman was and how this was going to play out. She was clearly well off, sophisticated, and certainly more travel savvy than I. Her approach to the situation had saved me from a difficult afternoon that would have escalated into an absolute disaster had I missed the train to London. She had looked out for me. Yet I was uncomfortable because she seemed to be attaching herself to me.

We sat together during the crossing. Her English was passable, much better than my impossible French. She told me that she was from a big family in Algeria. I inferred wealthy, politically connected, educated, liberal. She had determined to see Europe on her own, to the objection of her older brothers, but with the obvious support of her mother who got her father to pay for it. She would be traveling until the money ran out. That looked like it would be a long time to me. I asked her if such travel was typical. She said that it was not, but that some of her friends had done it and she was going to do it as well. I'm sure there was a story in why she was alone, but she never told it.

When we got to Dover our roles reversed. She was disconsolate that we had missed the last train to London. I tried to tell her that there had been a time change and that we still had a few minutes to make it. She didn't seem to understand. I grabbed her hand and dragged her and her luggage up the entrance stairs to the train station ticket window, bought the tickets for both of us and ran us out to the platform. I was angry because I had to deal with this woman. I almost missed the train because of her, but I could not just leave her.

We ran out on the platform just as what looked like the last passengers were boarding the train. I caught the conductor's eye and he signaled us to a car with its doors still open. It would later dawn on me that they knew the ferry had just arrived. It would be several minutes before the train left the station, and many more passengers would follow along after us. But at that moment, I was the hero. The woman was delighted, thanking me profusely. I just walked away and boarded the train, leaving her to wrestle her luggage aboard by herself. I felt cruel and guilty for it. She had helped me, but I had returned it in full measure. I could not accommodate a companion, especially a woman companion. As I walked away, she looked hurt and a bit bewildered but then resolutely she walked to the other end of the car and boarded the train.

The car was packed by the time the train pulled out of the station. Every seat was taken and the aisle full of luggage. It was more a South American image than an orderly British one. I wondered if I had done right. A married American man, a single, apparently liberated Algerian woman—what was the situation? What costs? What returns? What risks? Was I fantasizing in soap opera melodrama? Was I misreading her openness as forwardness? Perhaps she wanted only my presence; two are safer than one. It could be great fun in London with such an exotic friend—if it could be managed, and it would have to be managed carefully. In the end, I could not get out of the cultural narrative—those discourses of men and women together—that surrounded, enveloped, and finally suffocated this man and that woman.

We are, indeed, submerged in our cultural relationships—relationships to the cultural other of gender, ethnicity, and the like, relationships to the discourses that speak our truths. We may decry that captivity as a diminution of the spirit, but the discipline of every relationship exchanges power. One gives up potential in order to achieve the actual. Every relationship both

PRINCIPAL CONCEPTS

Any relationship is a constitution of power between its members. We are entered into cultural relationships including gender, ethnicity, and all the other cultural marks of self. Those relationships activate the dialogue of power with and control over that make up the culturally dominant and subordinate. Though it is also an instrument of subjugation, cultural membership provides the system of speaking, doing, and being in the world.

diminishes and enhances; we are less than we could be but more than we are. There is no Rousseauvian natural state in which we can reach the fullness of our existence. Without cultural membership, we have no system of speaking, doing, or being in the world. The truth of our cultural (and as we shall see our organizational) subjugation is its constituting necessity. If we are to have any power at all, we must submit to and be constituted by the relationship of self to other. Though there are certainly terrible inequities that each of us must take care not to enact (and if one is not openly resisting them, she or he is probably enacting them), *no cultural membership is without power, and there is no power outside of a relationship.* Our complicity in these power relations immerses us in the ethics of our expressions.

The "politics of identity" is a good example of the exercise of this power of the cultural other. On the other hand we do not want this writing to allow self-congratulation by the dominant. Power though reciprocal is most often unequally expressed in forms of control. Those dominated may not be aware of the means of their ability or if knowledgeable, may be suppressed by fear of failure or threats of force (Barnes, 1988; Clegg, 1989).

ORGANIZATIONAL STRUCTURATIONS OF CONTROL

Every organization is constructed out of relationships, from the simplest of member to membership to the most complex matrix of coordinated action. The organization is a system of mutual obligation and reciprocal power that is itself embedded in the ever-extending concentrics of society and culture.

Organizational structurations, however, typically work to enhance and naturalize the expression of power by some and to abridge and abnormalize that expression by others. These structurations are encoded in the moral or immoral practices of *control* that are initiated and sustained through the process of organizing itself. For example, some time ago a friend wrote:

> I have the perfect example for your writing on structurations. I was a member of the inaugural board of directors for a nonprofit service organization. This organization was to represent its members politically and to provide training and resources for them. Sounds pretty benign, right. State law requires an annual general meeting of any incorporated organization at which members elect the board and conduct any such other business as the board determines or the members get on the agenda. The issue in this evening discussion was who was eligible to vote—all members, or only those in attendance. One of the attorneys at the table was arguing that it should be only those in attendance. "They," he intoned, "are the only ones who have earned the right to vote by taking the effort to come to the meeting. If you don't care enough to come to the meeting, you don't deserve to vote." "Yeah," someone else said, "and that way we can keep the voting clean." By which she meant that those there would vote in the interests of the board. "Wait," I said, "there are lots of good reasons why people might not be able to come to a meeting. They shouldn't be disenfranchised because they have to work or have some other conflict. And why are we afraid of our own members?" There was a collective gasp and then a sigh. People looked at me as if I would never understand and voted in the attendance requirement.

This example illustrates the general cultural understanding that organizations must necessarily be hierarchical, that authority and resources must be distributed in such a way that privileges certain members over others. This cultural understanding (rather than reading some personal advantage) is underscored here because these board members writing the bylaws of the organization knew they would not be board members for long. Every privilege they wrote in was a burden they would soon have to carry. That did not matter; their duty was to create a proper organization—one that had real leaders with "real power," that is, the means of control.

The example also shows that the consequences of organizing, in this case board-controlled voting, are hidden in other discourse—here, earning the privilege of voting. We do not need to imply duplicity as did our friend. We know that there will be no meeting without the board members in attendance. Each of them will earn the right to vote. It is reasonable to ask the same of any other member. At the same time no one expects more than a small percentage of the membership to show up at the meeting. (The regular meeting room will hold only about a third of the membership and is never full.) Board members and their supporters will routinely be there in attendance.

Finally, the example shows how the organizationally authorized voice is protected. It will take a special and knowing effort by ordinary members to "take on" the board (assuming this board knows how to act as a proper board, of course). Ordinary members will have to find some method for coming together in concerted effort—something that the board does as a function of its regular activity. Ordinary members will have to break into their routines to produce this action. They will have to become knowledgeable of the bylaws—something that is an initiation requirement for board members. Board members will know more, know it sooner, and be better rehearsed simply as a function of regularly meeting as the board. Their statements will be viewed as competent, significant, and authoritative (as defined in Chapter 4) even by those who oppose them because they—designated as board rather than ordinary members—are given practical rights by all members to be extraordinary. (We call this leadership.) All of this was done when the relationship between ordinary and board members was created in the practices of the bylaws.

The outcome—that this privilege is that gift of control—is hidden away, concealed by what appears to be a mundane decision of voting eligibility. Organizing necessarily creates difference. It is after all a relationship between self and other. That difference is expressed morally across rights, duties, utilities, relationships, and virtues. A leader is positioned differently in these moral dimensions from a follower. This difference is not unethical but helps define our subject position in moral judgments. It is the cultural delegation of privilege to this difference across its seven systems that raises the ethical question. At present we see imbedded privilege as a cultural practice that is not necessarily unethical, but one that could be is used to create inequities for some while promoting the interests of others. For example, it is ethically uninteresting that some earn more than others as long as the others reach basic standards of self-expression and physical well-being. But the ethical spotlight is very much on the overprivileged if by earning more they reduce the level of educational opportunity, health care, legal service, and so on of the underprivileged.

We now step back into our service organization, which has 7 board members and about 350 ordinary members. The board controls an annual dues income of about $5000. More importantly it controls the certification of its members that makes them eligible for different and often higher paying jobs. At any particular annual meeting it would take a group of about 30 members to completely control the voting. That has never happened despite some years of significant dissatisfaction with board actions. All these members, board and ordinary alike, are, after all, colleagues who will often find themselves working together on some job. It would be unseemly for any segment to make a blatant move for control.

The metaphor of sedimentation develops out of the idea that each time one performs an action a trace is laid down that leads one back to that performance. As regularized performance develops, those traces form a force of enactment just as each footprint creates the trail to follow. The concept of sedimentation is used to talk about performance knowledge and its often unmarked consequences. Sedimentation does not yield to rationality and hence is frequently described pejoratively by rational theorists.

What we are looking at is how decisions made several years ago became sedimented in, secured in their position by the repeated expressions of the practical understandings of the relationship between member and board member. This sedimentation, however, obscures the power of the ordinary member and primarily illumines, celebrates, and legitimates only the leadership side of the equation. A board such as this should be aware of the legitimation of leadership and the ethical consequences attached to the various practices.

This process of revealing and hiding, authorizing and abrogating, legitimating and discrediting creates the organizational stage on which we see the "rightful" expressions of leadership and command—those sunlit virtues of the organization. Consequently we often divide the power equation into the empowered leadership in command and control on the one side and the disempowered followership who can offer only weak opposition and shadowed resistance on the other. The one side is considered legitimate, the other suspect. This view is deceptive, as we have seen, because power does not belong to one side or the other but is a product of the relationship. The control and other expressions of power that we see are the result of what is authorized for us to see and what is not.

The potential and the actual of the hidden, abrogated, and discredited, nonetheless, remains. These expressions often occur tactically with little fanfare and intending no trace. For example, a product developer ambushes his boss to tell her that he needs a particular piece of equipment or the job won't get done. No proposal, no memo just a stop in the hallway to say, "I gotta have this; here are the specs and the price. Let me get Leo on it." The request

> ### PRINCIPAL CONCEPTS
>
> Any organization involves a distribution of authority and resources that may privilege certain members over others. Organizing necessarily creates difference. The difference itself is not unethical, rather it is the cultural delegation of privilege to this difference that raises the ethical question.

is reasonable enough, the price small enough, and the risks in saying "no" are high enough. The boss says "yes" because it is not worth saying "no."

But what of the employee who does not know the ambush tactic, who believes the mantra of "no money," or who works for a boss who is willing to take the risks of saying "no." Certainly she lacks power. Actually, we would argue that she retains the power of the relationship *but does not know the means of exercising it.* The immediate consequences to her are the same, but the possibilities for her and the analytical approaches for us are quite different. For an ethical management style, the boss would need to acknowledge the different methods of manipulation and work for a climate of fairness with all workers.

RELATIONSHIPS, POWER, AND OBLIGATION

We put this chapter in motion by considering the basis of power. We found it in relationships. A relationship is defined, in part, by the reciprocal production of power. We can recognize the presence of a relationship by the expression of power. The other grand marker of a relationship, as we saw in Chapter 2, is obligation, the prior condition of ethical responsibility. Therefore a relationship gives us both the power to do something not otherwise available and the obligation to do certain things not otherwise required.

Relationships themselves develop within cultural frameworks. (Any relationship has to start with some common basis and that basis is always initiated culturally.) For example, your authors' relationships with their spouses develop within the cultural-social framework of marriage. Certainly that understanding has migrated during the years of our respective marriages, but it is still something different from a partnership or a live-in relationship. The character of the marital relationship is different from any other, and that character mediates the performance and our understanding of that performance. We cannot, for example, have casual sex with our own partners. The marital character of those relationships preclude that designation of our sexual activity whatever else it may be.

Finally, the marital relationship mediates all other friendship relationships, particularly cross-sex relationships, as well as all other sexual activity. This mediation declares what's right and what's wrong within these other relationships and activities (but clearly presents no guarantees). Members of other marriagelike relationships can attempt to produce the same mediated understanding of what's right and what's not and to extend the influence of that understanding beyond the face-to-face supervision of the other, but such relationships remain outside the social-cultural jurisdiction of the marital relationship. Such efforts are always vulnerable to the reply, "It's not like we're married or something!"

The belief that a long-term partnership or a live-in arrangement or a marriage with extramarital sex is the same as marriage is necessarily a *belief held under explanation*. The practical explanations go something like this: "Well, we're committed partners. It's better than being married." Or, "The sex is OK. Bill and Hillary have an open marriage." The tag sentences give away the understood difference. These examples are not judgmental. They are an attempt to show the force of ethical and unethical social-cultural understandings upon the practice of relationships. Persons may declare themselves to be brave, superior, free-thinkers, contemporary, independent, or whatever in their rejection of marriage, but they are dependent on the cultural standard of marriage to make that declaration. The standard mediates our understanding and valuations of the behaviors that fall within it.[4] And it does so in precisely the same way that scientific paradigms influence the observations conducted within their purview. Such was the argument of Chapter 2.

If we are to more fully understand what is granted and what is imposed with the dual character of power and obligation that is the product of a relationship, we also have to pay close attention to the cultural ideologies that mediate it. Consider the following possible relationships:

> Mary and John are having dinner and discussing joining forces to lease a car, a subject that Mary introduced. (a) Mary is John's boss. (b) Mary is John's

---

[4] We may be tempted to discount the force of these cultural understandings, but a recent Harvard Medical Newsletter reports sex as being less a strain on the heart than many routine household tasks. Nonetheless, 78% of those sexual encounters in which heart attacks occurred were with extramarital partners.

PRINCIPAL CONCEPTS

Relationships develop within cultural and organizational frameworks. A relationship gives us both the ability to do something not otherwise available and the obligation to do certain things not otherwise required. Relationships also set the terms of our ethical analysis.

---

business partner. (c) Mary is in a bowling league with John. (d) Mary just picked up John in the bar across the street. (e) Mary is John's wife, partner, live-in. Presuming she asks, what advice would you give Mary concerning the transaction, given that you are (a) Mary's boss, (b) in the same bowling league, (c) a long-time friend of Mary, (d) recently divorced from Mary.

Everything in those lists, of course, makes a difference in both the meaning of the discussion Mary and John are having and in the advice that you would give. The cultural expectations that are implicated in the first list lead us to consider the basis of the relationship. The discussion about the car lease makes the most sense under conditions (b) business partner and (e) wife. We might feel that John is most at risk in condition (d) a bar pick-up. The advice that Mary gets from you is likely to be most secure across all conditions from the long-term friend relationship and least secure from the recently divorced one.

It is certainly possible that Mary and John can successfully negotiate the conditions of a joint leasing of a car and enact those conditions happily over its duration. None of us, however, could give that simple advice across all those relationships and not be vulnerable to charges of advanced cultural naiveté or outright unethical behavior. We simply do not believe it to be true that the power that we exchange and the obligation we shoulder is the same across those relationships and that those differences make no difference in the promises we keep. "You leased a $35,000 car with some woman who picked you up in a bar?"

POWER AND OBLIGATION
IN ORGANIZATIONAL RELATIONSHIPS

A relationship is not something that two or more people simply negotiate on their own. Relationships have cultural identities that have consequences for the subject position of the members and the terms of exchange that govern. Culture is not monolithic, however. It develops out of the joint enactment of meanings, action, and language. That you, the reader, and we, the writers, share a common language (though not necessarily as native speakers), much of a common technology of living (systems of food, transportation, housing, media), a common political system, and many common narratives and symbols locates us in a common cultural space that makes this discussion of power and its expressions possible. But there is also much that we do not share. We do not have a joint history with you. We all have different families; work for different organizations; have, perhaps, different or no religious traditions; enjoy different sports; volunteer for different social causes; and so on. In these differences, this discussion devolves into the separate practices of writing and reading as we fail to accomplish the joint enactment of the text that is communication.

One of the first tasks of organizing, then, is to put into place enough communality that whatever else needs to be done, can get done. In establishing this common space, organizations first draw upon (and must be responsible to) this vast cultural reservoir that will motivate the division of hierarchy, space, time, and labor that the members will enact. But more than that will be needed and will necessarily develop out of deliberate efforts in the performance of the self, in discourse production and symbol use, in conventionalized practices and the like, as well as out of the sedimentations that will occur as the history of regular practice develops. Organizational ethics will develop out of both policy and practice—out of the rules we make, the stories we tell, the things we do, and our readings of them all.

In most of our organizational experiences the start of those rules, stories, and actions will be lost to us, as we will step into some historical moment of their performance as the latest embodiment of their intersection. Our experience of organizing, then, is of a process of discipline governed by a coherent ideological framework expressed in member-to-member relationships, shared meanings of discourse, and action (a.k.a. language and action rules), and the methods that referee rule-directed language use and action—all of which defines the doing, the done, and the could-have-been, that form the evidence of the moral.

The first goal of this discipline is the reproduction of the ideology that frames that action through the naturalized performances of its members. This reproduction is prior to any other instrumental action and all instrumental action sustains the ideology under which such actions are sensible.

These ideological practices are themselves initiated and sustained through instruction, rehearsal, supervision, modeling, mutuality (our joint recognition of each other's work), structuring of environments, and resource allocation (the controlled distribution of authority, information, and other resources).

Typically we enter into an organizing process that is well-established, rich in complex narratives and thematics, and well-sedimented in highly recognizable and well-rehearsed practices. These elements aggressively mediate the relationship among members by clarifying subject position in the performance of *self* and *other*. They also exquisitely detail the hierarchical rights of power expression by the dominant interests and the requirements of obligation of the subordinated. If we are to achieve that order set of relationships that is an organization, we cannot all be equal. We manage the paradox of reciprocity and inequality through concealment and in the differentials of subject position.

In the practice of concealment, the power of the one is shown by obscuring the other. In this play of light and shadow, we clearly see the rights of the dominant and the duties of the subordinate. What is hidden is the reciprocal obligations of each.

Relationships work across what are called embodied subject positions—sociocultural locations that are occupied by particular people. None of us can be engaged independent of our subject position. We are always culturally defined.[5] When ideological practices create subject positions that are filled differentially—the one-to-many equation of hierarchical control—power is distributed unequally across individuals. It is, however, still reciprocal across subject positions.

For example, most classrooms have a teacher subject position occupied by a single individual and a student subject position occupied by several individuals. The teacher/student relationship is maintained across these subject positions, not across the individuals. If one student resigns, the teacher remains as a teacher, but that student is no longer a student in that class. If all individual students resign (or even a significant number) the relationship of class collapses and the subject position of teacher disappears.

Teachers have to have students; managers have to have workers, otherwise they cannot be teachers or managers. Power reciprocates across these

---

[5] And even on the Internet we are understood culturally as a web denizen, a poser who ultimately must be met to build a "real" relationship.

Instructor   Instructor/Student   Student

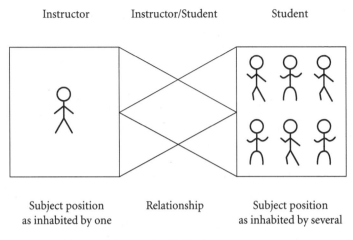

Subject position   Relationship   Subject position
as inhabited by one   as inhabited by several

Fɪɢᴜʀᴇ 7.1   **Subject Positions and Individuals.**

subject positions. Hierarchical structures, however, fractionalize the power of *individuals* who jointly occupy the same subject position within those structures (Figure 7.1).

Finally, organizing processes routinely violate the Habermasian communicative ethic (Habermas, 1979, 1984) in which members are to be equally trained and skilled, equally informed, equally given voice to question until satisfied, and equally valued in the process of consensus. Training and information are methodically withheld. Even if allowed to speak, there may be few who listen, and bargaining is much more the norm than consensus building. Organizational command and control, as well as the answering resistance and opposition as particular forms of power expressions, emanate from this inequity. Given this organizational inequity, it is surprising that our families, social and volunteer associations, religious groups, businesses, and workplace are not more often stages of hostility and enmity. What mediates this inequity into more or less tranquility is our commitment to the ideological premises that provide for it. It is this local hegemony—a set of understandings to which both the dominant and the subjugated subscribe—that sets the conditions of organizational control, resistance to that control, and the issues of right and wrong. We turn to these topics next.

PRINCIPAL CONCEPTS

Organizing must first establish the common ground of communication. Part of that common ground are practices and their rules of conduct that will in turn form organizational morality. This morality is not based on equity. Members are unequal in subject position occupancy and in their access to the expressions of power and furthermore accept this inequity. What mediates this inequity into more or less tranquility is our commitment to the organization.

ETHICAL ISSUES IN ORGANIZATIONAL POWER

Organizational power (like cultural power) is the product of the relationship between the individual and the ideological framework that in its expressions mediates subjectivity, discourse, and action. It is this ideological framework that establishes not only the effectiveness of commands to "do this," but also the very admissibility of the command itself. Resistance in organizations is defined within this relationship between individual and ideology. Resistance seeks to undermine some part of the means of its production, that is, transforming the ideological work of member-to-member relationships, shared meanings of discourse and action, and the judicial interpretation of those meanings to counter its reality constitutive force. Because of the inequity of resource distribution, organizing is global and strategic. Resistance is local and tactical (de Certeau, 1984).

The harms of organizing are, therefore, typically prior. Like the deliberate disenfranchisement of those who cannot attend the annual meeting of our service organization, the immoralities of organizations are encoded and sedimented well beyond the particulars of the given person enacting them at our moment of observation. John Frogley is enacting the immorality of an organizing process that defines the rights and duties of the mechanics and their supervisor. He may well see himself as righteously defending the company against the misconduct of these men (expressing what LaNuez and Jermier, 1994, call a high corporate identity). Frogley does not hear himself demeaning and debasing others. He hears himself properly administering the discipline of work. Frogley, the man, is not the problem; the supervisory rules of Intraxs are the problem. (We are not dismissing Frogley's responsibility to be ethical. Given the supervisory rules, however, he can

---

PRINCIPAL CONCEPTS

Ethical and unethical organizational practices originate in ordinary decisions that have declared and undeclared and intended and unintended consequences. Though we may not have declared or intended a result and may not have even participated in the decision, we are nonetheless culpable of their results. Members, by their membership, are complicit and implicated in organizational actions they do not resist.

---

effect but minor improvements on the shop floor [be empathetic rather than disgusting]. His ethical moment occurred when he discovered what the supervision entailed.)

In the very recent past, legal action has unfolded two spectacular cases of unethical corporate behavior. One involved the tobacco industry in which not one, but several, companies apparently colluded in a pattern of deception and deceit. The strength of the internal standard of "us against them" was shown in the consistent rejection of generally accepted scientific claims of harm by those who could have been respected scientists in their own right and in the fact that people had to leave the industry before the truth could be told.

The second case involved a multinational oil company that systematically discriminated against people of color. Building on the already prevalent Eurocentric racism, this company justified its racial stratifications on competency. But it was a set of recordings of "insider speech" by an employee forcibly retired that laid out the actual practices. Managers were recorded speaking of bags of jelly beans in which all the black ones were "glued to the bottom" (Roberts, 1998 as quoted in *Time*, March 16, 1998, p. 50). Coded speech of this sort works because the insiders all know what it means. Its reference to organizational structurations is clear.

In general organizational conduct derives from structurations of policy and practice. Organizational structurations of misconduct include those that:

♦ Encode discourses that diminish or deny obligation
♦ Disallow the considered evaluation of action

- Constitute subjectivities of disadvantage
- Deceptively devalue or overvalue the worth to the organization of forms of work
- Encode practices that put people unnecessarily at risk, particularly if those risks are disguised
- Disenfranchise or silence those with a legitimate stake in outcomes
- Require workers to violate laws or community expectations of moral action
- Debase or hold the individual up to ridicule

We will spend a few lines with each.

DISCURSIVE MISCONDUCT

It is important to note that while we have separated discourse and practice analytically, in reality they are inextricably intertwined. Discourse, as we remember, is any extended language use, whether in speech or writing, that does cultural or organizing work. The ordinary speech of the shop floor is recognizably different from the ordinary speech of the halls of management. Each has its own cadence, vocabulary, and syntax in use; each references different symbols and values. Discursive performances are both the mark and test of position. A patient who speaks in medical terms is likely to be suspect, as is a physician who cannot.

The importance of discourse here is its justificatory effect. If we continue to speak of the femininity of women, we are justified by that speech to exclude women from masculine domains. If we continue to rehearse the importance of race, we are justified in making distinctions based on color. The importance of focusing on unethical discourse is not the trivialities of "bad words" or the oppressions of political correctness, but the subjectivities and structurations in which it participates. Through structurations in discourse the unethical practices go unchallenged and unchanged.

Discourses of Diminished Obligation

Pat stared at the memo and then read it one more time:

For the past several wage increase cycles we have taken extraordinary efforts to bring staff wages up to national averages. While we have made some advances, we are still substantially below that average. Nevertheless, I can no longer approve of budget changes that move funds from contract personnel to hourly personnel. We are not justified in putting our faculty at risk in order to solve the staff problem.

"So," Pat sighed, "the faculty finally got to the Dean." She could hear the arguments: Faculty are more important, more valuable; staff are more expendable, replaceable. Staff also are not unionized and can't bring a dean down like faculty discontent can. It was a weakling's decision, Pat thought, but fully justified in the insistence on titles—staff are addressed by their first name; faculty by "Professor" and last name. Silence is imposed upon staff—staff have no standing in departmental meetings (or even presence except as note takers). Staff have no meetings of their own and must bring their concerns like a child to a parent. Staff are the problem, spoken of as the reasons for "our" difficulties in dealing with students or getting work done. These subjugations are practiced by a faculty that routinely has spent hours in emancipatory defense of those who suffer less injustice. Staff are the silenced ones, not to be heard, much less listened to. What obligation could we have to such as these?

Phrases such as "It's the customer's lookout," "pesky little brother," "The government's a conspiracy," "lazy students," "incompetent staff," when institutionalized in organizing discourse provide the unethical means for discounting the obligation for honest dealing, loving care, following the law, producing effective teaching, or giving a living wage.

Discourses That Disallow Reflection

Totalizing discourses such as "It's only the bottom line that counts," "winning isn't everything; it's the only thing," or the stereotypes in the form of "all X are Y" generate the "of course it's true" claims for the rightness of action by disallowing the opportunity of other positions to be authentically expressed. The operation of the bylaws committee (in our story on p. 174) gives us a good example of how this works. It is not that objections cannot be raised. It is that the language of the objection is not accepted as member language. This is clearly an "outsider" speaking because none of us would talk like that. Outsider speech does not need to be heard and equally important is listened to only at risk of being declared an outsider. Totalizing discourses produce efficiency but at the cost of reflection. This practice becomes unethical when it is used to prevent us from asking, "Is there a better way?"

Discourses of Disadvantaged Subjectivities

Remembering that one's subjectivity, as we use the term, refers to those collectively constituted resources for the expression of the self, the discourses of disadvantaged subjectivities are those that position the self in the domain of the less. Here we find an immorality in the discourse of "those people," the ones that can't be trusted; the ones that are too young or too old to do the job; the ones who are too emotional, too insensitive, or too something not like us.

Joanne Martin (1993) has commented that U.S. corporations that have highly integrated cultures (common and well-known rules of action and language) also show little diversity in the make-up of upper management, which tends to be repressively white male. Her conclusion was that phrases like "team player," "a regular guy," "one of us" were the predictors of another white male in management. Women and the ethnic other will need to prove themselves to be "just like us" in order to succeed. All too often their case will fail on the face of it rather than on the merits of it.

Discourses of Work Valuation

In an earlier era it was perhaps true that organizational leadership developed out of on-the-job competence (Clegg, 1975). The individual who could do the job best was pushed up the ranks. By the time s/he reached the top s/he had full knowledge of what the work of the organization was. The contemporary picture is much different for any but the smallest organizations. Now leadership is in the hands of professional managers who typically have no direct knowledge of work other than managerial. Managers can change industries or product lines with little difficulty because the principles of production and rational management are pretty much the same whether it's widgets or thingies that are being produced. Robert Quinn's (1988) eight leadership roles— facilitator, mentor, innovator, broker, producer, director, coordinator, monitor—speak not to the crafts and skills of the shop floor. Robert Jackall's (1988) powerful description of the world of corporate managers points to the more global separations than those of work. He describes the differences by education, religion, income, lifestyle:

> These managers take pains to separate themselves socially from workers. They mock what they see as workers' preferences for "stock car racing, drinking beer and watching girls' rear ends." They speak disdainfully of the crude, arm-waving "Assembly of God" Protestantism that many workers favor in contrast to their own high Baptist or, better, Presbyterian leanings. Especially if they are from the working class, they see workers' poor education and stumbling inarticulateness around authority figures as shameful, indeed disgusting. (p. 124)

> **PRINCIPAL CONCEPTS**
>
> Discursive misconduct occurs within ways of speaking and writing that deny our responsibilities, move toward totalitarianism, legitimate a domain of the less, and create the conditions by which the dominant remain the dominant.

It is in these discourses that value of work is established. The climate establishes the moral as the "rational" principles of management. Managers are always worth more than line workers. It is the "long hours" at the office that always wins out over the crushing boredom of labor. It is the stress of responsibility that is more heroic than the physical costs of embodied work. (See Banta, 1993, for an excellent analysis of these sorts of narratives.)

But we should not limit ourselves to considering just corporate life. With the majority of two-parent families now being two-career families, the struggle over who works harder, whose work is more important, whose work grants exceptions to the daily tasks of being a family is a familiar household battle. "I make more money," "I work more hours," "I'm a professional," "That's women's work," "That's a man's job" are all discourses that seek to hold in place a certain understanding of what's moral. They also serve to close down discussion and careful analysis.

Misconduct through Performance Rules

Action is the sign of what is being done. As a sign, action is a named performance that is recognizable to self and other as a pattern of behavior that is under cultural, societal, and local governances. In the United States, drivers keep to the right by a cultural standard encoded in law. Utah drivers reflect their societal differences from Vermont drivers, and Jim's driving is distinctively different from Elaine's. All of us, in our own ways, however, keep to the right, which is one of the ways we recognize driving from fooling around in an empty parking lot.

Performance rules represent the cultural, societal, and local governances that are reproduced in the action we recognize. The mechanics of Intraxs recognize the difference between cracking a bolt as an unpredictable event in the repair of a machine from cracking a bolt as an act of resistance according to these performance rules. Performance rules are not words; they are not instructions on how to do something, although words and instructions may be implicated in them. Performance rules are the embodied knowledge of how something is done.

Unethical conduct enters performance rules when the ordinary understanding of how things are done includes acts that put self or others in harm's way. That harm ranges from a reduction of self to a reduction of life span. We take a look at a few examples in the next section.

Unnecessary Risks

The waters of "risky or not, necessary or not" are difficult to chart much less run. The following example may help us.

Any U.S. university that accepts funds from the federal government is required to have an Institutional Review Board (IRB) for both its medical and nonmedical research. The nonmedical board reviews all social science research and other forms of scholarship that involves "human subjects" that seeks university sanction. The original motive for such boards was to safeguard the well-being of those people who would appear in those studies as the human subjects involved. The primary task involved is to assess the risks to the participants presented by the study's protocol and to ensure that those risks are fairly presented to the participants who agree to accept them.

In the conventions of cognitive science, respondents are often presented with some stimulus form (some image, content, sound, odor, etc.) to determine its effect on some outcome as mediated by some cognitive structure such as attitudes or values. The standard form of explanation is that "given the stimulus, persons with mental state Y will be more likely to do X." People who do Z instead of X, given the same stimulus, are presumed to have a different mental state. In very broad and oversimplified strokes, these are the performance rules of "doing a study."

In a recent meeting, there was animated discussion about the ethical implications of a proposal that sought to establish the norms of a paper and pencil test by comparing it to physiological measures. The test was a measure of pedophilia; the physiological measures were male sexual arousal to narratives of desire toward child objects. The value of having a measure that would indicate the presence of a sexual disorder that put children in harm's way was clear. The problem was how to protect the young men who would be exposed to the narratives from distortions of self or being haunted by memories of the narratives themselves or their arousal by them.

The board rejected the proposal because there was no way to predict or contain the risks posed by the study. To some members of the board even one man who went away with lingering doubts about himself was one too many. Others thought this danger might be mitigated by extensive debriefing and the availability of counseling afterward.

The proposal also foundered on its ability to obtain informed consent. Respondents need to know what they are getting into and the attendant risks. But how do you inform someone what a narrative of desire for an object-child is, when they may have had no experience with such narratives? And how do you do it and contain the very risks that the subject itself poses? Board members argued that the only way to truly inform someone unfamiliar was by an example, but that example might also harm.

In the fairly recent past, it was possible that none of these issues would have been considered because the rules of performance in the social sciences routinely privileged the knowledge gains of a study over the risks posed to the subjects. It was the potential and actual unethical conduct allowed by these rules that, in fact, led to the review boards themselves. Those of you who participate in scientific studies are safer because of them, but there are no guarantees of harmlessness. Risks to you are acceptable to science.

Risks that are potentially unethical to the other are acceptable in nearly all organizational settings. Parents put children at risk in sports activities, most often with little or no discussion of whether the child wants to take those risks. Sports after all are "good for them." Jim in his role as an official has seen coaches commit all sorts of misconduct under the normal practices of team discipline, particularly demanding that injured players get in the game. In one case, a cast was removed from a broken hand so that the child would be permitted on the field. It would have been a wonderful story for the player as a man to tell in 20 years as he pointed to his distorted, arthritic fingers. The child, of course, was anxious to play, having no idea and probably little care for the lifelong potential damage.

Industries such as timber, construction, and mining continue to have high-risk jobs, balancing the costs of further risk reduction against profits for ownership. Ethical issues abound when the consequences of their labor are not known by the workers, are exacerbated when what is known is withheld from workers (as apparently in the asbestos and tobacco industries), or when known safety measures are not supplied or enforced because of cost or reduced productivity. In these cases, the worker becomes an expendable resource.

A friend writes:

> The guy doing the attic insulation showed up at the remodeling site, wearing a T-shirt, shorts, and running shoes. No gloves, body protection, or mask, he goes up and spends over an hour in that enclosed space blowing in fiber-glass insulation. When he comes down, I get him something to drink and start a conversation. He's a college student working this job for the summer. Doesn't like it much, probably won't do it again. No, he didn't know anything about the dangers of insulation to skin, eyes, or lungs. They just showed him how to load and run the machine. He said there were lots of days when he didn't feel very good though.

Performance Rules That Silence

In the traditional hierarchy of medicine, it is the physician who establishes the regimen of patient care. While this example could easily go to the relationship between physicians and their corporate handlers as health maintenance organizations (HMOs) look to promote cost reduction over the best of care, it actually looks at the work practices defining the relationship between physicians and nurses. These relationship practices are laden with ethical implications. As professionals in their own right, nurses are partners (not equals, but partners) in patient care. They are independently liable for malpractice suits should they participate in a faulty regimen. The actual practice is that physicians sharply defend their authority. "I will get them to do what I want done," is how one put it. Pitted against responsibility and authority, the nurse is in a double-bind. Speak up and get a mark on the work record as well as a reputation for being difficult. Remain silent and violate one's professional ethics and face the risk of legal action. The problem here is not the nurse's silence, but the larger, intended or unintended unethical organizational practices that silence the nurses.

Performance Rules That Violate Legal Standards

The practical necessities of getting the job done often overwhelm the niceties of law, regulation, and policy. Laws and regulations are seen as unreasonable, impractical, burdensome, or "really not applicable to us." Policy is often written with the "worst case scenario" in mind, establishing requirements to "catch the thief" while impeding honest effort. Our concern here is not with the trivial, not with the construction boss who tells a worker to "go dump that little bit of solvent in the bushes." Our concern is with the construction firm that as a matter of practice buries 55 gallon drums of used solvent out in the back lot. Both break laws; the environment recovers quickly in the first case, but, perhaps, never in the second. In the second case, the firm's unethical practices entangle the backhoe operator and crew in a conspiracy of deceit and malfeasance. They know the violation, or if not, can probably guess that digging holes in the dead of night to bury waist-high drums is not quite right. But from what position do they act and speak? The solution is not to exhort workers to courageously risk their jobs. We might applaud those who do so (and at the same time be reluctant to hire them). This is unethical organizational behavior.

Formulating and adjudicating policy is one of the more difficult tasks of any organizing domain. Good policy is appropriate to the work to be done and can be adjudicated to accommodate particular circumstances. The more distant the policy maker from the practitioner, the less likely good policy will result. We see the results of bad policies and bad policy decisions daily in our corporations where disconnected managers make rules for work they don't understand. But it happens in our families as well where curfews, dress codes, or other rules undercut the very permissions granted. (Yes, you can go to movies, but you'll have to leave 10 minutes early in order to make our 10 o'clock curfew.) Such policy making invites resistance, and the policy maker is the culpable agent.

Performance Rules That Debase or Ridicule

There are unethical practices that are deeply embedded in work rules. These include regulations that deny individuals access to toilet facilities or other practices of normal hygiene; a mind-numbing, constant repetition of tasks; a relentless pace devoid of social contact; and all work that debases the individual, while exploiting a small proportion of ability and discarding the rest. The job may be putting on the driver's side door trim on 54 units per hour. But it doesn't have to be a lifetime sentence served 4 hours at a stretch, without locker facilities, work clothes, reasonable breaks, meal times, and the places to enjoy them. Whether on the line, in the clerical pool, or in the cubicles of middle management, the design of work has to provide a life worth living. It is easy to understand that unethical conduct has occurred when the worker is treated as less than a human being and viewed more as a piece of machinery.

It is not unusual for organizations to have hazing rituals of entrance, retirement, or dismissal. Those of the first two can actually be helpful in managing the transition from nonmember to member and back again. The rites of dismissal are often something else. In the opening scenario of Chapter 1, Bill suffered a personal crisis in his release from the firm. In many respects, however, the process was humane. The services Bill would need were provided and immediately available. He was protected from public embarrassment by the conveniently called staff meeting. He was treated firmly but with courtesy. Consider this dismissal rite, reportedly practiced by Disneyland:

> Dismissal began by being pulled off the ride after my work shift had begun by an area supervisor in full view of my cohorts. A forced march to the administration building followed where my employee card was turned over and a short statement read to me by a personnel officer as to the formal cause of termination. Security officers then walked me to the employee locker room where my work uniforms and equipment were collected and my personal belongings returned to me while an inspection of my locker was made. The next stop was the time shed where my employee's time card was removed from its slot, marked "terminated" across the top in red ink, and replaced in its customary position (presumably for Disneylanders to see when clocking on or off the job over the next few days). As now an ex–ride operator, I was escorted to the parking lot where two security officers scraped off the employee parking sticker attached to my car (Van Maanen, 1991, p. 76).

The Disneyland ritual was clearly designed to enforce discipline on the remaining employees by demonstrating the terrible consequences of violating the rules. This clearly unethical process sacrificed the dignity of the individual for corporate ends.

Finally, it appears as though Salt Lake City is moving steadily closer to Gomorrah, at least according to some local social commentators. A recent city council meeting in the suburb of Midvale approved the business license for an outlet of the restaurant chain, Hooters. Hooters, like other such sexually inflected enterprises, represents a problem because it deliberately presents its serving women as objects of gaze and desire. In the chain, service women wear white boots, hot pants, and midriff-baring tops that are tight across the breasts. The word "Hooters" and the owl logo are stenciled across the bust line, strategically placing the eyes and Os. There is little question as to the intended effect. Some social commentators consider the display pornographic, and some scholars consider the costuming another act of subjugation by masculine interests. At least some of the women, however, are quite pleased to make what is reportedly good money by celebrating their attractiveness. They do not consider their ability to manipulate more dollars into the tip their subjugation, but rather their power. (Emancipationists hate this sort of declaration by those they consider subjugated, calling it "false consciousness.")

How would we analyze this situation? We could begin by setting aside the costuming altogether and look rather at the total conditions of work. Does the job provide a living wage, one that could meet local requirements for housing, clothing, food, entertainment, and education? Do the service women have standing in the organization? Are their concerns listened to and responded to? Is there an opportunity for advancement? Is there work, opportunity, or some provision for life after youth and beauty? What risks are entailed in the work? Are those risks clearly understood and accepted? Are work practices in violation of laws or regulations or establish unwarranted expectations? Is the job part of a life worth living?

We (your authors) don't know the answers to these questions, but they are attainable through careful study. What we do know is that if the organization and its members pass these tests, then the problem of debasement and ridicule is located in the very people who intend the moral high road. Remembering that the meaningfulness of action is socially constructed, it is the effort of the commentators and scholars that debase and ridicule the chosen work of these service women. They do so to exploit them for their own agenda. This exploitation is simply one more act of subjugation.

On the day that Jim and Elaine visited Hooters, the Salt Lake County Sheriff's Department of Special Operations (the county SWAT team) was holding some sort of celebratory rite. The women of Hooters presented themselves athletically, similar to a beach volleyball team. Their uniforms revealed no more than the attire of female students attending a summer school course at a public university would and further were professionally designed to reveal less. Their clothing, nonetheless, was intended to invite the masculine gaze. The special operations men (we saw no women) wore tight-fitting, black T-shirts, camouflage trousers, and a weapon's belt slung low on the hip. Their attire is clearly intended to express strength, discipline, ability (and perhaps to invite the feminine gaze). It was a wonderful cultural intersection of gender.

Unethical organizational practices, as with all organizational conduct, emanate from ideological, discursive, and actional structurations that are constituted and maintained through the organizing processes themselves. Our culpability functions in the same way as it does in cultural misconduct.

> ## PRINCIPAL CONCEPTS
>
> Performance rules that promote misconduct include those that permit unnecessary or unrevealed risks, silence those who have the right to be heard, violate legal standards, or debase or ridicule the other.

That is, each of us participates in the racism, ethnocentrism, sexism, ageism, and objectifications promoted by our culture to the extent that we do not actively resist them. So it is with unethical organizational conduct: Each member participates to the extent that they do not resist. In each of us our membership declares the rest. But there are clear limits. We cannot choose our culture. By the time we are able to choose, it is too late. We cannot choose every organization to which we belong. In many cases, we are not free to choose where we work, or, once immersed, we are not free to change. The backhoe operator participates in the environmental destruction the construction firm wreaks. The operator's redemption is in resistance.

THE ETHICS OF RESISTANCE

We used the prior paragraph as a novel introduction to the concept of resistance in order to allow us to think about both sides of the ethical question of resistance. Most often we think of resistance as some wrong: Resistance to God's word is a sin. Resistance to one's parents is disobedience. Resistance to one's teacher is disruption. Resistance to one's supervisor is cause for dismissal. Ah, but resistance to tyranny, injustice, intolerance—such resistance is to be applauded. So the ethical value of resistance depends on what is being resisted.

We begin again by restating the process of organizing: Organizing is a process that disciplines individual performance to be accountable to and understandable within a coherent ideology of member-to-member relationships and collective practices of discourse and action. In so doing, organizing constitutes the doing and the done, the possible, the right, and the true. The goal of this discipline is the reproduction of the ideology that frames it through the naturalized performances of its members. Those performances are the expression of ideological practices that are themselves initiated and sustained through instruction, supervision,

PRINCIPAL CONCEPTS

Resistance in an organization is a disruption in the relationship between a member and the organizational ideology. Resistance is the
shadowed twin of command as both refer to the same power expressions but from different standpoints.

mirroring or modeling, and resource allocation—the controlled distribution of authority, information, and material resources, and structuring of
environments.

Organizational power is the product of the relationship between the individual and this ideological framework, not an attribute of a title or a person. Resistance in organizations is defined within that relationship and
seeks to undermine some part of the means of the production of that organization, that is, transforming the ideological work of member-to-member
relationships, shared meanings of discourse and action, and their judicial
interpretation. Resistance is the shadow twin of leadership in that both
refer to the same processes in power expressions. Each set, however, is nominated differently from the exnominated (the assumed and deliberately hidden) position of the dominant. Leadership is on the side of *good;* resistance
is a *problem.* They also function differently. In the system of organizing, administrative leadership is global and strategic, whereas resistance is local
and tactical.

ACTS OF RESISTANCE

What follows is a compilation of "acts of resistance," acts that intend to undermine the processes of organizing in which these acts participate. We pose
them not to put a list of techniques in print but to consider the instability
of their ethical character. From the exnominated position of what is declared to be right, these actions are wrong, a problem to be dealt with.[6] But

---

[6] The phrasing here is deliberately in the negative to emphasize the contrary nature of resistance; the actions we describe, however, could be both intended to be and be read as appropriate organizational work. The action text is not self-evident; it has to be interpreted. The
same can be said of the "supervisory misconduct" that follows this list.

if the organizational action is immoral, these acts of resistance may not only be justified, they may be called for. Consider these tactics:

- **Competition:** Poaching on the territory of others, doing someone else's (usually a supervisor's) job and claiming to do it better
- **Disruption:** Methods of persistent questioning, delay, sidetracking, raising irrelevancies, excessive ruminations, story telling and the like
- **Distancing:** Methods that limit one's engagement of and immersion in the ideological framework (e.g., rehearsing other ideological standards, limiting time in place, violating resource or environment codes)
- **Instrumental Incompetence:** Deliberately failing at an unwanted task
- **Masking:** Generating the appearance of authorized effort or using an authorized activity as the basis of a preferred activity
- **Overperformance:** Doing the job beyond reasonable need (four-color memo, landscaping leaf-by-leaf) or so well as to call the enterprise into question
- **Sabotage:** Producing defective work; ridiculing organizational beliefs; undercutting authority
- **Selectivity:** Methods of aggressive self-interest in choice situations
- **Simplification:** Reducing work procedures to less than the standard; unauthorized stockpiling; control of resources, tools, and/or methods
- **Specification:** Doing no more than what is specified in instructions or job descriptions (e.g., a "work to the rules" strike)
- **Surveillance:** Calling to question the performance of others; insisting on the literal performance of organizational proverbs; unjustified whistle blowing
- **Underperformance:** Deliberately slowing work; reducing productivity; doing just enough to remain below the horizon of supervision

SUPERVISORY PRACTICES OF RESISTANCE

What is often called supervisory misconduct or sometimes coercive power is also a form of resistance to ideological power. It involves the tactical appropriation of relationships, shared understandings, and methods of interpretation for unauthorized ends. While the action is generally recognized as unjust (called "bad management") the enactor cannot be removed without calling the ideological framework into question. It is this double articulation that distinguishes this form of resistance from the more simple ones listed above. Again, the ethical character of these tactics (as opposed to their instrumental value) depends on the manner in which they are interpreted. Forms of supervisory resistances include:

- **Appropriation:** Representing the work of others as one's own
- **Arbitrary Work Rules:** Extending one's authority into dress, conduct, or performance that have no organizationally justified consequences. Often includes oversupervision
- **Burden-shifting:** Moving an unwanted task to someone else without recognition or compensation (although sometimes under-the-table compensation is provided)
- **Disassociation/Isolation:** Actively sequestering the other
- **Double Binding:** Setting up requirements that guarantee failure
- **Harassment:** Harassment (sexual or otherwise) includes any inappropriate quid pro quo, marking or comment upon the individual, ground-shifting of understanding, interference in authorized or "off-duty" performance, and the like
- **Nonjustified Evaluation:** Unstudied claims about the abilities or performances of the other; use of hidden criteria, false deadlines, more stringent requirements
- **Nonrecognition:** The failure to account for justified activity, legitimate authority, and or discernible contribution
- **Overrecognition:** Providing praise, rewards, work rule exceptions, emancipations not authorized by organizational practices
- **Oversupervision:** Interference through surveillance requirements; supervising non–task-related activities
- **Reperformance:** Redoing the work of others, especially that which has been done well enough (often includes appropriation)
- **Sinecurism:** Creating positions of profit with no responsibilities
- **Suppression:** Refusing the work of the other; eclipsing acceptable performance; denying, belittling, or demeaning the extension of effort
- **Unannounced Changes:** Changes in performance rules, job descriptions, or criteria; methods that enlarge tasks or reduce responsibilities that are not revealed in a timely fashion but are used to evaluate performance

The Ethical Character of Resistance

The question we posed at the beginning of this section asked if forms of resistance could ever be justified. Our answer was, "Of course." In fact, we argued that sometimes it is demanded. We grant great approval to acts of resistance against tyranny from childhood stories of the bully, to tales of the resistance against fascism and soviet domination. In ordinary organizations resistance stills the ideological drumbeat, interrupts naturalized practices, calls into question the taken for granted, and allows us to interrogate the quality of organizational life with no agenda, no bid for higher position necessarily in mind.

At the same time, we need to consider the ordinary way we reconcile resistance in our families, classrooms, social groups, and work places. Our typical response as parents, teachers, participants, and leaders is to punish and suppress it. Resistance to our rightful authority is clearly wrong. (Honor thy father and mother, after all.) Failing that, we move to co-opt it—take it under our control, put it to our service—long before we accommodate and acknowledge its value.

Postmodern sensibilities toward the domination imposed by any organizing ideology, no matter how benign, further complicate our analysis of resistance. Any act of becoming happens in some ideological framework that disciplines potential into actual. As we have said, any expression of the self entails giving up what else the "I" could be. Even as the "I" becomes, the desire to be what the "I" is not continues. This desire resists the self. As a result we find ourselves resisting the very things that appear to give us what we want.

As there are no utopian solutions to organizing—an organization of absolute equality is no organization at all—and because there is no final resting place of the self, resistance is a necessary part of existence. Resistance need not seek to correct, improve, or transform. Any correction, improvement or transformation is simply a difference elevated in character by its standpoint of engagement. We resist because we will.

We separate resistance from the idea of opposition. Opposition, as we theorize it, has an agenda, and it functions inside the practical ideology in which it arises. The "loyal opposition," for example, is a central tenet of a liberal philosophy that believes that opposing ideas, while upholding a common ideological framework, will produce stronger results. Unfortunately, opposition is often two political parties vying to be the one that brings us "good government." Opposition does not question the internal operations of power as resistance does. It questions only who should hold the rights to them.

PRINCIPAL CONCEPTS

Resistance has a bipolar reputation being considered both problem and solution. As problem it calls legitimated authority into question. As solution it battles tyranny or creates the needed space for new ideas and practices. In the postmodern framework, resistance is the generalized response to the discipline of becoming. Its value accrues from its denial of certainty, totalitarianism, and unitary concepts of the true, the good, and the beautiful.

The ethical achievements of resistance are in its denial of certainty; its continual undermining of the totalitarian impulses of any organizing ideology; its rejection of any unitary projections of the true, the good, and the beautiful. Resistance always forces us to redo the work by which we constitute the reality in which we live. Therein lies the possibility of such refurbishments we might advance.

TRANSITIONS

This chapter conducted an exploration into the nature of power; its differentiated expression in acts of control; and its shadow, resistance. Power, we saw, was not the attribute of an individual or an office. It is not something to be held. Power was seen as the necessary outcome of a relationship through the reciprocity of obligation. Power is a relational characteristic within the recognition of self and other. It is the terms of the relationship that sets the terms of the expression of power. We concluded that no cultural membership is without power, and there is no power outside of a relationship.

We also concluded that power is reciprocal, but its differentiated expression is not equitable. Ideologically we manage the paradox of reciprocity and inequity through what is revealed and what is concealed. We reveal the rights of the dominant and the duties of the subordinate; we conceal their opposites. Practically, this paradox is managed through access rights to material and semiotic resources, to the stages of authority, to discourses and action.

Preparatory to considering acts of resistance, we revisited the nature of organizing. We repeated the description of Chapter 3, that organizing is a process that disciplines individual performance to be accountable to and understandable within a coherent ideological framework of member-to-member relationships, practices of discourse and action, rules of performance, and the judicial procedures of each. We then looked at resistance as those acts that work to undermine this discipline. We examined the acts of resistance from subordinate and supervisory positions. And we considered how their ethical character was in doubt, a doubt typically resolved through the exnominated practices of the dominant.

We now have enough of the moral and organizational elements of theory in place to profitably conduct the standpoint analysis that was presaged at the end of Chapter 6. This analysis starts with a case from our consultant files.

CASE STUDY

An executive vice president with a *Fortune 500* company is caught cheating on his expense account. The executive makes in excess of $1 million per year, yet the internal audit branch finds that he has been consistently abusing his expense account by about $2000 a month. The board of directors of the company determines that it is in the best interests of the corporation to allow the 56-year-old executive vice president an early retirement. The board also establishes this explanation as the "official story" of the corporation to be told by all.

A *Wall Street Journal* reporter learns of the early retirement and questions the corporate vice president of public relations. The reporter is sure that the executive vice president would work to age 65 on his million-dollar-plus salary. All executives he questions are firm with the story, yet they know the fabrication.

1. Who is protected by the lie?
2. Explain how access to information is a mechanism of control within the corporate structure.
3. Why is the truth denied the *Wall Street Journal*?
4. Explain organizational control within this case.

8

THE PRACTICE OF ETHICS

We begin this chapter with an extended case upon which to practice the sort of ethical analysis we have endorsed. Following the case presentation we analyze the acting agents as the standpoints of the case. We then consider the domain of agency as it positions these agents in a field of choices. Finally we begin to consider how we can address the questions of right and wrong.

THE HARASSMENT GRADES CASE

John Gordon is a 27-year-old, recently married, claims adjuster for a major household insurance company who is also finishing his degree in business administration. His job involves going out to the homes of policy holders who have claims for water damage from leaky roofs, broken pipes or for broken windows, wind damage and the like. John has pretty much seen it all when it comes to people "manufacturing" a claim. So he is careful, tries to get all the facts to protect the company against fraudulent claims. A 6-foot 2-inch, hard body, he uses his physique to intimidate those he thinks are lying to him. He has great hopes of moving up in the company once he finishes that degree.

But John has a problem. Last semester he finally got around to taking that required class in business communication. John was pretty successful in all his presentations. His work, however, caused him to miss a lot of classes. He got his friend to cover for him in the group work. But the instructor, Traci Johnson, one of the business communication (BizComm) teaching fellows, had this technique of giving unannounced pop quizzes to make sure that everyone was current on their reading. The instructor refused to indicate if a quiz was planned even when students checked in prior to a planned absence or to allow make ups for these quizzes saying that make-ups wouldn't be fair because "you'd know the quiz was coming and could prepare for the test."

John missed five of these quizzes, which counted for 25 percent of the grade. He ended up getting a "D" for the course. Because the graduation rules require a grade of "C" or better in every required course, John now has to take the course over, delaying his graduation by more than a year, or he has to get that grade changed.

John went to talk to the instructor about how work had made him be absent and that there was nothing he could do about that. His instructor listened politely to his problem and then pulled out the syllabus to point to the section where the rules of the quizzes were stated. "These rules are a contract between me and the students in the class," she intoned. "If I violate these rules for you, I cheat everyone else in the class. You have to make choices, John. School and work are part of those choices." "Come on," John replied, "you're a student just like I am. You must understand the pressures we're up against." Traci wouldn't budge. John was frustrated and left angry.

Evelyn, John's wife, listened to him complain about the meeting with his instructor. "That instructor was just plain mean," she commiserated. "You should talk to the dean or somebody. I think she has it in for you. Did you ever do anything to make her mad?" "I don't think so," John answered. "She did ask me to go to a graduate lecture, but I had to work, so I turned her down. You don't think that had anything to do with it, do you?" "I don't know," Evelyn teased, "you're pretty cute." John decided to make another appointment with the instructor. He got one for the following Monday at 6 in the evening.

On Monday, John drove back to the university around 4 P.M. to meet with his friends to do some work on a group project. He had been stewing about that communication grade all day. How did it happen that those five quizzes were given just on the days I wasn't there? If she wanted to get back at me, she could just give those quizzes on the days I was absent. It's a perfect system. John saw his friends at the cafeteria between classes and told them about his analysis. "Guess she could have done it that way," Rick answered. "I know I heard her say once, 'Well, John's not here again,' just before she handed out the quiz. And how come she wants to see you so late in the day? She got something planned for you, Johnny boy?"

When John met with the instructor later that evening, he went right to the attack. He told her that she had treated him unfairly and that he was going to file a sexual harassment case against her unless she changed the grade. When asked for his evidence, he replied, "You came on to me, you asked me out, and when I refused, you made sure to give the quizzes when I wasn't there. I have other students who will testify that you made remarks about me in class. And what were you planning to do tonight?"

◆◆◆

Traci Johnson is a 30-year-old, single, graduate student finishing her doctorate in communication studies. She sees herself as a bit overweight, "a Renaissance woman," she jokes. Traci is very structured and has a well-ordered approach to the many demands of her degree program and of her teaching assignment. She has been teaching business communication for 3 years now. She loves to teach, is always prepared, and expects her students to be prepared as well. She has a "thing" about students who come late or are absent. Most of her students hold her in high regard, but she does get complaints about being too rigid, too unrealistic about people who have to work, have family or other responsibilities besides school, as most do in this urban university.

When Traci discovers a bright student, she likes to appoint herself as an informal mentor, getting that student involved in the scholarly activities of the department. She is proud of two of her mentees who were accepted into the master's program.

Today, she has a 6 P.M. appointment with John Gordon. John works and Traci is in class until 6:00, so that was the only time they could meet. Traci has met with John before and knows that he is upset about the "D" he earned in BizComm. Last time she tried stonewalling him to make sure he was serious. But she likes John, even cares for him. This time, she'll try to work something out—extra work or something so that he won't have to take the class over. She tells her instructor, Dr. Williams, that she will have to leave 2 minutes early to meet with a student. Williams agrees and thinks to himself, "That sure is Traci, never make a student wait and know exactly the time it takes to walk across the hall to open the door."

The grad class goes well. Everyone seems comfortable with the material, the discussions are engaging, good humor abounds. At 2 minutes to 6 P.M., Traci stands up and starts to excuse herself when from across the hall comes the sound of someone pounding on an office door. "Oops," Traci says, "that sounds like my student. I better go."

Twenty minutes later an ashen-faced Traci stands in the doorway of Professor Williams's office who is sorting through the last of some student papers before going home to dinner. "I've got to talk to you," she anguished. She told the tale.

"Did this student say what he wanted?" Williams asked.

"Yes," Traci answered, "he said he thought a 'B'-minus was fair."

"A 'B'-minus?" Williams exploded in laughter, "He didn't even have the guts to ask for an 'A'? What a petty extortionist."

"I know he's wrong, but I'm going to change that grade, Dr. Williams, first thing tomorrow."

"Hang on, Traci. Let's wait a day and think this through. Nothing is going to change between now and Wednesday."

John got home feeling pretty good. "Man I sure showed her, Evelyn."

"What do you mean?" his wife replied.

"Well, I met with Rick and the guys, and they think she was coming on to me. So, I told her I was going to file a sexual harassment case if she didn't change the grade. I was honest though. I told her that I thought a 'B'-minus was fair. I think she sees what was going on now and she'll change that grade."

Professor Williams tried to reach Traci off and on for most of Tuesday, finally reaching her late Tuesday afternoon. "Listen, Traci, you simply cannot let him get away with this. I checked with some folks who work these cases. They said that if you change the grade, it may be seen as an admission of guilt. If his side sees it that way, he may go for more than just a grade change. That could be real expensive and not just for you. We're going to make him file his complaint. In the meantime, get your ducks in order; go over everything you did, and make sure that you have a plausible explanation for everything."

METHODS OF ETHICAL ANALYSIS

Any ethical analysis begins with three determinations that must be applied to both the action and the evaluation: (a) who were the acting agents, (b) what was their domain of agency, and (c) what system of values was in play. These determinations form the evidence for the answers to the questions we raised in Chapter 1:

◆ Who (what self or authorized entity) was the acting agent?

- What motives (elements of desire, freedom of choice, autonomy of selection) were present?
- What ideological framework was in governance?
- What resources (ideological, semiotic, social, and material) for action were available?
- What action (the interpreted sign) was performed?
- How (its competence, coherence, quality) was it enacted?
- What were the declared and undeclared, intended and unintended consequences (the attributed signs of outcome)?
- What resources (ideological, semiotic, social, material) for further action were sustained, created?
- What self is the evaluating agent?
- What standpoints are in evidence?
- What are the means of our evaluation–criteria, evidentiary process, warrants for our conclusions (the terms of reflexive analysis)?

The complexity of these questions demonstrates the difficulties of "doing ethics on the fly" in the midst of the action; why a record of ethical conduct is often predicated on one's prior prudence in the choice of circumstances, relationships, and repertoires of discourse and action; and why such analysis is most often practiced on the done. In our analysis of what has been done by John, Traci, and the others, we will undertake answers to the first two of these questions—the agents and their domain of agency. We leave the final construction of the third answer to you, but begin the process by extracting some materials for it from the case. We begin with the agentive standpoints of the case.

STANDPOINTS IN THE CASE

The analysis of standpoints allows us to look at the case from the various ideological positions that function to change the meanings of the facts of the case and of the interpretations that can be carried by those facts. For example, it is a fact that Traci asked John to attend a public lecture, but what was the intent of the asking? John might frame it as a bid for a different kind of relationship, Traci as part of her teaching function, Professor Williams as an inappropriate but good-intentioned move by a junior faculty member. Whichever of these interpretations is declared to be true becomes the basis for subsequent disciplinary action.

John

Standpoints are quite often synonymous with individuals, but it is the individual as located in the particular production of the self within culturally defined subject positions. John is a standpoint whose consistency across the action is his membership as a student at the university in the particular expression within the terms of the relationship with instructor Traci. At different times in the case, however, we see John dealing with the action from the domain of work, his marriage, and his friendships. We also see that John's gender is a resource in the narrative he attempts to construct around the facts of the case. John's body gives him power. So the standpoint is never just plain John; it is always John as he is contingently materialized in the self-in-action.[1]

Traci

For her part, Traci is multiply articulated within the case. She is Traci the instructor at the start of the case and Traci the student in the middle. In the very same location, she must reproduce herself in quite different ways. At the end of the case she is no longer instructor or student but employee whose actions have brought the potential of harm to her employers and to the organization. In the final sentence of the case, we see that Traci has lost control of the outcome and its declaration. There is, of course, more. As a self-described, culturally declared overweight woman teaching a business class, she is positioned within multiple stereotypes. Her body type and gender render her vulnerable to social judgments as to her authority and competence.

Evelyn

We know little of Evelyn other than her positioning as wife of John. We do know that she enacts a culturally derived "stand by your man" performance that creates a critical moment in the action. It is her relationship to John that permits that performance. She sees John as hardworking, trying his

---

[1] If we accepted "just plain John," we would be agreeing to a theoretical position of the human self being a unity that always has the opportunity for right reason and proper action. This essential self can be misled by desire or biased by ignorance, but it always has the capacity to reach for the true. We hold to a much more pragmatic "what you see is what you get" position.

best; she also understands that her success is coupled with his and views the degree as a goal to be reached in order to improve their lives. Traci's class is not a learning opportunity but a hurdle to jump. You get over it in whatever way you can. She also sees John as attractive, perhaps encourages his working out to maintain that attractiveness. She recognizes his value as a commodity.

Rick

Rick, John's friend, is positioned within his acts of resistance against authority. He allows John to "beat the system" by covering for him during his absences from group work; he is, in fact, a coconspirator in John's misbehavior. Because Traci is the visible expression of authority, he encourages John to "take her down," taunting, nearly daring him in their exchange. Their friendship relationship establishes the opportunity of the joint performances we encounter, but friendship does not seem to be the governance of Rick's actions.

Professor Williams

We see Professor Williams in his three vested roles in relation to Traci—teacher, advisor, and supervisor. He moves very quickly from advisor to supervisor the moment Traci declares that she is going to change that grade. At that moment Traci's interests are no longer the driving force. His interests as supervisor and those of the organization command his action from that moment. He can no longer see the problem as one simply involving Traci and John. The problem is the potential of a lawsuit, which he intends to win by the artful construction of "what actually happened."

And Behind the Scene

There are two and possibly four other standpoints in this case. We, the authors, are one; you, dear reader, are another; the possible third is the instructor of the class in which this book is a text; and the possible fourth is the other students in that class. As the authors we are attempting to contain the case to force it to the conclusions we wish to make in our argument. We want it to do our work in support of our joint vision of organizing and ethics. You, the reader, may have your own position on organizations and ethics, on how to construct argument, on the interpretation of the characters

> ## PRINCIPAL CONCEPTS
>
> The characters in the case represent different standpoints in the field of what is known and valued in the action described. The actual action text is a set of small pieces of activity. The analytic action text is those small pieces arranged in a mosaic that makes sense of them. Further, any analysis must move forward on incomplete knowledge and through assumptions that hold uncertainties stable.

in the case. We, of course, would be delighted as that is exactly our point. You certainly have a different set of responsibilities to the text than do we. You meet the text in the action of reading or, perhaps, studying; we in the process of writing. The relationship between us over this text becomes complicated with the introduction of an instructor and other students. The instructor, within the domain of the traditional classroom, gets to declare what is true and not, what is sound and not within her or his authority as the instructor. Other students can contest that declaration (as can you) or they may contest or complement your own. The facts of the case are a resource for all of us, and the story is for each of us to tell within the different domains of the telling.

THE DOMAIN OF AGENCY

John, Traci, Rick, and Williams all inhabit a common domain of agency, albeit as different standpoints.[2] Their membership is in their common knowledge of the choices, enactments, and evaluative terms that describe the domain and in the sharing of the consequences of action. Each is a stakeholder in the construction of the domain and, at some level in the scale of things, participates in the action of the other. Chapter 5 set the terms by which this domain can be analyzed. Those terms are memberships and relationships, hierarchies of action and discourse, thematics, and location.

---

[2] Evelyn is intimately connected to this domain through her relationship to John, but even though she can benefit or be hurt by what goes on there, she is not a member.

ETHICAL IMPLICATIONS OF MEMBERSHIPS

John

John is a student at Intermountain University (IMU). He carries a token of that membership in his billfold in the form of a student ID card. His membership gives him certain rights, privileges, and obligations. He can enroll in classes, check out library books, use computers, buy sports tickets, have access to recreational facilities. He must be enrolled in some class, pay his fees and fines, and maintain a minimum grade point average. Equally important, he must pay tribute to the hegemony of the educational contract. That hegemony sets the terms of the emblematic action and discourse of his membership.

John is also a member of Traci's class. (Note the hegemonic discursive assignment of class ownership to Traci, the instructor. The class does not belong to the students.) He can be in Traci's class because he is a student. (Being in Traci's class does not make him a student, though according to IMU policy, he must be in some class to maintain his student status.) As a member of Traci's class he comes into the assumptions of that membership. Such assumptions would typically include that students are under the governance of the instructor, that students are motivated to succeed and will accept the discipline of success, and that the instructor has the right to set the terms of that success, all, of course, within the purview of "good educational practices."

Membership is a significant grant of power, and in any rational system, where there is "give" there has to be a "get." The "get" in education is a mixture of tangible credits, allegedly measurable learning, and the intangible promise of a better life. In more crass terms, membership entitles John to a grade and the chance of a good grade. (One pedagogical premise is that students should have the means of their success and the right to fail.) We can see, then, that the issue for John is not sexual harassment, but the entitlement of his membership. His claim of sexual harassment is simply a means toward that end.

John has another significant membership to consider. That is his membership as an employee at Ranch and Home Insurance. John embodies the action site where the demands of these memberships must be managed. It is a unique site in these memberships in that neither John's employer nor John's instructor has the knowledge of the consequences of their separate demands in the way that John does, and often, neither cares because one is not a stakeholder in John's success in the domain of the other.

Traci

The standpoint of Traci is marginalized in this case by her membership as a graduate student and as a member of the faculty. She is neither clearly "one of us" nor clearly "one of them" but can be declared as either or neither according to the demands of the action. John had attempted to evoke Traci's membership as a student in his first negotiation. When that didn't work he invoked Traci's membership as a faculty member to establish the conditions of a sexual harassment claim. Williams begins as a colleague, but it is clear that he is not going to follow "some graduate student" to financial ruin. Traci does not seem to manage this marginalized position well. She attempts to exert more force in her relationships with students than she has the authority to sustain.

THE EVOCATIONS AND INVOCATIONS OF MEMBERSHIP

A standpoint becomes the self in action partially through the membership processes of *evocation* and *invocation*. Given the necessary resources, member action can evoke (call forth) the conditions necessary for a particular expression of the self, and enactors can invoke particular expressions to move action in particular ways.[3] Any of these callings could have ethical implications for all agents involved. For example, Traci in her calculation of the course syllabus establishes the conditions under which acts of resistance are not only possible but also encouraged. It is clear that absolute rules on tardiness and attendance cannot be sustained except through considerable effort and that they will be a target for subversion. Traci, in declaring those rules, may be in the thrall of the highest educational values, but the character of the rules exceed her ability to contain their consequences. They evoke resistance.

Agents can also invoke a performance from their repertoire. John gives an example of an unethical invocation when he declares himself to be Traci's sexual ambition. He invokes himself as the "innocent desirable," using the cultural standing of his gender, age, and body type as resources in that performance. Traci has contributed to that performance by her invitation, but that invitation is open to multiple interpretations. John has

---

[3] For example, Jim *invokes* his masculinity by dressing in his power suit prior to class; his masculine self is *evoked* as he chooses which restroom to use in the ordinary design of public facilities.

chosen one, a choice that finds support in the comments of Evelyn and Rick.

Evocation and invocation provide us a glimpse into the contemporary moral understanding of agency. This agency is not characterized by independence, but rather by choices that are embedded in complicity and implication. Students in Traci's class are provided choices within the realm of a recognizable system of relational power. Assuming that she has the ability to enforce that system, students, if they are to be students, will be complicit members of the system. They will also be implicated by it as they conform; work for change; covertly resist; or, as in John's case, attempt to unethically manipulate the system. The result is that whatever we are, we will be forced to make the choices that are allowable within that realm of existence. These choices may be harmful or helpful to others, but our understanding of them and our culpability for them are within the ideological framework that makes them sensible.

So, is conforming to Traci's rules the morally right thing to do? That is, if people are going to be students in Traci's class are they ethically bound by her rules? Though many would answer "yes," our answer is "not necessarily," although anyone might chose to follow those rules. As we have seen in Chapter 7, acts of resistance may be legitimate in the presence of the unethical expression of power. The start of the answer to whether this is such a case is to consider the standpoint in the choice: what defines individuals as students; why are such students in Traci's class; and what does conforming to her rules do to them, to Traci, and to their fellow class members? One cannot simply assume that Traci is right, the rules are right, or that all must follow. That assumption denies Traci's obligation.

RELATIONSHIPS

Rick and John

Rick and John may elsewhere be the best of friends, but in a typical educational setting they are competitors for the scarce resource of good grades. Instructors of typical U.S. college classes cannot give all the students "A" grades. So, one "A" earned is one less to give out. Rick's success can be to John's diminishment. It is to Rick's benefit, therefore, for him to encourage John to "take on" Traci. He is not acting as a friend, but as a member of a competitive class. It is his relationship with John, nonetheless, that gives him access to John's confidence. He takes advantage of that relationship in daring John to action.

That action raises questions considering the character of Rick's friendship. If that friendship has developed out of contiguity—being mates in the same class—the entire history of the relationship may be encompassed by school activities. In effect, John and Rick are business acquaintances because their joint performance is bounded by their work as students and does not achieve the complexity of engagement that friendship requires. Their lives are not mutually entangled. Using Aristotle's standard of friendship, Rick is not committed to the betterment of John. He is, rather, in an opportunistic alliance of two people in a common realm of action. John makes a substantial error if he assumes the quality of Rick's advice is based on that Aristotlean standard. John is either fooled or a fool if he believes the easy efforts of coffee in the student union are the stuff of friendships.

Evelyn and John

John should be able to expect a higher standard of commitment to his success in his relationship with Evelyn. As his spouse, she has entered into a contractual relationship in which they are to share the gains and losses incurred by each and both. It is to her personal advantage to be knowledgeable and to give good advice. In our case, she is working from the assumption that Traci, as the teacher, has control over John, the student, and that Traci can misuse that authority for caprice or personal satisfaction. She asks if John had made Traci angry, knowing that grading procedures and grades can be manipulated. Traci, for Evelyn, is an institutional object, a figure of oppression, and a barrier to her partner's success. The consequences of a sexual harassment charge are considered only from the viewpoint of the resolution of John's immediate problem and not from the consequence for Traci or the long-term consequences to John should he be sued for damages.[4]

Evelyn and John, however, were engaged in an ordinary conversation, action where the flow of talk is more important than what is said. Had she been involved in a problem-solving session, she would have been expected to be more considered in her responses and certainly should be held to a higher standard. It is well beyond practice to hold every turn of talk to be

---

[4] Awards of over $1 million have been given in such damage suits.

fully representative of one's full expertise. Evelyn is not speaking as a harassment specialist, although she may be one. Her teasing at the end of the conversation shows her speaking as a partner easing the troubles of the day. John has not asked her to be anything more—or less.

Professor Williams and Traci

Professor Williams is an expression of direct and indirect authority for Traci. He is the instructor in a class in which she is a student. As a senior faculty member, he is involved in the governance of the department and therefore has quasi supervisory authority over her performance in the classroom. But central to this case, he serves as her mentor—an advisor and confidant— with an acknowledged obligation to give good advice and support. Throughout the dialogue we see Williams enacting the different elements of this relationship, although Traci seems firmly located in the teacher/mentor dimensions. In the sentence that begins, "Hang on, Traci," Williams reveals the shift to his supervisory role.

The shift in that relationship recalibrates the ethical equation. He is no longer operating as one responsible for Traci's well-being. Although he might not intend to do harm to Traci, his and the organization's safety are now paramount. What happens to Traci is now of secondary concern. If Traci doesn't hear the shift, she may mistakenly interpret the character of the advice Williams subsequently gives. That may be to Williams's advantage. Even though Williams may be justified in moving to a supervisory role, his undeclared advantage raises the shift to an ethical concern.

Traci and John

John defines the terms of this relationship as strictly bounded by the classroom. He has no interest in an academic career and sees school as a stepping stone to the "real world." Although he might remember her, once the class is over, he may literally never see Traci again. Traci, on the other hand, treats her students as "projects"—people to be both nurtured and disciplined into superior performers. She sees John as a comember of the university, a student with promise who might go on to follow in her footsteps. It is this difference in view that creates the conditions by which the case becomes a case.

John is just passing through on his way to something else. Traci wants John to stay around and participate in the intellectual life. This difference resonates with the cultural center of the classic masculine/feminine conflict.

Although we can work to limit their influence, we cannot escape the cultural narratives that operate to make life sensible. It is not surprising that John moves to an interpretation of sexual desire and, consequently, to an explanation based on sexual harassment for his grade. All the resources are there for him to do so.

Every relationship entails risk; Traci sets the parameters of the risks she takes by overreaching her status as a teaching fellow in attempting to establish a mentor/mentee relationship with students who would be justly confused by her credentials for that role. Traci's invitation and John's refusal were likely a very awkward moment. Traci was probably chagrined, but she also very likely "wrote John off" from that moment. John was likely irritated by being asked to do something outside the classroom for which he had little interest. In Traci's eyes, John was less of a student; for John, Traci turned weird and her actions from that time on were tainted by that judgment. Both worked from a different set of assumptions and both failed to test the validity of those assumptions or to recognize the evidence of their defectiveness.

Off-Stage Relationships

There are, of course, any number of off-stage relationships for which we have no information in the case. We can certainly predict something between John and his boss and between Traci and her teaching fellow colleagues. But we don't know what part they play in the actions taken. Such is always the circumstance in evaluating action. We are always working from incomplete knowledge. Our judgments always need to be tentative and open to new information and interpretations.

We need also remember that each of us is positioned in relationships (as well as all the other elements in a domain of agency) that bear upon our judgment. There is no Archimedean standpoint, no place sufficiently distant from the reality we live in to reflect without influence upon that reality. So, in making a judgment we necessarily impose a point of view, not a foundational moment of truth.

Hierarchies of Action and Discourse

We begin this part of the analysis by noting that John has ceded power over his action and discourse to the institution of the university in exchange for the opportunities of a college degree. Because of this grant, he does not control either the choice of the BizComm course in his curriculum or the conditions under which he can succeed in it. He is forced to work either through approved channels of negotiation and appeal or through channels of resistance. We have seen John choosing both methods. His attack on Traci is a legitimate, if somewhat tainted, means of controlling the grade to be recorded. It is tainted, not by the validity of his claims (which do not appear to be supported) but by a number of institutional and cultural codes that surround superior-subordinate relations in general and sexual harassment cases in particular. These issues will be taken up under thematics. His acts of resistance have to do with his subversion of the rules about group work.

John wants to be successful in both work and school (among other arenas). He has to finesse the conflicts that arise between the competing demands that success in these arenas impose. Instead of maintaining the pretense of group work (his and Rick's deliberate acts of deception) could John simply openly declare that he cannot do the group work and if no substitute could be allowed that he would take the penalty? That depends on how Traci has set up the class. Many instructors will insist that the curriculum is a unit and everything must be done to accomplish the complexity of learning necessary for a grade. Others allow deviations but impose secret tests of what a good student is. ("Those who skip group work cannot be good students.") Some empower students to select the elements by which they will succeed. In any case John's choices are set by what the instructor designates. The instructor, therefore, is complicit, though not necessarily culpable, in the choices John makes.

We can understand the hierarchy of discourse in play here by considering what John can say to mount a successful appeal of his grade. The issue here is not the group work, because apparently he didn't get caught in his deception, but in the lost points from the in-class quizzes from which he was missing. Traci defends her intransigence with the canon of fairness.[5] Presuming that her belief is authentic,[6] the only way John can succeed in getting her to waive or substitute for the tests is for Traci to declare herself

---

[5] She is, of course, confusing similar treatment with fairness. She could be fair by treating each student according to her or his circumstance. It may not be fair to treat people who have to work to earn the tuition by which they can attend school the same as those who do not, across the criterion of available time.

[6] The case shows that her belief is not authentic.

"unfair." John's negotiation should have been conducted following the announcement of the requirement and continued after every missed test. At the beginning, Traci's supervisor could have been brought in within the boundaries of a friendly discussion. At the end of the course, it is John's potential for trouble versus Traci's authority to grade that are pitted against one another. As the course proceeds, the discursive range narrows tightly to where an attack appears to be John's only recourse.

So why didn't John negotiate in a timely fashion? For the answer we would look at two places. First, we might consider the institutional response: How do students feel about talking to instructors? How do instructors feel about students negotiating their curriculum? Although we would not speak for everywhere or any place, your authors' experience in teaching in both Eastern and Western cultures would suggest that common institutional practice discourages students from entering into discussion much less a negotiation. Again complicity appears on this analytical scene.

Second, consider John's work practices. When he meets resistance, he uses pressure, bluff, and intimidation to get his way. He is encouraged and rewarded in doing so. It is a "naturalized" practice, one that is "at the ready" and easily performed. Traci may know none of this, of course, but her initial bluff (stonewalling to see if John was "really serious") played right into John's naturalized practice of response.[7]

Consequently, there are institutional, cross-venue, and Traci's complicit contributions to John's adversarial stance. So is John merely a victim of circumstances? Well, no, it is still John's choice, but the alternatives to attacking are more difficult to recognize and to select. Given Traci's rigidity, John would have had to be a supplicant rather than a negotiant. It would have taken unusual, maybe even extraordinary, effort for John to come pleading in pursuit of relief early in the course. Further, at the beginning of the course there was no actual problem. It is only at the end of the course, when the cumulative effects of chance events are clear, that the problem emerges. The result is that we see John would have had to anticipate a problem that did not then, and might not ever, exist and to advance this possibility into a relationship institutionally resistant within a plea for unknown relief when this action had been signaled as unacceptable by the agent of that relief.

---

[7] In the language of officiating we would say that Traci has participated in John's misbehavior. Officials who allow a preventable action, and then penalize it as a foul, participate in the player's misbehavior.

> ## PRINCIPAL CONCEPTS
>
> Memberships and relationships underscore the processes of complicity and implication. None of us is solitary. We are complicit in what others do and implicate others in what we do. This complicit and implicative fabric of connected lives is a significant element in the choices available and the reasons for selection.

Given the hierarchical structure of action and discourse that characterizes the performances within this case, it is not surprising that we end in an adversarial conflict. The topic or content of this conflict does not come out of this structure. John wants a passing grade; Traci wants to maintain the integrity of her instructional responsibilities, but they will fight across a topic provided by a contemporary theme.

LOCATION

There are four significant locations in this case: John and Evelyn's home, the student union, Traci's office, and Professor Williams's office. John takes on a different persona in each of them. At home, he is a member of the wrongfully abused; in the union, a member of the cadre but expendable; in Traci's office, he is a complainant and student; and in Williams's office, he is a threat and a miscreant. The terms of the case take on substantially different interpretations in the different relationships supported by these different locations. Consider that John goes to Traci's office (in proper deference to Traci's institutional standing). In that office, John and Traci are naturalized in the power relationship of student and teacher, and the meeting will be played out in some form appropriate to that relationship. But how might the action have gone if they had met by chance in the Union? The chance of a negotiated solution seems higher there. And how might the action have been played out if Traci had gone to John's home? You can just hear Williams exclaiming, "You did what!?"

For an action to be considered criminal sexual harassment by the courts, the following three tests must be met: (a) the action has to be pervasive and egregious, (b) the action has to be declared unwelcome by the targeted person, and (c) it has to be because of the sex of the participants.

THEMATICS

Sexual discrimination, sexual harassment, and gender harassment[8] are themes that made their official entrance into organizational discourse with the passage of Title VII of the 1962 Civil Rights Act. Those themes have been developed in over 400 court cases, additional legislation, as well as in the political correctness of identity politics to the extent that no organization can afford not to have a policy on these and related issues. Our boxed analysis of John's likelihood of success in a criminal sexual discrimination case (which is what he has despite his calling it a sexual harassment case) shows that such cases carry a heavy burden of proof. Our judgment is that John is far from success. But the difficulty in mounting a successful legal challenge is not the same as what might be required for applying pressure in an organizational complaint or even being successful in a civil suit. Organizational policies are often far more aggressive than the courts. Individual actions that might not rise to a legal standard can easily rise to the standard of dismissal. For example, in a "hostile climate" claim individual acts contribute to the whole character of the climate. Ostensibly harmless actions (like hugging a coworker or inviting a subordinate to an outside event) may in the larger view be seen as contributory factors in creating a hostile climate that rises to the actionable. Organizations often decide that any action that could be seen as contributory is not worth the risk.

Traci has put herself at risk, first by retaining all her grading authority and thereby establishing classic quid pro quo possibilities and second, by her unusual invitation. While Traci would not be found liable for either criminal discrimination or harassment in a court (she can always be sued), her department may find her in violation of policy.[9] That is John's pressure

---

[8] Sexual harassment and gender harassment distinguish between two conditions of a hostile climate. In sexual harassment, the hostile climate is sexually motivated. That is, sexual desire is its source. In gender harassment, the hostile climate is motivated by gender of the target. For example, *The Salt Lake Tribune* (September 20, 1997, p. B1) reported an out-of-court settlement between a department store and a male cosmetics buyer who claimed that he was harassed and ultimately fired because he was a man in a "woman's world."

[9] A recent NBC *Dateline* had a corporate expert on such matters testify that any physical contact other than a standard handshake, implication of a non-work relationship, or talk about such implications puts the person at risk within many corporate policies. If person A puts their left hand on the arm of person B while shaking hands and person B complains about "inappropriate touching," the organization must take some action. Person A is often reprimanded and for repeated incidents even fired.

PRINCIPAL CONCEPTS

Knowledge and understanding are not states of being but practices that are performance dependent. The manner of their recognition and authentication, where they are performed, with what resources, and under what governances all count in what we know and understand at the moment of choice and at the moment of evaluating the choice once made.

---

point. But instead of carefully applying it, John resorts to extortion and triggers an organizational alarm.

There are other thematics being sounded here: fairness, obligation, responsibility, earning a grade. Traci has to be fair to all her students. John was irresponsible and did not meet his responsibilities. But to John, he earned a "B−" and was entitled to it. Somehow learning and education do not often appear as themes in such discussions, however.

APPARATUSES, DISCIPLINES, A LITTLE ECONOMICS, AND HEGEMONIES

Apparatuses

John's ability to apply pressure by calling out sexual harassment is the result of decades of political action, litigation, bureaucratic regulation, corporate policy making, and media dissemination. It has been the work of these apparatuses to "rewrite" a portion of the hegemonic code implicating cultural practices across gender. Before this recodification, Traci's invitation might have raised an eyebrow but never an alarm. John would have carried a substantial burden to prove the connection between the invitation and the grade. Now, however, the presumption has shifted, not perhaps in a court, but certainly in corporate policy. What was harmless in an earlier time has now become questionable.

Disciplines

Two interlocking disciplines, that of the classroom and that of the workplace, mark this case. Regardless of the emancipation of education, the classroom's first lessons are those necessary for a docile workforce trained to submit to authority with sufficient control of body functions that long hours in regulated conditions can be sustained. A friend writes:

> My wife is a preschool teacher. In the beginning of each school year she regales me with stories of her latest hellion who refuses to submit. Be it a boy or girl there is usually one in the class who won't come to the circle for story time, listen quietly, or play cooperatively. The most recent throws toys, temper tantrums, and fists. He runs out of the room and chases down the hall. Her language is both of professional concern and personal exasperation, "a dysfunctional family," "that kid drives me crazy," "I've got to strategize my approach." I'm always a little saddened by these stories because they always end the same way. Slowly, carefully, with intelligence and skill, little Charley, little Mary, will be brought to the circle, will be taught the joys of listening and playing with others. They will be broken to the saddle of disciplined action. Oh, I know how much we have gained through this discipline, but I mourn what we have lost.

John has long before been taught to defer, and Traci is learning the limits of her authority. In all of this, though, we hear the echoes of "Now, John, come to the circle and be a good boy. Do what teacher tells you." Traci cannot teach if John does not come to the circle, but is John ethically obligated to come?

A Little Economics

Two major economies are in play in this case, the labor economy and the sexual economy. The labor economy, as the standard by which we evaluate student/teacher relationships, is pretty clear. If the student does the following *work*, she or he *earns* such and such a grade. John's sense of injustice occurs inside this economy. He felt that he had earned a "B−." When he did not receive that grade, he began to investigate the means by which he could gain economic justice. We can assume that in the first meeting with Traci, he argued the work that he did do to justify his claim. Traci, however, would accept as work of value only that set by the provisions of the syllabus. That John learned something was not an issue on either side. The issue was the terms of the work contract. John has no collective bargaining power. Traci has no reason to give up any of hers. Having no strategic force in the face of authoritarian injustice, John has to turn to tactics of resistance.

He finds those tactics in the contested grounds of the *sexual economy*. The term "**sexual economy**" refers to the relationships between genders.

It assumes that the feminine and the masculine each have qualities scarce in the other and therefore of value to the other. Clearly with a biological foundation, this economy, nevertheless, is most concerned with the social conditions of gender—what it means to be a man, what it means to be a woman. The issues have much more to do with identity than with intercourse. In the current standard of nondiscrimination, this element of identity is to be rendered invisible in superior/subordinate relationships. From our reading of the case, we would claim that neither Traci nor John nor the relationship itself is ever under the direct governance of this economy. But John always presents himself as a man and Traci always presents herself as a woman. Consequently they are never outside this economy either. It is the fact that each day we do the work to present ourselves as one gender or the other through dress, style, body decoration, and the like that the interpretive force of this economy is so readily at hand.

In the United States' white, middle-class expression of this economy, John has good value as a productive, well-buffed image of the masculine. Traci presents the more maternal of the feminine and is probably of lesser value in this economy.[10] John's claim that Traci "hit on him" in the invitation gains believability within this differential of value. John gains a tactical advantage by invoking it.

Hegemony

Hegemony describes the terms of the implicit system of power relationships. That we agree biologically and culturally, for example, to organize power in our social system using gender, among many other elements, creates the conditions for a sexual economy to arise. The power structures in this case are pretty clear. Education is a class-based system (no pun intended) that began in birthrights and has been overlaid with market capitalism. Prior to the public school movement, education was the purview of landed gentlemen. It was a mark that separated the noble from the crass, the masculine from the feminine.

Education still retains that character as a "meal ticket" or "union card" that is often necessary to gain access to the more valuable positions within society. We get that degree to get ahead, to become that doctor, lawyer, or

---

[10] As the writer of these words, one can sense the irritation at their crassness. One's value within a particular sexual economy is not the worth of the person, however.

PRINCIPAL CONCEPTS

The analysis of harm shows the effects of complicity and implication. There is no innocence among the agents in this action. It also shows that culpability, responsibility, and accountability are conferred rather than factual states. No action reported here predicts a sexual harassment charge. Those we hold culpable, responsible, and accountable are often the most vulnerable, expendable, and insignificant elements of the ideological frame.

merchant chief. Most people do not hold college degrees (in the United States, more than 70 percent do not). Several apparatuses (e.g., accreditation and licensing bodies) are in place to ensure that the degree remains valuable and that most will not attain one. The educational institution represents one of the ways by which privilege is constituted, and it is charged with guarding that system. The source of the institutional power comes from that system. The institution owns the rights to a marker that is required or useful to achieve certain social levels. If you aspire to those levels, you have to come to the terms of the institution. So John is a student in Traci's class. Within what might be articulated limits of the institution, she sets the terms, polices the performance under them, and judges the value of that performance—executive, legislative, and judicial powers in one person. Pretty heady stuff for Traci; pretty disempowering for John.

MOVING ON

In commenting on the corporate world, Robert Jackall writes:

> In the welter of practical affairs, . . . morality does not emerge from some set of internally held convictions or principles, but rather from ongoing albeit changing relationships with some person, some coterie, some social network, some clique that matters to a person. Since these relationships are always multiple, contingent, and in flux, . . . moralities are always situational, always relative. (p. 101)

Traci is musing to herself as she prepares her syllabus for her course in Business Communication, "Last time students were not prepared to discuss in class because they hadn't read the material. So, this time I'll use pop quizzes to make sure they read." John is remarking to his wife Evelyn, "Hey, I finally got into that stupid BizComm class. It looks like I'll graduate this year after all." Well, Traci, John, maybe, maybe not, but in this very ordinary manner Traci and John are joined on a path marked by simple choices, whose consequences can be seen only after the fact, and leads to the potential of a life-changing situation.

They get to their destination according to their cultural position within the categories of men and women and their vested rights and obligations as teacher and student; within their value in labor and gendered economies and the discipline of work; within the oversight of regulatory view and the themes of harassment, justice, fairness, and learning; within the conventions that govern their discourse and actions toward one another; and within the demands of other relationships and the terms of their memberships. Our analysis of the domain of agency within the case gives us a pretty good idea of the recognizable alternatives and *how* they made their choices (not *why*, notice). Though we now understand how Traci and John got to their situation, we recognized that it certainly could have been different. The ethical question is: Could it have been done better? That is the question we next address.

THE ETHICAL QUESTION

Ethics hinges in half on the question of harm. Its study enables us to consider the possibility of harm, to whom, to what degree, the possibility of eliminating harm, the possibility of knowing that harm might occur, and the balance of harm across participants and over time and forces us to consider what harm is.

John Gordon's current job as a claims adjuster revolves around protecting his company from fraudulent claims. Yet, with the help of his wife and the goad of his friends, John constructs a fraudulent claim against his BizComm teacher in hopes of getting a higher grade. Our analysis has shown why this claim has come to pass and why we would call it "fraudulent." The question is, what does John believe? He has only the slightest evidence of either sexual harassment or sexual discrimination. He has an overwhelming desire to graduate, which his grade in the BizComm course prevents. At no point do we see John reflecting on his actions, considering the value of the evidence, the force of other desires, or the consequences of the events that might follow. As ethicists, we want John to enter into this reflection. We know that without it, John's belief is merely convenient and not justified. And justification is the answer to the moral question.

In the absence of this reflection, John breaks the basic rules of morality. He knows what his actions have been in his BizComm class, that he has indeed violated the rules of the course. He should know that his claim of sexual harassment is tentative at best. He knows his friends won't support the claim in court. He knows he is using his claim against the teacher in order to get a higher grade, not to redress some sexual injustice. Any grade change would not be based on his performance according to the requirements in the course syllabus.

Traci as the instructor is also morally at risk. She has set up an authority system in her classroom that is immovable. She refused to understand personal circumstances of students, insisting that they all had similar lives and must be similarly devoted to education. Morally, has she set up requirements that create conditions of harm for her students? It appears that in John's case she has, and therefore, she participates in his immorality. Does Traci understand that John has passed the knowledge competencies for the class with a much better grade than a "D" grade? At an earlier point could she have negotiated a more appropriate grade for John? Clearly she does not believe that he needs to be punished to the extent that he should stay in school an additional year. Why then the power play of stonewalling? She too does not reflect on the justification of her actions, choosing merely to invoke her authority in the paradigm of "teacher."

John's wife is a moral negative in this case. She listens to John's story, but is also apparently looking for a way out of an additional year before John's diploma is in hand. Evelyn decides that she and John are being harmed by Traci. She next takes another illogical leap to suggest that it is sexually based. She appears to be an advocate of deception or "win at all costs." Ethically, Evelyn's logic should be rejected on the same moral grounds as was John's logic and behavior.

There may also be some sexism at play in her response to John. Had this been a male professor, John's wife probably would not have suggested sexual harassment. Indeed, she would need to manufacture another type of claim to help her husband graduate on schedule. As some philosophers would counsel, "One shouldn't want something so badly that the soul is sold for it." John and his wife are both close to breaking this moral advice.

Morally, John's friends bring an interesting complication to the case. The friends have been attending class and taking the quizzes. They are probably going to pass the class. Now that classmate John may have to retake the class, they teasingly support John's manufactured claim. Would the friends really defend John in court? Probably not. The friends appear to tease John just far enough to goad him into improper behavior. Now they can sit back and watch the fireworks without personal danger. The friends did not give ethically sound advice.

Professor Williams also has some moral responsibility in this situation. He wants Traci to go along with traditionally established rules. Traci is trying to solve the problem as quickly and as easily as possible. She is capitulating to John's immoral demands. Williams lets her know that capitulation does not fit within the institution's interests. A system of rules and behaviors exists at the university. Most students, faculty, and administrators fit within this system of behaviors. John threatens the system and Traci's membership in the system by stating that he will press sexual harassment charges against her unless she changes his grade. One individual is not allowed to "blow the whistle," and disrupt this type of system. Williams wants Traci to go through the embarrassment of the charges to protect the overall system. His call to Traci could now be seen as an authoritative directive. Traci could be held with insubordination if she doesn't comply with his suggested role of behavior. Traci now finds herself in collision with the institutional system.

In the end a moral action calls for the competent application of an adequate moral code. You and I are not given the privilege of determining the terms of the moral code to which we will be held accountable. Those terms are a cultural production under constant social management. We are, nonetheless, given the responsibility for its competent application to the extent that we can control or govern that application. As we mentioned in Chapter 4, we are born into a functioning moral code (which may be deemed more or less adequate by others) and learn its competent application in the uncounted moments of relational obligations. Part of our identity appears in these naturalized practices of our morality.

The problems for us in this enactment, nonetheless, are many: (a) The moral codes we live are dynamic, complex, inconsistent, and often at points incoherent. (b) Our intentions are not always consciously addressable. (c) Action can be guided by many intentions and even by the force of its own significance. (d) Action is a real-time performance that is often recognizable only when it is done. (e) Deliberate analysis and reflection have to be a part of our moral practice because we cannot always connect our intentions to our acts or foresee the consequences of our action in the processes by which we constitute that action. John and Traci particularly need to stop to consider what they were about. That consideration may change nothing. But it is their only chance at reaching a morally justified position.

We have stopped to consider John, Traci, Evelyn, Rick, and Professor Williams at some length. That consideration has led to a partial listing of the conditions of the case in which an ethicist might find harm and its components. We end this chapter here for you to consider it.

- At no point in the scenario can one predict the sexual harassment charge. That does not happen until John adopts harassment as the explanation for his predicament. It is John's interpretation and use of the facts (facts themselves can never be agents) that creates the charge.
- John's charge has the potential of much greater harm to both himself and his instructor than his failure.
- John is not adequately knowledgeable about the charge of sexual harassment or of the consequences of the charge.
- Traci is complicit in John's unethical behavior by her rigidity.
- Rick fails to discharge his duty as a friend but rather uses John to advance his own ends.
- Evelyn does not consider the consequences of her remarks for either John or Traci.
- Professor Williams maintains the pretense of being a "mentor" when in fact he is no longer acting in the interests of Traci.
- Traci is willing to surrender what she believes in, on the threat of loss of position.
- Traci deceives John by stonewalling in their first meeting.
- John refuses to be accountable for his own actions in missing class.
- John lies in his group work.
- Rick lies in support of John's group work deception.
- The institution puts workers at risk by an unenlightened harassment policy.
- The department puts Traci at risk by inadequate supervision and training.
- Traci's inadequate supervision and training put her students at risk.
- John's and Traci's failure to reflect on the character of their actions puts themselves at risk.

EPILOGUE

Professor Williams caught sight of Traci at the copy machine. He loitered there until she was finished. "Got a second?" he asked. "Come on back to my office."

"You know we had that conference about that student and his grade right at the end of the school year. It all seemed to disappear. I've been wondering what happened."

"I gave him an 'A.'"

"An 'A'!? I thought he was asking for something like a 'B'-minus."

"He was. I gave him an 'A' so that every time that he thought about it, every time he saw me on campus, he would remember how evil he was."

"Sort of heaping the burning coals of kindness upon the head of your enemy, eh?" Williams commented.

"You got it."

◆◆◆

"Evelyn, guess what. I just found out that instructor gave me an 'A.' Isn't that great?"

FURTHER QUESTIONS

Evaluate the case in this chapter. Focus on these terms from Chapter 7:

1. Double-binding
2. Burden-shifting
3. Harassment
4. Nonjustified evaluation
5. Unannounced changes

9

THEORETICAL PRINCIPLES

PREVIEW

Imagine your authors sitting around the kitchen table looking at the pictures taken from their journey through the writing process. The pictures are familiar but each offers some new view, a little surprise, perhaps in what wasn't or couldn't be seen before. This book started as an effort to bring four concepts—the self, morality, the organization, and power—together into a coherent theory of the organizational self and ethical conduct. In the process we were drawn to a fifth concept—resistance. In this chapter, we revisit those concepts, guided by the pictures of our writing, to tell the story of our journey.

This chapter is designed to gather the theoretical constructs that we have developed throughout the narratives, to bring them to a single place, and to investigate their implications for the analysis of ethical conduct. It offers nothing new except through restatement, but is given as a teaching and learning aid, so that the whole of the theory can be seen in one place. Again we would caution you against modernist expectations of a secure, linear theory, tidy in every aspect. The theory is excessive and irreducibly contentious even with itself. But it is consequential. It influences particular ways of thinking about organizations, organizational members, and their actions.

PRIORS

This book is centered on the relationship rather than the individual. It rejects the epistemologies of naive empiricism[1] and methodological individualism, as well as the Cartesian view of the independent, right thinking person. In their places, we offer social constructionism, methodological holism, and the view of the person as an intersection boundary in the web of connected lives, well colonized by the collective's semiotic resources of language and action. Reality does not present itself; it is both mediated and produced. One cannot study the social by examining its parts. We are human in our collectivity and not in our separateness.

Having rejected the foundationalism of a directly addressable reality, we also rejected the foundationalism of universal values of right and wrong and that of the rationally self-evident. Right and wrong and the good reasons for them are, for us, cultural productions. This position means no more than it is social practices and not genes or an infusion of the soul by which values are crafted and maintained and by which right reason is attained. We may all agree that something is right or wrong but it is the social process of the agreement, not the intrinsic quality of the thing, that makes the judgment universal (Eagleton, 1996).

Our rejection of the self-evidentness of reality and reason requires that action too must be interpreted through collective means to declare its character and quality. As our opening scenario of Chapter 1 related, the command, "thou shalt not steal," begs the question of what action would be designated as stealing and demands the social practices of ownership to find the answer.

We have adopted Anderson's (1996) **activative individual,** that "artful coconspirator who materializes collective resources of action in local and partial performances within the realm of his or her own agency" (p. 90), to manage the tensions between individual action using collective means within a joint **phenomenology** of what is and ought to be. It is the individual who must act, but cannot act alone. She will improvise on culturally given action routines made sensible within collective understandings.

---

[1] This rejection is not of all empiricism. Your authors are empiricists of the interpretive sort. Nor is the term *naive* pejorative. It refers to an epistemology that holds experience to be innocent (not complicit or implicative) and, hence, *naive*.

This position promotes an existentialist's focus on behavior. This focus rejects the mentalist distinction between intention and action. The formation of an intention is an action in its own right that occurs over time and uses collective resources in both the means of formulating and in the creation of the intended. Intention does not cause subsequent behavior. We appropriate prior and discipline subsequent behavior to maintain the intention. Intentions, therefore, are not fixed agents but are organically coupled with the attributed action they make meaningful and that sustains them.

Our character, then, is revealed in action not archived in interior mental states. There is not a good woman or good man among us except that she or he acts like a good woman or good man. But what is revealed in that action is a set of signs full of potential in their significance but indeterminate in their meaning. That good woman/good man is a conferred state executed by agents authorized by the conditions; of such, meaning is made. The *I* may claim what the *I* means to do, but others may have more authority to make that declaration.

The real time, particular enactor, contingent phenomenology, and actual enactment requirements of action leaves the doing in doubt. It is the done that becomes the text of our interpretations. We most often come to know who we are and the quality of our action in the interpretations of a different time and place. The defining postmodern effort is the struggle for meaning in defining who we are, what we are doing, and the qualities of each.

The Principal Concepts

We have addressed five concepts from the foregoing axiomatic framework: the self, morality, the organization, power, and resistance. In each case we have maintained the centrality of the relationship. We found the self emerging in the relationship between identity and subjectivity and expressing itself in relation to the other. Morality rested on obligation or the moment of recognition that a relationship exists and found its character in the duality of complicity and implication. The organization was offered as a set of ordered relationships that created the provenance of action, that phenomenological framework of coherence that forms the member's domain of agency. Power appeared in the reciprocal exchange of obligation. Power was seen as a joint production. Power *with* was contrasted with control *over*. And finally, resistance arose in the relationship between indeterminate desire and determinant existence—in the longing to be, but the refusal to be only. We take up each of these concepts in their turn.

THE SELF

This section is divided into two parts. The first walks through the five axiomatic claims we make about the self: (a) the self is an ideational object and therefore a social invention; (b) the self is a sign of the person not an entity; (c) the self is an expression that **actualizes** the potentials of identity and subjectivity; (d) the self is in the continuous state of becoming in action; and (e) the self is possible only in the web of connected lives. The second section reworks these ideas exploring examples and drawing further implications.

An Analysis of the Five Axioms

THE SELF AS AN IDEATIONAL OBJECT   We have argued that there is no physical structure that we could point to as the self. One cannot discover the self in the absence of the other. The self, therefore, has no material reality, but is rather an *ideational object*. As an ideational object, the self is a collective achievement. It is a *social invention*.

THE SELF AS A SIGN   The self is a semiotic—a composite of signs, iconic (of the body), actional, and discursive, both persistent and not, and only partially under local control. This composite is kaleidoscopic, the pieces in motion presenting different views, different signs of the self. It is those signs that we read as the person.[2]

THE SELF AS AN EXPRESSION   The self is an expression, an action text if you will, that actualizes some set of the potentials of identity—those durable signs of the particular person—and subjectivity—the invoked and

---

[2] This concept of the self as the sign of the person is probably the most contraintuitive part of our theory, particularly for those whose environments are relatively stable, performance demands consistent, and engagements regular. These steady state conditions allow for the repetitive appearance of the same semiotic formations, giving the sense of a centered unity. As the regularities of family, occupation, education, religion, and memberships fall away, the self becomes more and more in doubt. The answer to the question, "Who am I?" is an uncertain reading of the signs (Foster, 1987). Any answer, of course simply raises the additional question of who does the reading in endless recursion.

evoked cultural resources of the subject.[3] The elements of identity begin with the instrument of material action, the body. The body is obdurately material; it is both in language and beyond language. We submerge it in discourse, but it has its own knowledge. Identity continues in those over-rehearsed, naturalized practices through which the body and the mind manage their material and discursive presence. They are our characteristic ways of moving, thinking, speaking. These naturalized practices are themselves read into the self-images we maintain. Iconically, symbolically, discursively, we sign the self into its ideational identity. Finally, as the self is a product of self and other, our long-lasting relationships form part of the anchor of identity.

Issues of identity are carried in the body but are read and located culturally. Those cultural readings and locations provide one's subjectivity. Our subjectivity begins in the cultural marks that the collectivity places on us—the marks of ethnicity, race, gender, age, caste and the like that can be evoked by others and invoked by us. Our subjectivity is further expressed in our subject position—that recognizable persona of Foucault's (1986) anonymous discourses, Bakhtin's (1986) dialogics, and Nietzsche's (1967) symptomatic modes of existence. In these subject positions, we are reproduced as some paradigmatic figure (hero, victim, lover, squire, manager, worker, teacher, student), located relationally across societal interests (important or not, powerful or not), and expressed practically in the action at hand (author/reader, here). The action in hand further defines us through its structurational characteristics as recognizable routines—the signs of what is being done. These routines carry their criteria of performance, and we are called to their account as we enact them.

THE SELF AS A STATE OF BECOMING   The expression of the self is a local appearance in action, in time, and in place, but beyond local control. One cannot be just anyone; the body refuses, the durability of identity resists, and culture demands. On the other hand, one must act and, therefore, will be someone in the expression of this necessary action. The expression is an act of becoming; it materializes the self. The self appears in the present

---

[3] This argument is informed by Anderson & Meyer, 1988; Banta, 1993; Du Gay, 1996; Edwards & Potter, 1992; Gergen, 1991, 1994; Goffman 1959; Harré 1991, 1992, 1995; Jacques, 1996; James, 1988; Laclau, 1990; Lears, 1985; Pearce & Cronen, 1980; Potter & Wetherell, 1987, among others.

moment which puts it at risk, but the present moment, as Hawes (1999, p. 242) puts it, is "the past-becoming-present and the present-becoming-future," which gives the self its anchorage (see also Bogue, 1989). It is this continual process of becoming in which the past extends into the future through a present moment that must be produced that gives both the vision of continuity and the specter of doubt in the question of who we are.

The self appears as a recognizable expression contingent on the real times and places of its manifestation. Each of these times and places is under collective influence of varying intensity. We are the partners, parents, and children of our families; the workers, peers, subordinates, and managers of our workplaces; the team members, volunteers, performers, audiences, congregations, classmates of the many other venues of collective practice. We are these persona not by the force of our will or by the strength of some inner core or by stepping into some preordained role, but as a result of the ongoing complicity of others whom we, in turn, implicate in our action. We are the agents of the duality of the recursive complicity/implicature of self and other.

We are simultaneously the agents of this duality in the multiplicity of the action lines we enact. We are partners, parents, children, workers, peers, subordinates, managers, and the rest at once not serially, although a particular performance will most often be the surface of one rather than another. A performance does not mark the start of action. The multiple action lines of who we are continue even in apparent absence of performance.

THE SELF IN THE WEB OF CONNECTED LIVES   Our conclusion from this analysis is that the self is possible only in the web of connected lives.[4] There is not much required of this claim, coming as it does out of our denial of a foundational entity and out of our claim that the self is a social invention. The work it does, however, is worth examining. The claim speaks to the self as agent, attributable, accountable, culpable, and it puts that agency in doubt. The traditional, Cartesian/Kantian solution offers a much easier answer to the question of "What am I doing?" That solution offers an **a priori** entity, independent and complete, using "natural" or at least

---

[4] We sometimes get asked about "hermits" and "recluses." Both hermits and recluses are recognized subject positions that carry certain culturally imposed lifestyle requirements, reciprocal obligations, and so on. Even a hermit has to be a hermit in relation to "not being a hermit." Their sodality may include reduced physical contact, but they remained immersed in language, action, and the technologically archived presence of others in tools, architecture, and so on.

universally available means of singularly right reason addressing a compliant reality that yields its secrets directly and truthfully to enact the will. This person is fully responsible for her or his actions as she or he has all the means to contain error and, by extension, there is a well-defined, proper action to be discovered and taken. In this formulation, there is a single science, a final truth independent of human intelligence that is yet discoverable by it. There is no complicity, implicature, or reciprocal obligation; there is simply an objective standard of right or wrong that each of us can enact.

The postmodern attack on this position reaches across all fronts. We as individuals are cultural products, embedded in language and action; reason and science are multiple, reality is both material and socially constructed and always mediated through signs that are not simply referential and in discourse that is not simply representational; our actions are not inventions but improvisations on collectively recognized routines; the self is not foundational but a relational expression in a web of connected lives that pre-exists all of its members.

In this latter day formulation, what the *I* is doing is indeterminate because the *I* is never singular and the "what is being done" is never closed to other interpretations. The questions of who and what can always be reopened. In the end, the agent of any action is an attribution whose causal force is made apparent by ignoring all the other contributing elements in both cause and consequence. Both who did it and what was done are social constructions.[5]

Reworking the Issues

We have argued that the self is an expression in action rather than an essence. We have defined the self as an interdependent expression derived from long-standing and short-lived individual and cultural resources contingently assembled in the coherence of action and rejected the notion of a singular unity that moves across time and place. The self as an expression rests within the network of cultural understandings and enacted relationships that produce the framework of understanding and the coherence of

---

[5] We both argue for and resist this formulation in our everyday practices, generally excusing ourselves and condemning others.

practical action in which the self appears. As an expression, the self comes into existence at the moment of its performance. At the same time we have acknowledged the persistences and consistencies of identity and the widespread resources of subjectivity. The self, then, is not a moment-by-moment invention without history or predictability. What it is, however, at any moment of its expression depends on something else.

That "something else" is the *other*. This dependency is a key construct. Developmentally if we are to become a person, we must first come to recognize the other. We live in the sodality of a congregation, not in the collection of an aggregation. The individual, therefore, is not self-sufficient. We not only interact; we must interact if we are to be human.

The interdependent character of human life can be seen by considering the human mind. We follow the lead of Karl Popper (Popper & Eccles, 1977) and reject the identity hypothesis of the physicalists (Anderson, 1996) by saying that the mind is different from the brain. The brain is the result of genetic processes, but the mind is a social invention, depending on the social products of language and action, discourse, and performance. There is no question that the brain is the physical foundation of the mind and by whatever means the brain functions, the mind is affected. The relationship between the brain and the mind, however, is like the relationship between clay and a brick. The quality of the brick is dependent on the characteristics of the clay from which it is made. But there are no "natural processes" of the clay itself that will produce a brick—a uniform product with interchangeable characteristics that can participate in the coordinated action of building. So too, there are no "natural" processes of genetics or biology that will produce the human mind—that more or less uniform semiotic system that provides interchangeable ideational objects through which we can communicate.

The clear evidence for this claim is the immense social investment we as a society make in signs and their use that produces the cosmologies of language and action. The argument here is that both language and action are semiotic systems that are social inventions whatever their biological support. No individual brain can produce or sustain either language or action. Language and action provide the basis by which we contact and interact with the material world, ourselves, and others. In this way we live mediated lives. Because language and action are collective enterprises, we live lives outside of ourselves. This "outsidedness" entails an extension of the human brain into processes and capabilities well beyond its biology. The human mind is not simply "behind the eyes." In fact much more exists between us than within us.[6] What exists between us, rather than within us, is the discourses and performances through which the self becomes its materialized expression in the actualization of the coupled potentiality of identity and subjectivity.

Communality in signs and their use requires our continued joint effort. It is not a given. What can be held in common has to be covered by the span of this joint effort (such is the import of media's global distribution); nothing can be held in common except through joint effort; and joint effort of any sort produces common understandings.

The self is an ideational object, rather than a material one, that appears in action signs and their interpretation. The self is, therefore, a product of joint effort and contingent upon the terms of its appearance. To underscore this notion of dependence consider: No individual can think a single exchangeable thought or enact any recognizable performance except through collective resources. The self requires the common semiotic resources of language and action for its expression. The self must use the social in order to produce the personal. Jim cannot be of any gender; of any color; of any age, height, weight, handsome or not, ethical or not except that the resources of gender, color, age, height, weight, handsomeness, and ethicalness be provided to him.[7] Self and other are artful coconspirators in the production of the individual.

But that production is never fixed or final; it is always ongoing. The self is an expression, a sign to be produced and interpreted whose only certainties are its object properties. It is the self, however, that is the acting agent. There is no transcendental agent; no monolith of genetic unity. The self is a sign that stands in the place of "who" in the question "who am I?" As a sign its interpretation is always open, never final.

AN EXAMPLE IN JUSTICE   Consider now that we wish to point to a self that is just. We have presented ourselves with some difficulties in doing so by putting into flux the concept of the self that is to be an expression of the just. We will give ourselves even more difficulty by putting the concept of justice into flux.

---

[6] As an individual I (your keyboardist) am situated in various collectively encoded environments that provide me the terms for how to think, speak, and perform. I cannot type except that I use collectively agreed upon technology. I cannot reason except that I meet collectively enforced standards of normal rationality. My fingers are disciplined to and extended by the keyboard that extends the capability of my body. My arguments are disciplined to and extended by the conventions of writing argument that extend the force of those arguments.

[7] Gender, color, age, height, weight, handsomeness, and ethicalness are all ideational characteristics and, therefore, semiotic. Elaine cannot be 6 foot tall without a measurement system that provides that definition and cannot be recognized as a "6 footer" without a cultural system that marks that height as recognizable.

Justice too is an ideational rather than material object. Justice has to be enacted by social agents in each time and place of its existence. The justice scholarship of John Rawls is made possible by the scholarly community to which he belongs. His ownership is of the particular expression, the particular arrangement of ideas, words, and sentences, each of which is made possible by his community.[8]

There is, consequently, no transcendental ideational object called *justice* with fixed boundaries and brute characteristics. Justice, as it appears in word and action, is part of an enacted ideology. My mindful understanding of justice is itself a joint effort. If justice is not transcendental but its truth is in the consensus of joint effort, then what justice is depends on that consensus, the parties to it, its solidity, its coverage, and its application to the expression in hand. If the self is to be just, it not only must solve the question of what is justice, but also the question of what is its proper expression within the action at hand. Not only do we ask "who am I?" in moral analysis, we must also ask "What am I doing?"

We follow the existentialist claim here that one cannot be just and act unjustly. As there is no transcendent self, there is no transcendent quality (a notion that we have also rejected) that can be attached to it.[9] To act is to become, so that who and what come into view in the process of doing. Consequently, if the self acts unjustly, the self is unjust in that action, but such action does not signal a flawed character, rather it signals the constitutive processes of agent, agency, action, and judgment.

The self as the acting agent appears at the moment the action is to be taken. It is not some average of performance or what has been or might be. Consider that you are taking a test, and you come upon a question the answer to which you knew last night but this morning cannot remember. Alas, the acting agent does not know the answer. But, you might argue forgetting is a temporary condition, the true self knows the answer. But clearly remembering is also a temporary condition, comes the reply. In fact all of our conditions are temporary. Why is the self that remembers any more true than the self that forgets? Agency has to be determined by what is available at the point of action, not what should have been available, not what had been available or could be available in the future.

---

[8] This is true of our own scholarship as well.

[9] This principle can be applied to all such qualities, leadership, productivity, mean spiritedness, etc.

If we have exercised proper care, we have not overstated our position. We have not denied the persistences of identity or the fact of intentionality and its planful execution. What we have argued is that the self—the acting agent—is not fixed from within but is in play in action. The self is formulated in action; it is not foundational. The self, intentionality, the domain of its agency, and the execution of action each has to be produced and sustained from the first stirrings of the will to its consequence.

The agent of any act is not secure either in the acting or the analysis. As a manager, firing a given person may seem to be the appropriate move for the bottom line of the organization. As that person's friend, that same act may seem to be a grave injustice. There is no reconciliation of these competing positions. It is indeed right for the manager and wrong for the friend.[10] We justify the action by declaring which self is the agent.

MORALITY

The postmodern effort at the recuperation of agency plus its refusal to separate the questions of *is* and *ought* in a mediated and socially constructed reality require us to reintroduce the issue of morality at all levels of the discussion. Ethical analysis is demanded if we grant any ability to make a difference to the corseted and speculative self we just visited. Ethical analysis is also demanded when it is held that no truth claim is independent of the processes by which it is held to be true. In this framework, every truth claim does political work in the service of the standpoint that makes the truth of the claim possible. The claim is, at least in part, true because it ought to be true for the good of the collective effort that makes it possible.

The moral framework for this ethical analysis can scarcely be the unmarked traditions of duties, rights, utilities, and virtues given the postmodern ravages of the Cartesian/Kantian self that forms the necessary foundation of these traditions. Something else will have to appear. The something else that we have offered is obligation, complicity, and implicature. We review these next.

---

[10] One might hear the echoes of a typical proverb that one should never act as a friend in making managerial decisions. The opposite is equally true: one should never make managerial decisions when being a friend. I cannot be a friend and make decisions that damage my friend or be a manager and make decisions that damage my stewardship. The action determines what I can be. The reader might wish to take this principle of the self as acting agent and reconsider the scenario of the vice-president and the manager that was presented in Chapter 5. The confusions there are clearly about "who" is acting.

Here is an example from what some would call "bad" (and therefore correctable) science: A psychologist proposes to draw a sample of African-American students to participate in a study on the cardiovascular effects of performance stress. Subjects will each be required to prepare and give a speech that will subsequently be evaluated negatively. Subjects will then be able to "vent" their feelings by writing a report on the experience. Cardiovascular measures will be taken throughout the process. It is clear that whatever findings appear, they will be attributed to the "race" of the respondents (else why study African-Americans?) and necessarily compared with the exnominated, dominant interests. The study serves primarily to further validate the concept of race for a society that depends upon it.

Obligation

Caputo (1993) considers obligation to be a given, a fact of life (p. 6). He also considers it to be "a spontaneous causality, a cause without antecedent that breaks in upon the unbroken regularity of phenomenal succession, with a power to move heaven and earth" (p. 13). Obligation, then, as used here, is not some hard-edged Kantian duty, universal and transcendental. In our argument, obligation is a duality with relationship. As is the relationship, obligation is culturally informed and locally negotiated. It is the evidence of a relationship. It defines the character of the relationship, whereas the relationship defines the terms of obligation. It is the self that is obliged. The self is obliged because of the necessity of a relationship with other. The moment, therefore, the self makes its appearance, it is already under obligation. But what is the self obliged to do? The simple answer is "whatever it is doing." If, as we have argued, the self is a manifestation of identity and subjectivity in action, then relationship and obligation are conjoint with action. The self is obliged to continue the relationship, to continue to provide for its own manifestation.[11]

That we are obliged by a relationship means nothing more than if we are to continue the relationship, we must somehow meet the obligations of it. The significance of the relationship and its performance, nonetheless, is in who we are. The absence of obligation is an absence of self, so the failure to meet one's obligation is an erosion of the self.

---

[11] This argument is similar to Luhmann's (1990) claim that any autopoietic system has only two choices—to continue or not.

Obligation is not simply of the self, however. It is the relationship that sets the terms of obligation and those terms are mutually managed and supervised by the members. A relationship is a conjoint necessity. Self constitutes other as other constitutes self. For self to be, implicates other, and other is complicit in that implication. Other is complicit in what self is, and what self is implicates other. Our obligation is intertwined. It cannot be sorted out univariately. Obligation is, therefore, complicitous and implicative.

Complicity references the background field of enablement that allows the self to materialize in action. We are complicit in whatever our memberships provide. Implication references the foreground of action. It considers how action crosses the boundaries of self and other to confirm their mutual interdependence. As complicity says the *I* is never enough for its action, implication says the *I* is never alone in its action. Complicity draws the self into the action of the other; implication draws the other into the action of the self. Complicity and implication are the necessary conditions of living in the web of connected lives. And it is to the issues of complicity and implication to which we now turn.

Complicity

The fact that the self is an interdependent expression of what could be that finds its domain of agency in the product of joint action, as well as our arguments that there has to be consensus on what is to be vice and virtue and upon what is vicious and virtuous performance clearly establish the concept of complicity. One cannot do good works, commit crimes, be a great leader, make a great contribution to knowledge, or have any consequence beyond that of any other material object without the complicity of others.

The principle of complicity has very local implications as well. Mary cannot break a promise to John unless John accepts the pledge. (She can violate her own intentions, of course.) If John accepts the promise, he is then complicit in Mary's performance or nonperformance. He participates in Mary's behavior and puts her at moral risk, depending on her performance. The morality of every action is dependent upon the terms of obligation that the relationship imposes. It is these terms of obligation that establish our moral character. Obligation is the necessary requirement of quality.

Understanding the complicity of obligation in the moral quality of the individual appears to shift the target of moral analysis from the character of the individual—the good or bad person—to the terms of obligation under which an action is to be judged. One cannot cheat on tests that are not given, for example, or falsify records that are not taken. It is useful, but difficult, in that fit of umbrage over the failure of one's partner to consider how you participated in that failure. At the very least, your act of declaring *it* (whatever *it* is) a failure constitutes *it* as a failure.

None of this is to say that we are free to negotiate locally what is imposed globally. It is to say that obligation is a social rather than a biological process and that its terms create the conditions of moral behavior. The social character of obligation and its complicity in morality helps us to understand the failure of ethicists to finalize any list of rights, duties, goods, virtues, or practices that constitute morality. The terms of obligation are always in process, never fixed. There can be no definitive discovery of what they are. Further, the professional work of ethicists is a part of these social processes. As we study and write, we create further resources for difference.

Complicity also leads us to understand that moral judgments are situated judgments. There being no Archimedean point, no ideologically independent location from which to dispose, moral judgments (and quality assessments of any sort) must necessarily depend on the conditions under which they are made. But what of right and wrong and good and bad—the universals of action and value? For us, right and wrong as well as good and bad are determined in cultural/political processes. Moral standards are cultural texts that must be maintained in social practices. Those practices produce, sustain, interpret, and apply the consequences of our cultural beliefs. Commendation and condemnation alike are ideologically located, economically motivated, and politically intentioned to produce some consequence. Our moral judgments are at work to produce the world we wish to live in. As a consequence, we must be aware of whose interests are being best served.

Let's work an example common to student life and one we nodded at earlier in this section. We mentioned that instructors who give tests put students at risk for cheating. (One cannot cheat if the conditions for cheating are not made available.) The question we might ask here is whose interests are being served by putting students at that risk? Is the traditional testing procedure of each person working separately at some task necessary for either teaching or learning? The answer is clearly "no." While this traditional testing procedure might be useful, we can certainly teach and learn without it. So what does the procedure do? It disciplines and differentiates students for social purposes other than learning and teaching as part of a "human resource" economy.[12] Grades are important not only because they signal intelligence and mastery but also because they point to the compliant and subjugated—those who do what they are told and do it well. Grading is a hegemonic instrument. Grading celebrates the authority of the instructor, promotes the myth of individual meritocracy, enforces competition among students, and thwarts collective action, all very useful training for the workplace.

You may entirely disagree with this description. Our point is not to enforce an Althusserian analysis (Althusser, 1971), but to show how little work it takes to uncover what is potentially concealed in our agreed upon—complicit—performances and their descriptions. Individual grading, even if entirely indicative of subject mastery, is part of an economy that involves students, instructors, universities, funding institutions, and corporate interests. It archives a collective way of thinking about learning and knowledge. We are willing to put students at risk, and students accept that risk in order to preserve it. As participants in this economy, we are complicit in its methods and consequences.

In fact, we are each—perpetrator and victim alike—complicit in the oppressions practiced by the organizations to which we claim membership. As members of the dominant interests we are implicated in the racism, sexism, ageism, and such other discriminatory hierarchies except to the extent that we actively resist. Holding the conferred status of white, I, your keyboardist, have benefited from the racial discrimination of others if in no other way than its absence from my life. A person of color who practices the politics of racial identity is equally complicit (McPhail, 1998a, b). These are hard conclusions that assail the sensibilities of good women and men and strike violently at the moral tradition that we are each responsible for what we do, but only for what we do. Here we are also responsible for what we enable, permit, ignore, or do not resist. The only relief is in the fact that our responsibility in no way lessens or mitigates the responsibility of the other. Our ownership of property makes the thief possible, and we are ethically bound to consider those consequences, but the thief is responsible for his or her choices.

---

[12] A most accommodating pedagogical theory would hold that tests can measure general knowledge gain and therefore the success of learning and teaching. At best, tests can measure success in what they ostensibly test for, and even that is dependent on the skill of the test maker.

A case in point: Minority member A accused dominant interest member B of practicing racism because she used the Anglo pronunciation of a minority cultural term. B had never heard the term pronounced, having engaged it only in print. Nonetheless, when she chose to use it in class in her position as instructor, her responsibility included determining these issues. A, however, then proceeded to demand reparations in the form of reduced requirements because of her "crime" against his ethnicity. Both are complicit in racism.

Implication

We have noted that complicity references the background of enablement, drawing the self into the action of other and that implication references the foreground of action, drawing the other into the action of the self. Complicity and implication enlarge the traditional moral field of responsibility and shift the constitution of the acting agent from the single individual to an illuminated self and shadowed other.

In our examination of complicity we considered what the other provides; in implication we consider what the self entails. In zero sum games for example, Player A cannot actively work for her success without at the same time seeking her opponent's failure. This is the ethical defect of self-interest in conditions of restricted opportunity.

One of the few failures in feminist discourse was the slogan, "men just don't get it." It was used by the radical to justify a program of terrorism, by most to eliminate the male as a legitimate voice, and by the masculine as a release from any effort at reform.[13] As some feminists worked to constitute the truth of the slogan and their superior position as knowers of the truth, they worked for these other truths as well (that men have to go and that men have no standing in the discussion and no responsibility for sexist actions). Consequently this discourse left no place for men, but the genuine reform of the system of gender requires all parties.

Implication is more than simple consequence. It is about what has to be true of the other—true of the relationship—for our action to make sense.

---

[13] Masculinist programs are dedicated to showing that (a) the masculine is as much of a social production as is the feminine; (b) even though clearly privileged, costs are entailed by the masculine at the hands of the feminine that are the legitimate subject of reform; (c) there can be no genuine reform in gender unless the interests of the masculine are part of the discussion; and (d) there is no inherently superior position from which to undertake this discussion.

Implication declares what action, discourse, dialogue, and mode of being of the self hold to be true about others that are entangled within these actions, discourses, dialogues, and modes of being. Joan's corporate leadership implicates John's corporate followership. Joan's leadership makes no sense unless it implies John's followership.

That declaration is not trivial—it often carries mortal consequence—because we act to ensure the truth of those declarations. In our societally infiltrated relationships we put into place the mechanisms that naturalize what is implied. Joan's leadership and John's followership are both readily apparent because we have made them so. Because all such hierarchical claims are social constructions, we must look for the mechanisms by which this hierarchy appears. It is through these mechanisms that we become complicit in what is naturalized as true.

Implication generates its own contribution to the relationship. Organizations, for example, are often structured under the principle of the division of labor. Jeremy doing his job implicates Marie in doing hers and Marie implicates Jeremy. The work done moves forward in the joint effort and is greater than the sum of each because the implication makes its own contribution. The work of Margaret may depend entirely upon it.

Finally, changes in implicature force changes in what is assumed to be true. If we no longer enact gender, the truths (as well as their economic and political value) of the masculine and the feminine disappear even while the genetic differences of male and female remain. The persistent conservationist voice, for another example, has changed the nineteenth century vision of subduing nature through eradication and extraction. One cannot enter the conservationist discourse without admitting the questioning of these practices. The result is that one can no longer kill animals at will and property rights have been limited in favor of preservationist interests. But as another result, livestock operators have to withstand losses against increasingly narrow profit margins and landowners can no longer fully develop the value of their property.

The Relationship between Complicity and Implication

The relationship between complicity and implication can be viewed by starting with either complicity or implication. Theirs is not a linear relationship of one causing the other; neither can function without the other. Starting from complicity, the relationship can be stated as: If a given action (discourse, mode of existence) is recognized, accommodated, permitted, or not resisted by Y, then X produces that action through Y's complicity, and X implicates Y in the sense-making truths of the action. Starting from implication, the relationship can be expressed as: If the action of X implies a truth of Y, Y is complicit in the action of X in so far as Y enacts, accepts, permits, or does not actively resist that truth.

X and Y are in a relationship. Y is complicit in what X does as a product of that relationship, and X's action implicates Y. So, too, X is complicit in what Y does as a product of that relationship, and Y's action implicates X. This relationship can read at any level from the local to the global. It can be tracked in the actual performances of two particular people—who one hangs with matters—and it appears in this anonymous relationship that we have between author and reader. We, the authors, have implicated you, the reader. Your reading implicates our writing. We are each complicit in each other's actions.

There are several truths implied by our writing and your continued reading:

1. The necessity of a relationship that is shot through with complicity and implicature calls into question the acting agent. No longer is it possible to claim an independent autonomous individual as that agent. That agent is necessarily a constitution of some sort in which self and other participate.
2. The relationship between complicity and implication, however it is expressed, highlights resistance as the way in which the "of course it's true" character of relational action is broken into. Resistance, therefore, is necessary for a change in the morality of action.
3. There is no simple quality of innocence. Perpetrator and victim constitute a relationship. Without in any way reducing the culpability of the perpetrator, the victim may well be complicit in the crime. The co-dependencies of alcoholism, drug abuse, and marital violence are examples. When the relational action is considered immoral, victims have an ethical responsibility, mitigated by ability, to extract themselves from such co-dependencies.
4. To the extent that the action is a product of the relationship, the action of one member of a relationship constitutes a truth of the other. The one has an ethical responsibility in the claim; the other in the complicity. For action within the scope of the relationship, parents, for example, are complicit in the actions of their children and children's actions declare some part of what is true of the parents.

5. Complicity and implication are morally neutral. The relationship may move toward the right and the good as well as the wrong and the bad. Given that, implication may be used in the service of the good and render the uncommitted yet nonresistant complicit in that action. The relationship can raise the moral quality of its members. The quality of the organization is more likely to produce the quality of its members.

6. If the quality of the acting agent is dependent upon the relationship(s) in which that agent appears, moral character in one relationship is no predictor of moral character in another. X can be a paragon at home and a predator at work with no internal contradiction. The domain of action is more important than the enactor in understanding moral quality.

7. Given the importance of the domain of action for the appearance of moral behavior, our interests should be directed toward developing the morality of relationships—intimate, social, corporate, and political—rather than focusing on individual character. It is the quality of the organization that predicts the quality of its members. Members accede to that quality; a given individual is not the cause of that quality or the likely source of its reform.

The direction of these implications is consistently away from the Cartesian self performing Kantian universals in action and toward a relationally constituted agent engaged in collectively infiltrated action within the boundaries of an organizationally defined domain of agency. The questions of who is the actor and what is being done are not to be answered through introspection but in an inspection of the organizational conditions that provide for agent, action, and agency. It is, therefore, to the question of the organization that we now turn.

The Organization

We have defined *the organization* as a meaningful and significant set of ordered relationships that is the ongoing product of organizing.[14] We examine

---

[14] We alluded to the terms "significant" and "significance" when we introduced this definition in Chapter 3. Semioticians distinguish between the meaning and the significance of the sign (Noth, 1990). Meaning is the work produced by the sign in action. Significance is the potential of the sign to constitute meaning (Anderson & Meyer, 1988). Organizations are meaningful according to the normalized responses we have to the environments, objects, members that are recognized as part of them. Organizations are significant in so far as they provide resources—establish the potential for becoming and acting.

the organization under four principles: (a) its continuous production through organizing, (b) its meaningfulness as a bounded field of obligation, (c) its significant properties as the sites and resources for the expression of self and action, and (d) its coherence-producing properties in the justification of agency and action. We want to remind the reader that the term "organization," as we use it, is not synonymous with the "firm" or "corporation." The world of work is an extremely important site of organizing, but it is not the only one.

Continuously Produced in Organizing

The organization is not a material object, although it can have material objects attributed to it. It is, rather, an ideational object that is the product of the processes of organizing. We have defined *organizing* as a process that disciplines individual performance to be accountable to and understandable within a coherent ideology of member-to-member relationships, practices of discourse and action, rules of performance, and their judicial procedures. We do not redo the work of Chapter 3 here by recapitulating these principles item by item. Rather, we look to some of their implications.

DISCIPLINE   The principle that the self is actualized in performance indicates that in any performative domain (which is one of our descriptions of an organization), one both gains the right to be something and gives up the right to be something else. Our potential is disciplined into some actual. We embrace the opportunity to become, but recognize that it is at a cost. Further, we mourn the loss of what could have been, not in the sense of "I-could-have-been-district-sales-manager," but in the sense of the unrealized potential of identity and subjectivity. This loss stands in resistance to the complete surrender to the self we have become. In Marxist terms, this resistance is an alienation from the self.[15] This resistance provides us the perspective to read the text of the self we coproduce.[16] It gives a distance vital to the analysis of our own moral conduct. (We have considerably

---

[15] Young children provide spectacular exhibitions of this alienation as their resistance to the self overpowers their ability to constitute an acting agent and they dissolve into an uncontrollable rage of tears.

[16] It also raises the question of who or what does the reading. Our answer is not to retreat to some "inner self," some interior homunculus that directs our exterior performances. But rather to point to the excess of who we are. As with any sign, we are more than we can signify in any particular setting.

more to say about the relationship between resistance and morality in the last section of this chapter.)

Readers (analysts and reflexive members) of organizations will observe the discipline of the actual in what can be said and done in the various subject positions recognized by organizational members. A point to consider: the saying and doing are part of the rhetorical strategies of the subject. No performance is ingenuous (remember the slogan that we are neither cultural dopes nor dupes). Any performance is a sign of what is being done that is subject to all the tropes and figures of rhetorical strategies. Any performance can be performed in parody; with full disrespect, as in humor; in irony; in metaphorical reference, as synecdoche, and so on. The reading has to be as complex as the performance.

Second, organizational performance is never the work of a single individual. A single individual may make a bid for the saying or doing of something, but that bid must be confirmed by the collective effort that makes that "something" meaningful. It is not the actional facts that alone constitute the meaningfulness of action. The facts of the case do count, but alone they are always banal. It is their constitution as meaningful by the collective that establishes their standing. Again the center of the universe is the relationship.

IDEOLOGY   Ideology is the standpoint from which we make sense of things within a domain of action. Our use of the term emphasizes the socially constructed nature of all our knowledge about reality (which is Berger & Luckmann's 1966 thesis), as well as the social construction of the semiotic domain of reality (which Eco, 1984, would support). There may well be some domain of an objective, phenomenal reality, but our contact with it is always mediated by social processes. The vision of seventeenth century British empiricism unfortunately directs us away from a careful analysis of the practices of this mediation. Truth may be eternal, but knowledge is human. All of our knowledge is human; none of it divine. Further much of the world we live in has no foundation other than social practice. Our knowledge of those domains is part of the very process by which they come into existence.

Ideology, then, is not some false consciousness or defective understanding or biased view. Rather it is a Foucauldian regime of truth—a set of claims that allows us to act in certain ways to accomplish certain ends. Ideology is multiple, often competitive, and ultimately irreducible. In our analysis of organizations, it serves the same purpose as, but is more effective than, the term "culture." It serves the same purpose in that the term does the work of liberating understanding from a universal/foundational mooring and puts understanding into the hands of its practitioners. Ideology as a theoretical term is more effective than the term "culture" because our collective usage allows it to be seen in more local applications. That is, it makes more sense to move ideology down to the historical practices of measurable numbers of people. It makes little sense to move culture to this level (as we argued persuasively, to us at least, in Chapter 3), which is not to say that culture is not ideological. But culture depends on grand systems—those of the semiotic, epistemic, deontological, aesthetic, economic, political, and social. Organizational ideologies poach cultural truths and make use of cultural systems within their own practical framework of coherence.

For social action theorists, ideology is coded in practices that include discourse but are not limited to discourse. It is evidenced in the action of the collective not in the cognitive structures of its members (thus, methodological holism not methodological individualism), although body and mind play their part. Ideology is the epistemological structure (in the duality of structure and practice) that arises as motion becomes recognizable behavior, as act becomes action. Once some motion becomes part of the sign of what is being done, its recognition is its ideological status as an element in what is true. As our statement says, it is an ideology *of* "member-to-member relationships," etc.; it is not prior to or determining of those elements of practice.

MEMBER-TO-MEMBER RELATIONSHIPS   The ideological constitutive force of member-to-member relationships seems self-evident to us. What rescues the concept from tautology are the comparisons that can be made with member-to-nonmember and nonmember-to-nonmember relationships. If members are not differentially obligated (obligated to, obligated not to, and not obligated) from nonmembers, then the analyst needs to call the question on the process itself (or its point of observation). Not every collection of individuals, even if all are coded in membership, is an organization. It is, in part, the differential in obligation that moves an aggregation into a congregation.

Obligation, as we have said, demonstrates the presence of the relationship, and the relationship sets the terms of obligation. If we are claiming *member-to-member* relationships, then obligation has to be distinctive of membership.[17]

---

[17] Studies across ideological components (e.g., Vangelisti & Daly, 1997 [and their commentators: Wood (1997) and Burleson (1997)]; Deaux & Major, 1987) often show that the variance within a membership is greater than the difference across membership even though that difference is secure. Ideology is neither totalizing nor robotic. That one knows (has been trained in) what ought to be done doesn't guarantee performance.

practices, rules, and procedures   The requirement of difference holds true for the remaining constitutive elements of ideology (practices of discourse and action, rules of performance, and their judicial procedures). It is either not much of an organization or one is not much of an organizational member, if it makes no difference to the self—to who one is and to what can be done. Our interest in organizations arises because they represent material conditions that do make a difference. Nonetheless, the claim of an organization or the claim of membership is evidenced in the difference that is made in the processes of organizing.

If the process of organizing is authentic, and therefore effective, in making a difference, then that process participates in the formulation of the acting agent (the self), predisposes a menu of action, sets a basis for interpreting what is going on and what has been done, and indicates the criteria by which the doing and the done shall be evaluated. In short, it constitutes the domain of agency.

Organizational Meaningfulness

You have parked your car in the driveway of 135 Elm Street, a middle class home in AnyMidwestTown, USA. The house at 135 Elm is a well-kept, two-story home built about 30 years ago. As you step through the doorway there is the door to the coat closet on the left and a large, arched entrance to the living room on the right. But as a first time visitor, how do you know the names of these rooms? The answer is that the physical structure is already meaningful to you as a home. You step through the door with certain understandings in place about the environmental arrangements, the family membership or guest status of the people you meet inside, the ownership of the objects within, and your appropriate behavior to each. With no other indicators than those provided in this sketch, you would be amazed to step through the door into a butcher shop (but you also would immediately adjust your expectations about environment, people, and objects).

The basis of your understanding is not idiosyncratic. It is the normalized response to traditions in architectural design and family living that separate public and private venues and develop front stage and backstage areas. Any organizing process creates a similar meaningfulness. Living room or chat room, home or virtual space, the organizational site makes sense within its ideational status—a status that is constituted in the ongoing process of organizing. The lack of this status, the failure to coalesce a particular field of meaning, again, calls the organization into question.

The meaningfulness of the organization also locates *you* inside the field of organizing. You are implicated by your presence and assumed to be complicit in the organizing process—the signs of which surround you. Stepping through the doorway into the home, you are a family member or a guest; stepping through the same doorway into a butcher shop, you are a supplier, customer, "just looking," ("just looking?! What's to look at in a butcher shop?") or perhaps lost. You are understood and you understand yourself in relation to the meaningfulness of the organizational site.

Significance

We can state the general principle of organizational significance as: Organizing produces significance in the potential it provides for the meaning of acts, space, objects, persons, environments, relationships, performances, and so on. Some meaning will be put into place—some potential will be actualized—in the moment of engagement/enactment of any of these elements. The appearance of a policy manual, previously unused, on the desk of a supervisor, for example, represents a powerful potential for the course of an employee review session.[18] The prior production of that policy manual as a little used instrument of punishment creates its significance in that meeting. The performance of the meeting itself provides for the significance of its appearance and so on. In each of these cases, the organizing process creates not just a book or a procedure but the resources of meaning.

That some meaning can be produced from those resources does not imply that *a particular* meaning will be produced or that *any* meaning *whatsoever* can be produced. Meaning is a real time event of interpretation that requires enactment—it is not some cognitive spasm—and is limited by the significance of the resources available. The significance of the organizing process, then, is twofold. It provides specific resources for the production of meaning and it establishes a provenance of understanding that normalizes given interpretive strategies. The policy manual on the desk of a supervisor (specific resource) is engaged quite differently during a casual visit by a subordinate than during a review session (provenance of understanding).

---

[18] This example demonstrates that rates of performance (the proportion of times the manual appears) are only partially useful in understanding human conduct. The critical instance of a performance (the appearance of the manual at *your* review) is equally meaningful and often with an effectiveness far exceeding its frequency.

Though one is always meaningfully located in an organizational site, that meaningfulness has to be enacted in performances that can be accommodated within the organizational field. Even the most tightly practiced organizing process cannot determine performances or contain their semiotic excess. I, the keyboardist, must necessarily be the guest in a reader's home. But I must enact the guest that I will be. Performances are always improvisations on the demands of subject position using personal and organizational resources. This improvisational space may be the lowest level of autonomy, but it is irreducible. We always have choice in *how* to be, which implicates who we are.

Many organizing processes provide a number of subject positions and a great deal of improvisational space for the performance of self. There is greater autonomy in these processes, but there is also greater risk. The *I* can be many things, but it also has to be something. The choice of one means the loss of the others, even if only temporarily. The choice of one also means that the *I* must successfully negotiate that performance.

Coherence

The concept of the organization as a provenance of understanding arises from the idea that a product of the organizing processes is a phenomenological framework, an epistemological coherence within which meaning is produced and against which meanings are tested. Coherence theory, as an epistemological form, develops out of the writings of Keith Lehrer (1974, 1990) and Laurence BonJour (1985).[19] Its basic tenet is that what we know and what we can justify are held in the reciprocal relationships among a nexus of beliefs. It represents a rejection of foundationalism, the linear progression from one statement to the next that depends on the first statement being somehow foundationally true (Bender, 1989).

The work of Lehrer and BonJour looks to what we can universalize as knowledge. Our work radicalizes coherence theory by moving it out of universal governance and moving it toward regional and local governance. It is our claim that organizations, to successfully create boundaries of membership, must produce an internal coherence of beliefs in which the particular must make sense and the acceptance of which is a mark of membership.

---

[19] Other authors who informed this argument include Alvesson, 1993; Castañeda, 1989; Goldman, 1988; Hare, 1995; Sayre-McCord, 1996; and Walker, 1989.

In this last phrase we have taken ourselves back to the beginning of this discussion, back to the ideology that is the substance of the coherent relationships. Ideology establishes the truths of the organization, the propositions nominated for belief. Coherence involves the management of ideological claims and their justification as something to believe. The reciprocal relationships among beliefs that is coherence is not intrinsic to the beliefs themselves but is a production of the effort at coherence. This effort involves such productive practices as the glossing of contradictions among statements and among statements and practice, the maintenance of consistency in worldview, the containment of anomalies, the rehearsal of inferential connections, and the integration of new beliefs, as well as such protective practices as counteracting entropy and neglect, surveillance and defense against attack, celebrating instrumental successes, and co-opting instrumental failures. Coherence is not an epistemological state. It is an epistemological practice. That it can be achieved does not preclude its subsequent collapse.[20]

Organizational coherence, then, is a practice of particularized[21] sense making that justifies the ordered relationships, differential obligations, practices of discourse and action, rules of performance, judicial procedures, meaningfulness, and significance that are the marks of organizational membership.

THE RELATIONSHIP BETWEEN IDEOLOGY AND COHERENCE   Ideology and coherence produce, respectively, the truth statements of the organization and their justification for the organization. Real work has to be expended on producing and circulating what is true about the organization and its environment, the discipline of membership, the order and nature of relationships, the character of obligation, and the practices of action and discourse with their rules and adjudications. And real work has to be expended to form these truth statements into a structure of justification, otherwise their production and circulation is simply sloganeering, and statements become propositions without implicative effect. This is all too often the actual character of mission and policy statements. They are decorative rather than structural.

---

[20] The failure of the political will of the Soviet Union is a spectacular example of the collapse of coherence.

[21] The word "particularized" stands in opposition to "unique." Ideology and coherence—truth statements and their justifying structure—are not the wholesale invention of organizations. Organizational practices are both opportunistic in poaching solutions and under the larger governance of societal regulation and cultural beliefs.

Much of both kinds of work is naturalized out of sight, reproduced without supervision and review. This naturalization produces high efficiency. Members have a taken-for-granted understanding of what is true and right. But naturalization produces vulnerability to resistance that cannot be ignored. Families, for example, are often disrupted by members who just say "no" to what is assumed to be true and justified. Resistance forces the practices of ideology and justification out into the open and often motivates a better job of it.

JUSTIFICATION IN AND OUT OF THE FRAME   The organization is only one player in the collection of what is true, and the manner of its integration is a necessary preamble for what follows. We do not want to promote the idea of organizational membership being an entrance into an unrecognizable reality. No membership boundary is hermetically sealed. Nonetheless, organizational membership that has moral implications is more than a badge pinned to a lapel. Membership is a discipline, sometimes learned over years of effort. Some things are true and some things are justified only in the naturalized action of this membership. This sentence should not be read as declaring member knowledge to be parochial, rather it declares member knowledge to be a genuine contribution to the field of knowledge and a unique, authentic medallion of membership. This conclusion follows quite directly from a claim of knowledge as socially constructed. We hold social practices to be local, not universal. Therefore, knowledge has to be localized within some set of social practices (even if the practitioners are all over the globe). Further every set of social practices is productive of the knowledge that supports it and, to the extent of its integration, justifies that activity as well. The characteristic ways of being, doing, and speaking that evidence the boundaries of membership also evidence the boundaries of a field of knowledge and justification. Any organization worth its name, consequently, produces both some portion of what its members know to be true and manages some part of the integration that justifies those beliefs.

As you might suspect, this proprietary knowledge and justification cause us great difficulty in judging ethical conduct. A member can act from an uncontested belief in a justified manner within the phenomenological framework of an organization and yet be judged culpable from without. In Chapter 7, we gave the example of the hypersupervision of John Frogley. In the analysis of that example, we commented that Frogley probably thought he was doing the right thing by humiliating and degrading his subordinates. He, of course, would call it "proper discipline."

Further examples of management practices that reflect this in-and-out character of justification are plentiful. Recently, it was reported that a Utah school district refused to turn on the air conditioning in school buildings while teachers spent 4 days moving furniture, cleaning rooms, and preparing for the opening of school in 100+ degree heat. The justification according to the newspaper report? School was not in session. From the outside, this decision looks ridiculous; from the inside—and we do not know the facts of the case—it probably wasn't even discussed. It would not have been discussed because the decision was the "right" thing to do, given what is held to be true of the teaching staff, the work being done, and the primacy of cost containment.

The coherence with which these beliefs integrate justifies a decision to save money rather than to regard staff health and satisfaction. (It, of course, goes without saying that the administrators who made the decision work in offices that are air conditioned all summer long.) Administrators in this frame cannot see how they look to the outside and would likely consent to turn on the system only under collective pressure and certainly with complaints about wasting and coddling.[22]

On the other hand, the umbrage of this analysis derives from an ideology of different truths concerning the same issues of administrators, teachers, work, discomfort, and costs that are integrated to justify different conclusions. This coherent ideology emanates from separate organizing processes that nonetheless reside within the same titular organization. Who then is right? Is it better to spend $200 on the comfort and safety of the staff or to save $200 to put to work for the school children? Are the administrators petty martinets or courageous defenders of the taxpayer's dollar? The issue cannot be resolved by appealing to either of the standpoints we have presented because the issue cannot exist in either of them. The issue exists only in the comparison and can be resolved only in such standpoints that provide for that comparison.

In the meantime, the decision has been made, the work has been done with sweat and discomfort, school has started, and the air conditioning is on. The media voice that championed the teachers' cause was found too late

[22] Decisions such as these are typically made without consultation with those who have to suffer their consequences. In management lingo, it's called "thinking within the box." We need to act with an eye to the boundary and to step out of the frame to analyze the quality of the decision.

to have any effect. The ascendancy of one set of truths and their justification over another is demonstrative of control within ideological justifications the organization provides. The use of the media to complain is demonstrative of resistance to that framework of coherence. The complaint finds its standing by its expression in a different ideological frame where the decision of the administrators could be called into question. It is the decision within a framework of understanding that sets the quality of the decision, not the decision itself.

Moving to a Dialogic Community

Our analysis of the four principles of the organization—its continuous production, its meaningfulness for its members, its significance for discourse and action, and its ideological coherence—allows us to re-describe the organization as a **dialogic community.**[23] For us, this term captures both the sense of ongoing practices materialized in performance and the sedimented structurations that result as well as filling the void left by our objection to *culture* as an explanatory term. The dialogic character of an organization is a joint enactment, in continuous production, implicative of self and other, meaningful to its members, full of significance, and embedded in an ideological coherence. The structurations of the community of an organization are ordered relationships, reciprocal obligations, the supervision and governances of those relationships and obligations in policies regulations, customs and agreements, and the material sites of their enactment. And communities appear *in* cultures—not *as* cultures.

The conclusion of our analysis, therefore, is to claim an *organization* as a dialogic community whose membership is continuously produced through communicative achievements marked by specialized vocabularies and distinctive action routines with characteristic constellations of discursive and performative practices through which ordered relationships and reciprocal obligations appear, are furnished, and maintained. This conclusion is, of course, just the beginning of this argument, but its development awaits another time and place. In this time and place, we move to the analysis of power.

---

[23] The argument we briefly develop here is founded on the work of Bakhtin, 1981, 1986; and connects to Hawes, 1999; Martin & Nakayama, 1999; and Mumby, 1997a.

POWER

Our analysis of power is based on the prior condition of desire and its primal state of longing-to-be. Desire arises from our incompleteness. The self requires the other. The course of human life is a history of dependence. Each of us has spent years being carefully trained into it. We cannot be human except that we submit to the other. While thoroughly domesticated by this dependence, we are also given the recognition of our own existence by it. Once again we center on the relationship, and with that relationship, obligation, and in that obligation, the emergence of power.

Propositional Prepositions

We can begin our analysis of power by considering three propositional prepositions: (a) power *of,* (b) power *over,* (c) power *with.* If we use the phrase, "power of," we constitute power as an attribute of a person or subject position. Power is held singly not as product of a relationship. This is a formulation common to leadership studies. If we use the phrase, "power over," we again indicate that power is separately held and are directed to forms of analysis that use the traditional definition "A has power over B, when A can get B to do something B would not otherwise do." It is only when we use the phrase, "power with" that we are forcibly directed to consider the conditions of the relationship.

In our analysis of power, we reject *power of* as chimera, a false figure that is put in place by the careful staging of cultural interests. It is clear, for example, that leadership cannot exist without followership and that good leadership is, therefore, dependent on good followership. To consider power as an individual trait is to ignore the fact that no one can exercise power alone. We do not reject "power over" but do change its formulation to "control over." Our justification for this change is that the concept of "power over" conflates the concepts of power and control. For us, power is the potential and actual expressions of a relationship. Control is the differentiated means of that expression. Power directs us to consider the character of the relationship; control leads us to consider the material practices of its expression. We are left then with the phrase, "power with" as the basis of our concept of power.

Power With

The concept of power has two separate meanings both of which are in play in this discussion. The first meaning of power is about energy, an unrefined, nondelineated potential for change, similar to the electrical charge available at a wall outlet. The second definition deals with an ability to do something. In this latter definition, energy is harnessed into some service, as a power saw uses electrical energy to cut materials. In our theorizing, entering the relationship generates the energy of becoming, the potential to be. As that potential is realized, what one does in the service of the relationship is the expression of power. Just as the power saw, the relationship becomes the device by which the potential of energy is transformed into some actual expression. Both the potential and its expression depend on the relationship and have to be understood within its terms.

In thinking about power and its expressions, it is useful to distinguish between what Martin Buber calls "I-thou" and "I-it" relationships. Human relationships of the "I-it" type involve the objectification of the other and the manipulation of that object. In the corporate world, people become positions and commodities. A manager cuts six positions; she doesn't fire six people. In family life, a reluctant young child can simply be picked up and carted off. In "I-it" relationships, one can use force against another. But force is not the same as power. Pretty much any four people can use force against your keyboardist, but I am not in a power relationship with those four people. I am simply the object of their attention.

Authentic power—the sort of power we wish to deal with theoretically—arises out of a relationship and is always at risk through the termination of that relationship. This principle makes no claim that we freely/rationally enter or exit relationships. Choice is more often than not either absent or limited in the relationships of which we are a part. For most, it is a truism that we do not choose our mother or the cultural systems in which she is immersed and in which we will be so diligently trained. Upon birth a panoply of relationships with parents, caregivers, teachers, guides, mentors, bullies, friends, lovers, partners, the stronger, the weaker, the smarter, the superior, the subordinate, the more or less valued in all the ways of value stretch before us.

We will not enter these relationships as individuals, but as subjects— subjects of the relationship, occupying the subject positions defined by the relationships and enacting the terms of the relationship. We will not invent these relationships or their paradigmatic subject positions or their syntagmatic lines of action. These will mostly be given to us within the social/political systems of our culture. In all of these relationships, however, there will be a reciprocity of power—an exchange of the potential to be for some actual self—and a set of rules for performance—the means of realization of that potential in the expressions of the self.

THE RECIPROCAL OF POWER   An analysis of power begins in the reciprocity of the relationship. In a simple, dyadic friendship that reciprocal between subject positions may be one individual to another. Each member contains the power of the other, even though each may not have equal access to its performance. In a typical hierarchical relationship, a superior may have dozens of subordinates. Each subordinate defines the subject position of the superior. Should one subordinate break off the relationship, the subject position of the superior does not disappear as does the subject position of the friend. Hierarchical structures reduce risk for the superior subject position and amplify the effect of that position's actions by increasing the number of units that fulfill the subordinate subject position of the relationship. In this simple analysis, a *one* of the many who fill the subordinate position is the least powerful because she or he contributes only a part of the reciprocal position.[24]

POWER *WITH* AND CONTROL *OVER*   That power emanates from a relationship means that power is a joint production. Power involves an exchange of obligation just as dominance requires submission. Terminating the relationship terminates power. The question to theorize then is how do we move from the joint production of power—power *with*—to what certainly appears to be control *over*? We make that move by recognizing that we enter a relationship not as an essentialist self but as a subject position and that structure works to contain risk and amplify effect for some and to heighten risks and reduce effectiveness for others. We move from "power with" to "control over" by constituting differentials in performance—the expressions of power. Subject positions are charged with cultural and ideological significance. Consequently they have different potentials for performance. A boss is supposed to act and speak differently from a worker. A command, for example, is a discursive form appropriate to being a boss. Workers can guide the performance of other workers, but the appropriate way is through requests, a different type of speech act.

Signifying systems (such as subjectivity) work because of collective participation that has been naturalized through what Habermas (1979) calls

---

[24] This weakness becomes strength, however, when the relationship cannot be broken or requires great difficulty to break. Families, educational institutions, and civil service bureaucracies provide examples of these circumstances. In these organizations, subordinates can simply refuse to enact their subordination (hence, insubordination). The result is a resort to force or the development of a different sort of relationship where both parties have something to lose.

the manufacture of consent. Consent is manufactured through social processes in which the participants have little or no opportunity to question. Collectivized systems of training, such as families, schools, churches, sports, clubs, and the like, continuously reproduce and rehearse the truths of organizing—who occupies what subject positions with what discursive and actional rights. Capitalist, corporate ideology, for example, is introduced to children as young as 2 years old in standard U.S. school systems. By the time the child is 18, she or he will have had at least 12 years of training in a hierarchical, top-down structure that distributes awards across dominant interests. The greatest achievement of our school system is not the learning of facts of American history or good English grammar but a docile workforce.

The result is that the control of others by some and the submission of most is considered the way things ought to be. You can't be a boss unless you can give commands. Control then is not the local exercise of power over another. Control derives from the rights of performance collectively granted to different subject positions that are significant within the organizing process. It is Gramscian hegemony, not personal power, that generates control.

The differences between the sources of "power with" and "control over" are instructive. When Joe hires on at Corporation X, he agrees—his consent is manufactured—under various coercive forces (like withholding access to food and shelter) to fulfill the terms of the subject position of worker. He will learn what the specifics of those terms are as he goes along, extending his consent into the unknown. When he is introduced to his boss, Joan, he will enter a relationship, not as Joe and Joan, but as Joe the worker and Joan the boss. Joe and Joan will mutually constitute the relationship that provides the power of control, but they will do so within the culturally defined and ideologically marked subject positions of boss and worker. Power is local; control is global.

Both Joe and Joan will have to enact their subjectivity, and they will have substantial improvisational space to do so. Nonetheless, part of the means of recognizing who Joe and Joan are and what they are doing will be their separate culturally evoked subjectivities. For example, Joan, but not Joe, can make an improvisational move toward equality, granting bosslike rights to Joe, but only within the relationship between Joan and Joe. She cannot extend his rights in the company of other supervisors and will have to negotiate his status with other workers. Both Joan and Joe are at risk in this violation of cultural and ideological expectations.

The example of Joan and Joe illuminates the value of the distinctions we are making between power and control and their separate sources. Joan and Joe enter into a relationship, one that neither member needed to choose or necessarily wanted, that obliges them to one another. It is their subject positions, however, that supplies the expressive modes of that relationship. Neither Joan nor Joe is independent of that subjectivity. Each is bound to it, defined by it, and constrained within it. Again each will improvisationally enact the actual relationship but will do so with cultural and organizational resources. The self is directed to a particular agency with given codes of conduct and modes of expression.

We might profitably take up this theoretical lens to examine programs of "empowerment" such as Total Quality Management (TQM). In such programs, employees are empowered to take initiatives that reinforce organizational ideology (production, performance, quality, etc.). In most cases, such programs are simply co-opting moves that further conceal the means of control by having workers take on the duties of supervisors (what Tompkins & Cheney, 1985; Barker, 1993 call *concertive control*) with none of the rights. Job descriptions change, but subject positions do not. If we were to seek an authentic program of empowerment, we would look to changes in the fundamental character of the ordered relationships that constitute the organization. Such changes do not appear in the much ballyhooed empowerment programs. They may make us feel better about ourselves, but the work is still the work of the master.[25]

Resistance

Organizational theorists, with their nearly universal administrative perspective, have done little to theorize resistance. That job has fallen to continental sociologists (e.g., de Certeau, 1984; Bourdieu, 1984) and to U.S. performance study scholars (e.g., Scott, J., 1990, Butler, 1997). Our interest in resistance comes from the following argument: (a) Any organizing process is a discipline that must necessarily suppress options, and any hierarchical structure is necessarily a form of oppression. (This statement rejects the possibility of Utopian solutions and accepts a Foucauldian pessimism toward good intentions.) (b) The means of control within organizing is not

---

[25] There is a similar sham in calling workers "associates" or graduate students "junior faculty." Whatever is the diminutive of choice it is still a diminutive.

personal but cultural and ideological. (c) As such they are concealed hegemonically by being taken for granted. They are part of the "of course it is true" legacy that justifies action. (d) Control, therefore, is naturalized, performed without contention by dominant and subordinate alike. The result is that organizing conceals its injustices; works to justify dominant interests, and will move, if allowed to continue unchecked, toward totalitarianism. When organizing discourse and action become totalized—represent all that is true and good within the organizational domain—control becomes self-fulfilling. The system becomes self-organizing.[26] Such self-organizing systems offer repression without recourse because there is no resistance left in the system.

The necessity of resistance is an Enlightenment concept that has maintained itself in postmodern thought, albeit in a radically different form. No longer is resistance the "loyal opposition" of liberal democracy or the corrective counterarguments of a Habermasian ethic. Resistance is escape from surveillance (Foucault, 1980). It is tactical and temporary (de Certeau, 1984). It is nomadic (Deleuze & Guattari, 1987). It is a moment of self-mastery and mastery of the self (Best & Kellner, 1991).

We argue for the ethical necessity of resistance, not as a corrective in the path toward certainty, but as a disruption in the path toward totalitarianism. Resistance is more than the fool, more than the moments of carnival. Resistance is a celebration of what could be in a continual undermining of what is. It is a wildness, an uncultivated deconstruction. Resistance does not present "a better way." It is a refusal to entirely submit to the discipline of solidarity to give up all of our potential. It delays, distracts, disables, siphons resources, wastes time, dissipates energy. It pries the cracks and fissures of ideology; it hollows veridical foundations; it sheds gloss, presents ugliness, resents beauty. It denies the self that *is* in the name of the self that *could be*, all for no larger reason than it can. But in doing so it prevents certainty, celebrates indeterminacy, gives respite, reveals the concealed, forces reconstruction, all while demonstrating the domesticated pleasures of belonging, the very pleasures it opposes. Resistance is the necessary evil: the shadow to sunlight.

---

[26] It appears that a necessary consequence of autopoiesis is the elimination of resistance. If human practices become self-organized, they materialize a singular actual and suppress all other potentials, just as a cell can allow no variation within its boundaries. This consequence does not appear to be addressed by organizational scholars who see self-organization as liberation.

As our own critique, we find this theorizing bordering on the romantic. It could be easily read as ignoring the necessity of the collective for the self. Whatever we once were, we are now irretrievably social. Resistance has to be theorized within social processes. What rescues our theorizing from the Rousseauvian noble savage is its firm grounding in these processes by our posing a duality between resistance and control. Resistance works to justify control, just as control justifies resistance. Resistance is not rebellion. It defines the borders of membership, of sodality, of joint action, of productivity, of safety. It speaks the warning: "Look, if not *us*, then chaos."

Resistance will manifest itself in particular actions, some of which we listed in Chapter 7. The means of control will attempt to anticipate these actions through rules, regulations, and policies (Gottfried, 1994). The first response of control is suppression and containment. Failing that, the resistance will be co-opted, acknowledged, accommodated, assimilated, in short domesticated, put into service. ("Casual Fridays" is a good example of this sort of domestication that also had the added benefit of increased consumption by requiring two different wardrobes.)

Finally, our definition of resistance does not preclude a corrective, consequential opposition; in fact, in any organizing, we would expect opposition. Our definition does distinguish between the two. Oppositional correctives necessarily rely on the "taken for granted." They are inside the ideological system, within its cybernetic domain. They are already domesticated. Correctives present a different representation of the same dominant interests (see Fish, 1994, for example).[27] It is Democrats and Republicans working to create better government. Corrective opposition, then, is not resistance. It imposes the same discipline. It is not sufficiently primitive.

There is considerable work to be done in the theoretical development of resistance. What we have attempted to do is to bring it forward as a legitimate subject of organizational analysis. The characteristics that we hold to are that (a) resistance is part of the structuration of social action, (b) it is non-consequentialist (seeks no direction or set of goals), (c) it defines and illuminates control, and (d) its ethical service is the disruption of an ideology's manifest destiny.

---

[27] The logic is simple. If one is to correct something—make it better—then both what *is* and what is *better* have to arise from the same set of practices.

Concluding Remarks

This book has brought a social action, social constructionist perspective to bear on the organizational actor, using standpoint epistemology and postmodern sensibilities about the self as the acting agent, the organization as its domain of agency, and the moral judgments that can be derived from them. It has taken a strong stand against universalism while striving not to succumb to a trivial, narcissistic **relativism.** It has insisted on an empirical foundation of material practices as its evidentiary base. Nothing takes place behind the veil; no ideal types are invoked; no revelations implored.

On the other hand, nothing is put to rest either. Each narrative continues. Every judgment remains temporary, open to reinterpretation, until time and events pass it by.

While the question of moral conduct is the center of this book, it centers the answer in organizational life. It argues that organizations are the ongoing product of organizing and that organizing produces the phenomenological frame in which the actions of the organizational members make sense (Lanigan, 1990). This frame may be light and fragile, but becomes increasingly durable as the time and effort required of membership increases. The morality of any action depends on the frame of its judgment.

Because culture and organizational ideologies manufacture consent by being prior to the individual, by promoting the taken-for-granted, by withholding alternatives, by concealing the means of control, and by celebrating selected outcomes, societies and organizations become moral entities whose culpability can be greater than any of its members. There are immoral corporations, social groups, teams, and families whose members ensnared in the web of complicity and implication produce them in naive unawareness. Good organizations produce good members and immoral organizations produce members who are complicit in that immorality. The individual is not the building block. It is the relationship.

The glimmer of light in this potential repression is the irrepressible Trickster, the Raven of Resistance. Long reviled in organizational theory, it emerges here from its shadow of disrepute to play a requisite role in both individual redemption and organizational renewal.

GLOSSARY

Action Routine. A semiotically encoded and recognizable performance. Action routines make sensible the acts that compose them. Acts are under the governance of the overarching understanding that allows them to be recognized as a component of a routine. The action routine is the sign of what is being done. It carries rules of performance and implicates the character of the enactor within those rules. The enactor is necessarily an agent of the routine.

Action. A meaningful line of activity. All lines of action are dialogic and improvisationally enacted by local agents as a partial expression of a collectively held semiotic of action. Action is the performance of being in the world; it is the expression of the individual in each constitution of the self.

Activative Individual. The *coconspirator* who materializes collective resources of action in local and partial performances within the realm of his or her own agency. Through managing the tensions between individual action, the composite uses collective means within a joint phenomenology of what is and ought to be. It is the individual who must act, but cannot act alone. The individual will improvise on culturally given action routines made sensible within collective understandings.

Acting Agent. The accountable source of action. The acting agent, or accountable agent, can be but often is not an individual but a composite of self-other relationships such as parents in a family, a leadership group, or a corporate committee. In these cases, it is the composite, and not the individual members, that is empowered to act. The three elements of the acting agent are identity, subjectivity, and agency.

Actualize. To accomplish, achieve, or bring about a product.

Aesthetics. The philosophical reflection on a range of concepts relevant to art, such as beauty, harmony, structure, plot, texture, narrative, fiction, composition, and so on.

Aesthetic Systems.   The systems of beauty. Aesthetic systems set the codes of beauty, elegance, and style. Organizations from corporations to schools to families routinely govern the aesthetic expressions of their members through practical rules governing appearance, personal space, and requirements for performances and products.

Agency.   The ability to do otherwise. Agency requires some degree of freedom—the availability and recognizability of alternatives of action—and some degree of autonomy—one's self-governance. Agency is negated by the absence of choice.

Analysis.   The notion that ideas, concepts, and constructions are capable of being understood in terms of their component and sometimes conceptual parts.

Apparatuses.   The resources and practices of social structures. Political parties, class structures, government bureaucracies, industries, churches, and schools are all social apparatuses that go about the business of producing the society in which we live.

A priori.   Latin meaning "prior to" or "before" and used to refer to reasoning based on reason. Mathematical knowledge is frequently characterized as *a priori* because its truth does not depend on sense experience.

Autonomy.   The notion of self-governance. Autonomy is the ability to determine for oneself the rightness or wrongness of an action. Autonomy is the state of self-production or nondetermination of action. Autonomy allows authentic choice.

Axiology.   The study of value. A branch of philosophy concerned with developing a theory of value. Ethics and aesthetics are two main subdivisions.

Categorical Imperative.   An unconditional command or law. The unconditional instructs us to do something regardless of the consequences. According to Kant, we should act always such that our behavior could be a universal for all humankind.

Choice.   An action of the will. A power that implies an end or purpose that requires the exercise of judgment. Ethics is essential where there is authentic choice. Authentic choice gains its authenticity from what is possible at the point of the action. Choice, including the freedom to enact it and the autonomy to govern it, is the key in the analysis of ethical behavior.

Complicity.   A concept that enables the self to materialize in action. Complicity draws the self into the action of the other. The other must recognize the accomplishment of the self. Complicity links with implication. They are the necessary conditions of living in the web of connected lives. See also *implication*.

Consequentialism.   The position that a person's actions are right or wrong as a result of the consequences. This type of theory can also be termed teleological and can be contrasted with nonconsequential or Kantian theories.

Culture.   The system that provides for, mediates the process of, and is reproduced by human interaction. Culture is significantly greater than notions of shared values and meanings. It involves major systems of ideology and practice that constitute the conditions of our daily affairs.

Deontological. Pertaining to duty ethics. This term refers to ethical theories that stress the importance of the motive of doing one's duty in assessing the moral value of actions. For Kant, it is the motive for, not the consequences of, actions that count.

Dialogic Community. A membership continuously produced through communicative achievements marked by special vocabularies and distinct action routines with characteristic constellations of discursive and performative practices through which ordered relationships and reciprocal obligation appear, are furnished, and maintained. A term used to describe an organization.

Disciplines. Systems of practical training that provide for coordinated action.

Discourse. Any extended language use that is recognizable as its type and does work according to its type. A discursive type has a distinctive vocabulary-in-use, typical phrases, and more importantly encodes a particular standpoint on reality. Discourse is used metonymically in that a fragment invokes the whole.

Divine Command Theory. A belief that an action is morally right because God commands or wills it.

Domain of Agency. An arena of action, or a social location where objects, acts, and discourses are provided or denied states of meaningfulness. It is a sense-making frame that establishes many of the prior conditions of knowledge and belief and the ongoing conditions of freedom and autonomy under which choice can be practiced.

Duties. A system of ethics in which individual obligation is determined by moral rules. Duty ethicists include Immanuel Kant.

Economic Systems. Systems of valuation. Economic systems are the methods by which we sort objects and utilities into categories of greater or lesser value and in conjunction with political processes establish the rights to and distribution of such objects and utilities (e.g., ownership) and set the procedures of value exchange.

Empiricism. An epistemological theory holding that knowledge is somehow anchored in experience and that knowledge claims are verified by reference to sense experience. There are many variants of empiricism from brute-sense to perceptual to naive to constructive to hermeneutic (Anderson, 1996).

Epistemology. A branch of philosophy concerned with developing a theory of knowledge and truth.

Epistemic Systems. Systems concerned with publicly authenticated knowledge. An epistemic system focuses on the means by which proposition and practice are declared to be true. Within the organization there are methods by which organizational members authenticate or confer the status of truth on propositions and practices.

Ethics.   The study of morality and of moral behavior.

Evocation/Invocation.   A principle that relates to identity. Identity always carries the signs of the cultural value of the self; however, those signs are not always in use. An identity is evoked by others or invoked by self in different actions.

Existentialism.   A theory that each individual creates his or her own being through the choices made. The act of choosing and becoming is something more than the sum of all external influences.

Frame or **Frame of Meaning.**   Our action, discourse, relationships and notions of self take on particular values depending on the circumstances or setting. Frame or frame of meaning applies to the circumstances or setting.

Freedom.   The availability of authentic alternatives of action. An authentic alternative is one that can be recognized from the standpoint of the self and put into action within the domain of agency in which the self is then operating. If we are to choose, we must have something to choose from. Organizing, in its processes of ordered relationships, communication strategies, and coordinated activity, both reduces and increases freedom by manipulating the alternatives of action.

Habermasian.   Theory representing Jurgen Habermas (b. 1929), a German philosopher widely known for his rejection of positivism in favor of social theory.

Hegemonies.   The social contracts by which apparatuses, disciplines, and the other systems of culture are organized and maintained. They are the agreements by which we recognize the dominates and subordinates of a social system. They contain the codes by which we distribute resources across the polarities of gender, class, ethnicity, race, age, and so on.

Heideggerian.   Arguments based on the philosophies of Martin Heidegger (1889–1976), a German philosopher in the phenomenological tradition who spoke to the character of the self.

Hierarchies.   Practical rights and duties according to such social constructions as age, gender, ethnicity, caste, even birth order. Ethical responsibilities often accompany one moving through the gateway of one hierarchy to another.

Identity.   The persistent characteristics of the individual. Identity is invoked or evoked according to the cultural meanings of one's subject position. Identity and subjectivity provide for the self, the sign of the person. See also *subjectivity*.

Identity Agent.   The agent that is a particular and identifiable *agent of* action, providing some impetus or resource of the action. Identity and subjectivity appear together as the self. It is the self that acts; not identity alone; not subjectivity alone. See also *subjective agent*.

Implication. The foreground of action. Implication considers how action crosses the boundaries of self and other to confirm their mutual interdependence. See also *complicity*.

Instrument of Action. The first concept of identity. Identity as the instrument of action includes *material, biological,* and *semiotic* configurations. Each of these configurations occupies space and exists across time. The body is a *material* object. The material object of our body archives the markers of values and presents them, as, for example, in the way individuals drape, paint, dye, and otherwise modify and call attention to the material object or body. As a *biological* entity, it carries a genetic code that distinguishes aspects such as sex, age, and ethnicity. In its *semiotic* configuration, it explains the mental states of individuals in observable, social processes such as language, discourse, and action.

Justice. Justice is an ideational rather than material object. Justice has to be enacted by social agents in each time and place of its existence. There is no transcendental object called justice with fixed boundaries and brute characteristics. Justice, as it appears in word and action, is part of an enacted ideology.

Language and Action. Semiotic systems that are social inventions. Language and action provide the basis by which we contact and interact with the material world, ourselves, and others. Because language and action are collective enterprises, we live lives outside of ourselves.

Location. The stage for action. It is defined by material and semiotic boundaries and contains material and semiotic resources for the performances to be enacted. Location creates boundaries of thinking, acting, and being. It can influence the conditions of ethical communication and is one of the means by which organizing practices distribute resources of action and discourse. One's ethical analysis must account for location.

Membership. A reciprocal relational process. Membership involves the declaration or claim of *belonging* and the recognition of that claim by others identified as members. True memberships create domains of privileged action and discourse. Communicative practices provide for and sustain the domain of membership and its meaningful action.

Membership Field of Action. An action that could involve at least five elements including: (a) routines and their performance, (b) the declarations of and for action, (c) the resources to perform the action, (d) the reproduction of significance, and (e) meaning must be collectively validated.

Modernism. A method that has been characterized as the drive toward closure, control, and certainty. Modernist writing is objective, its authorship is concealed, its claims are essentialist.

Naturalized Practices. Part of the cultural and societal processes that provide a system of performance in which the self materializes. In their naturalized practices, individuals are an agent of culture and society, as well as sets of organizational memberships and interpersonal relationships. Naturalized practices are the second component of *identity*.

Objectivity. A view (objectivism) holding that there is a foundational framework for determining rationality, knowledge, truth, reality, and moral value. The opposite of *relativism*.

Obligation. The duality with relationship. Obligation is culturally informed and locally negotiated. It is the evidence of a relationship. It defines the character of the relationship, whereas the relationship defines the terms of obligation. If we are to continue the relationship, we must meet the obligations of it.

Ontology. The study of being. A major subdivision of metaphysics.

Organization. A set of ordered relationships and communication processes that is both meaningful and meaning-making. As a significant set of ordered relationships and processes, it is meaningful in that the organization is an ideational site. Regardless of its material attributes, or lack thereof, the organization serves to make sense of both the objects of its domain and the persons who inhabit it. In this text we have examined the organization under four principles: (a) its continuous production through organizing, (b) its meaningfulness as a bounded field of obligation, (c) its significant properties as the sites and resources for the expression of self and action, and (d) its coherence-producing properties in the justification of agency and action.

Organizing. A process that disciplines individual performance to be accountable to and understandable within a coherent ideological framework of member-to-member relationships, practices of discourse and action, rules of performance, and the judicial procedures of each. This discipline is produced through the reproduction, modification, specification, and enactment of culture.

Organizational Frame. The organizational provenance of understanding. Within an organizational frame, our action and discourse, relationships and notions of self all take on particular values that both are established by and serve to constitute and maintain the frame of meaningfulness. What we organize in the framework of organizations is the meaningfulness of who we are in what we say and do.

Other. A key construct in postmodern arguments concerning the self. The self is a cocreation with the "other." The individual is not self-sufficient or an essentialist unity. We not only interact; we must recognize and interact with "the other" if we are to be human.

Paradigm. A culturally defined persona or ideal type. The *hero, middle class, damsel in distress*, are all paradigms.

Paradox.   A false conclusion understood reasonably correctly from apparently true assumptions.

Patriarchy.   An organization of society or culture by men and women in which the masculine is privileged and dominant.

Persistent Characteristics.   The recurring aspects that help to define an individual organization or other entity.

Phenomenology.   The study of the formation of human consciousness and self-awareness as a preface to philosophy or as a part of philosophy. It is also a philosophical arena that represents the formal structures of the objects of awareness and the awareness itself from any claims concerning existence.

Philosophy.   The Greek word for "love of wisdom." Philosophy is the rational attempt to formulate, understand, and answer fundamental questions.

Politics.   The systems of allocation—the distribution of rights, privileges, entitlements, duties, responsibilities, requirements, rank, status, position, and the like. The particular political processes that are authorized to perform these distributions are clearly a hallmark of the society, organization, or social group in focus.

Postmodernism.   An epistemological method that avoids closure, seeks openness, denies certainty, offers standpoints, and attempts to reveal the methods and practices of control. Postmodernist writing declares its standpoint, reveals its authorship, and reflexively analyzes the constructed character of its claim.

Power.   The potential and expression of a relationship. Power is not the attribute of an individual or a hierarchical position. It is a quality of a relationship that comes into play at points of authorization. Power is reciprocal, but its expression is not necessarily equitable. The reciprocal nature of power does not imply that the expression or experience of power will be the same for every member of the relationship. *Authentic power* arises out of a relationship and is always at risk through the termination of that relationship. In all relationships there will be a *reciprocal of power* or an exchange of the potential to be—and a set of rules for its performance—the realization of that potential in the expressions of it.

Praxeology.   The study of action that answers the question of the methods and meaningfulness of what is done.

Quality Circles.   A concept of work teams within the theory of Total Quality Management. The theory emphasizes a cooperative effort and power sharing.

Relationship.   The moment of obligation. The relationship includes the reciprocal production of power as well as obligation and the condition of ethical responsibility. Relationship gives both the power to do something not otherwise available and the obligation to do certain things not otherwise required.

Relationship Ethics.   A theory of ethics that focuses moral decision making on caring and sharing within a web of relationships.

Relationships and Memberships.   Components of identity. Relationships and memberships are regularly exercised and have naturalized practices that define them. The nature of obligation in relationships and memberships acts as a basis for evaluating the moral character of action. Individuals are recognized through their relationships and memberships. Defined as the fourth component of *identity*.

Relativism.   A view of ethics and epistemology that denies the existence of objective, transcultural moral values and/or standards of rationality. The only moral values and standards of rationality that exist are relative to either individuals (*individual relativism*) or societies (*social relativism*).

Resistance.   A disruption in the relationship between potential and actual. Resistance is a celebration of *what could be* in a continual undermining of *what is*. Resistance does not present "a better way." It is a refusal to entirely submit or to give up potential. It prevents certainty, promotes indeterminacy, gives respite, reveals the concealed, forces reconstruction, all while demonstrating the domesticated pleasures of belonging—the very thing it opposes. Resistance is the necessary evil.

Rights.   A theory of ethics that focuses on the obligation of the community to the individual. The ethics of rights stands as a foundation to *social contract theory*, which is a theory of political sovereignty claiming that the authority of government derives from a voluntary agreement among all the people of a society to form a political community and to obey the laws laid down by the government they collectively select.

Self.   The self is a construction of identity and subjectivity that materializes the acting agent. In this text, the self is defined in five constructs: (a) the self is an ideational object and therefore a social invention; (b) the self is a sign of the person not an entity; (c) the self is an expression that actualizes the potentials of identity and subjectivity; (d) the self is in the continuous state of becoming in action; and (e) the self is possible only in the web of connected lives.

Semiotics.   A general philosophical theory of signs and symbols that deals with their functions in both artificially constructed and natural languages. It involves a system that manages significance and meaning in the processes of language and action. *Significance* is the referential and expressive potential of the sign—word, symbol, icon, sound, melody, odor, color, action, anything that stands for or connects to something else—what the sign can come to mean. *Meaning* is the consequential result of using a sign (word, symbol, icon action, etc.) in a particular time, place, and process.

Sexual Economy.   The factors within systems of power relationships that use gender to privilege or punish the other.

Social Action Theory. A theory that is epistemologically grounded in methodological holism and places an emphasis on the material practices by which human action are made sensible (instead of relying on physical determinants, biology, or mental states) on the social construction of knowledge, and on the necessary ethical presence of the scholar in society.

Social Constructionism. The view that the person is an intersection boundary in the web of connected lives, well colonized by the collective's semiotic resources of language and action. It includes the concept that reality does not present itself. Reality is both mediated and produced.

Standpoint. The position occupied by the acting agent. In this position we render judgement on the actions of others through the ontological, epistemological, praxeological, and axiological.

Structurations. Forms of hierarchy, definition, or enactment that are embedded or encoded within an organization.

Subject Position. A culturally defined location of the self. *Teacher, student, police officer, perpetrator* are all culturally defined locations in which a self can appear.

Subjective Agent. This is an *agent for* some recognizable intersection of cultural signs, such as parent, child, adult, worker, manager, customer, tourist, teacher, student, friend, etc. Identity and subjectivity appear together as the self. It is the self that acts; not identity alone; not subjectivity alone. See also *identity agent.*

Subjectivity. The cultural location of the self. Subjectivity is a cultural production that includes the cultural meanings symbolized in the marks of identity. Individuals necessarily appear in subject positions that are the intersections of cultural resources for the appearance of the self. These subject positions form the prior conditions of self-actualization.

Syntagm. A culturally defined line of action that has rules of performance and that positions its enactors. *Doing homework, enacting a rescue,* and *driving to work,* are all examples of syntagmatic lines of action.

Teleological. The study of ends or goals. The word comes from the Greek *telos* (goal, purpose, or end) and *logos* (word, reason, study) and is generally used to refer to theories that stress that the consequences or outcomes of actions are what determines their moral value.

Thematics. The organizational descriptions and stories members tell themselves in order to help make sense of what they do. Themes are not passive reflections of what is, but active elements in creating the organization.

Utilitarianism. A moral theory centered on the obligation to maximize happiness. Utilitarian analysis is directed toward the value of an action residing in its utility for the production of pleasure or happiness.

Vested Relationships.   The relational forms that enact one's title. It is a relationship vested by a conferred status.

Virtue.   A moral theory developed by the ancient Greeks that centers on the obligation to self and community.

Will.   The product and enactment of desire. It establishes the capacity for action. The will answers the prod of desire by constituting what is true out of the resources provided by the situation.

BIBLIOGRAPHY

Althusser, L. (1971). Ideology and the ideological state apparatuses (notes toward an investigation). In L. Althusser (Ed.), *Lenin and philosophy and other essays*. New York: Monthly Review Press.

Alvesson, M. (1993). The play of metaphors. In J. Hassard & M. Parker (Eds.), *Postmodernism and organizations* (pp. 114–131). Thousand Oaks, CA: Sage Publications.

Alvesson, M. (1996). *Communication, power, and organization*. New York: de Gruyter.

Alvesson, M., & Deetz, S. (1996). Critical theory and postmodernism approaches to organizational studies. In S. R. Clegg, C. Hardy, & W. Nord (Eds.). *Handbook of Organization Studies* (pp. 191–217). London: Sage Publications.

Alvesson, M., & Wilmott, H. (1996). *Making sense of management: A critical analysis*. London: Sage Publications.

Anderson, J. A. (1996). *Communication theory: Epistemological foundations*. New York: Guilford.

Anderson, J. A., & Meyer, T. P. (1988). *Mediated communication: A social action perspective*. Newbury Park, CA: Sage Publications.

Anderson, J. A., & Schoening, G. T. (1996). The nature of the individual in communication research. In D. Grodin & T. Lindloff (Eds.), *Constructing the self in a mediated world* (pp. 206–225). Newbury Park, CA: Sage Publications.

Anderson, R. (1997). Women, welfare, and United States media. In C. G. Christians (Ed.), *Communication ethics and universal values* (pp. 300–326). Thousand Oaks, CA: Sage Publications.

Anderson, W. T. (1998). *The future of the self: The making of the postmodern person*. New York: Putnam.

Apel, K-O. (1980). *Toward a transformation of philosophy*. (G. Adley & D. Frisby, Trans.). London: Routledge & Kegan Paul Ltd.

Baier, A. (1986). Trust and antitrust. *Ethics, 96,* 231–260.

Baier, A. (1985). *Postures of the mind.* Minneapolis: University of Minnesota Press.

Bakhtin, M. M. (1981). *The dialogic imagination.* (M. Holquist, Ed.; C. Emerson & M. Holquist, Trans.). Austin: University of Texas Press.

Bakhtin, M. M. (1986). *Speech genres & other late essays.* (C. Emerson & M. Holquist, Eds.; V. W. McGee, Trans.). Austin: University of Texas Press.

Bakhtin, M. M. (1990). *Art and answerability.* (M. Holquist & B. Liapunov, Eds.; V. Liapunov, Trans.). Austin: University of Texas Press.

Banta, M. (1993). *Taylored lives.* Chicago: University of Chicago Press.

Barker, J. (1993). Tightening the iron cage: Concertive control in self-managing teams. *Administrative Science Quarterly, 38,* 408–437.

Barnes, B. (1988). *The nature of power.* Cambridge: Polity Press.

Bateson, G. (1958). *Naven.* Stanford: Stanford University Press.

Bateson, G. (1972). *Steps to an ecology of mind.* New York: Ballantine Books

Bateson, G. (1979). *Mind and nature: A necessary unity.* Toronto: Bantam Books.

Beach, W. (February, 1998). *Conversational analysis.* Paper delivered at the Graduate Colloquium, University of Utah.

Bellah, R. N., Madsen, R., Sullivan, W. M., et al. (1996). *Habits of the heart: Individualism and commitment in American life.* Berkeley: University of California Press.

Bender, J. W. (1989). Coherence, justification and knowledge: The current debate. In J. W. Bender (Ed.), *The current state of the coherence theory* (pp. 1–15). Dordrecht: Kluwer Academic Publishers.

Benhabib, S. (1992). *Situating the self: Gender, community and postmodernism in contemporary ethics.* New York: Routledge.

Berger, P. L., & Luckmann, T. (1966). *The social construction of reality: The treatise in the sociology of knowledge.* New York: Doubleday.

Berman, A. (1994). *Preface to modernism.* Urbana: University of Illinois Press.

Best, S., & Kellner, D. (1991). *Postmodern theory: Critical interrogations.* New York: Guilford.

Bogue, R. (1989). *Deleuze and Guattari.* London: Routledge.

Bohm, D. (1980). *Wholeness and the implicate order.* London: Ark Paperbacks.

Bohm, D. (1994). *Thought as a system.* London: Routledge.

BonJour, L. (1985). *The structure of empirical knowledge.* Cambridge, MA: Harvard University Press.

Bormann, E. G. (1982). Symbolic convergence: Organizational communication and culture. In L. L. Putnam & M. E. Pacanowsky (Eds.), *Communication and organizations: An interpretive approach* (pp. 99–122). Beverly Hills, CA: Sage Publications.

Bourdieu, P. (1984). *Language and symbolic power.* Cambridge, MA: Harvard University Press.

Bourdieu, P., & Wacquant, L. J. D. (1992). *An invitaiton to reflexive sociology.* Chicago: University of Chicago Press.

Brockelman, P. (1985). *Time and self: Phenomenological explorations.* New York: Crossroad Publishing.

Brown, M. H. (1990). Defining stories in organizations: Characteristics and functions. In J. A. Anderson (Ed.), *Communication yearbook 13* (pp. 162–190). Newbury Park, CA: Sage Publications.

Burleson, B. R. (1997). A different voice on different cultures. *Personal Relationships, 4,* 229–241.

Burrell, G. (1993). Eco and the bunnymen. In J. Hassard & M. Parker (Eds.), *Postmodernism and organizations* (pp. 71–82). Thousand Oaks, CA: Sage Publications.

Butler, J. (1993). *Bodies that matter: On the discursive limits of "sex."* New York: Routledge.

Butler, J. (1997). *The psychic life of power.* Stanford, CA: Stanford University Press.

Calas, M., & Smircich, L. (1996). From "the woman's" point of view: Feminist approaches to organization studies. In S. R. Clegg, C. Hardy, & W. Nord (Eds.), *Handbook of organization studies* (pp. 218–257). London: Sage Publications.

Caputo, J. D. (1993). *Against ethics.* Bloomington, IN: Indiana University Press.

Castañeda, H-N. (1989). The multiple faces of knowing: The hierarchies of epistemic species. In J. W. Bender (Ed.), *The current state of the coherence theory* (pp. 231–241). Dordrecht: Kluwer Academic Publishers.

Chafe, W. (1994). *Discourse, consciousness and time: The flow and displacement of conscious experience in speaking and writing.* Chicago: University of Chicago Press.

Chisholm, R. M. (1982). *The foundations of knowledge.* Minneapolis: University of Minnesota Press.

Christians, C. G. (1997). The ethics of being in a communications context. In C. G. Christians (Ed.), *Communication ethics and universal values* (pp. 3–23). Thousand Oaks, CA: Sage Publications.

Clark, K., & Holquist, M. (1984). *Mikhail Bakhtin.* Cambridge: Harvard University Press.

Clark, M. (1990). *Nietzsche on truth and philosophy.* Cambridge: Cambridge University Press.

Clark, R. W., & Lattal, D. (1993). *Workplace ethics: Winning the integrity revolution.* Lanham, MD: Rowman & Littlefield Publishers.

Clegg, S. R. (1975). *Power, rule and domination.* London: Routledge & Kegan Paul Ltd.

Clegg, S. R. (1979). *The theory of power and organization.* London: Routledge & Kegan Paul Ltd.

Clegg, S. R. (1987). The power of language, the language of power. *Organization Studies, 8,* 1, 60–70.

Clegg, S. R. (1989). *Frameworks of power.* Newbury Park, CA: Sage Publications.

Clegg, S. R., & Dunkerley, D. (1980). *Organization, class and control.* London: Routledge & Kegan Paul Ltd.

Clegg, S. R., & Hardy, C. (1996). Organizations, organization and organizing. In S. R. Clegg, C. Hardy, & W. Nord (Eds.), *Handbook of Organization Studies* (pp. 1–28). London: Sage Publications.

Conquergood, D. (1992). Life in big red: Struggles and accommodations in a Chicago polyethnic tenement. In L. Lamphere (Ed.), *Structuring diversity: Ethnographic perspectives on the new immigration* (pp. 95–144). Chicago: University of Chicago Press.

Conrad, C. (1994). *Strategic organizational communication* (3rd ed.). Fort Worth, TX: Harcourt-Brace.

Coupland, N., Coupland, J., & Giles, H. (1991). *Language, society and the elderly: Discourse, identity and ageing.* Oxford, UK: Blackwell.

Crespi, F. (1994). Hermeneutics and the theory of social action. In P. Sztompka (Ed.), *Agency and structure: Reorienting social theory* (pp. 125–142). Yverdon, Switzerland: Gordon and Breach.

Csordias, T. J. (1994). *Embodiment and experience: The existential ground of culture and self.* Cambridge, UK: Cambridge University Press.

Daudi, P. (1986). *Power in the organisation: The discourse of power in managerial praxis.* Oxford, UK: Basil Blackwell.

Deal, T., & Kennedy, A. (1982). *Corporate cultures: The rites and rituals of corporate life.* Reading, MA: Addison-Wesley.

Deaux, K., & Major, B. (1987). Putting gender into context: An interactive model of gender-related behavior. *Psychological Review, 94,* 369–389.

de Certeau, M. (1984). *The practice of everyday life.* Berkeley, CA: University of California Press.

Deetz, S. (1992). *Democracy in an age of corporate colonization: Developments in communication and the politics of everyday life.* Albany: State University of New York.

Deetz, S. (1995). *Transforming communication, transforming business: Building responsive and responsible workplaces.* Cresskill, NJ: Hampton Press.

Deleuze, G., & Guattari, F. (1987). *A thousand plateaus: Capitalism and schizophrenia.* Minneapolis: University of Minnesota Press.

DeMarco, J. P. (1996). *Moral theory: A contemporary overview.* Boston: Jones and Bartlett Publishers.

de Saussure, F. (1910/1959). *Course in general linguistics.* New York: McGraw-Hill.

Du Gay, P. (1996). *Consumption and identity at work.* London: Sage Publications.

Dunne, J. (1996). Beyond sovereignty and deconstruction: The storied self. In R. Kearney (Ed.), *Paul Ricoeur: The hermeneutics of action* (pp. 137–158). Thousand Oaks, CA: Sage Publications.

Eagleton, T. (1996). *Literary theory* (2nd ed.). Minneapolis: University of Minnesota Press.

Eco, U. (1984). *Semiotics and the philosophy of language.* Bloomington: Indiana University Press.

Eco, U. (1992). *Interpretation and overinterpretation.* Cambridge; New York: Cambridge University Press.

Edwards, D., & Potter, J. (1992). *Discursive psychology.* London: Sage Publications.

Elliott, D. (1997). Universal values and moral development theories. In C. G. Christians (Ed.), *Communication ethics and universal values* (pp. 68–83). Thousand Oaks, CA: Sage Publications.

Emmott, C. (1997). *Narrative comprehension: A discourse perspective.* Oxford, UK: Clarendon Press.

Fairchild, H. H. (1985). Black, Negro, or Afro-American? The differences are crucial! *Journal of Black Studies, 16,* 47–55.

Faludi, S. (1991). *Backlash.* New York: Crown.

Finnis, J. (1983). *Fundamentals of ethics.* Oxford, UK: Clarendon Press.

Fischer, J. M., & Ravizza (S. J.), M. (1998). *Responsibility and control: A theory of moral responsibility.* Cambridge, UK: Cambridge University Press.

Fish, S. E. (1994). *There is no such thing as free speech, and it's a good thing too.* New York: Oxford University Press.

Foot, P. (1958). Moral arguments. *Mind, 67,* 502–513.

Foster, D. A. (1987). *Confession and complicity in narrative.* Cambridge, UK: Cambridge University Press.

Foucault, M. (1977). *Discipline and punish: The birth of the prison.* Harmondsworth: Penguin.

Foucault, M. (1980). *Power/knowledge: Selected interviews and other writings 1972–1977.* (C. Gordon; Ed.; C. Gordon, L. Marshall, J. Mepham, et al., Trans.). New York: Pantheon Books.

Foucault, M. (1986). *The care of the self: The history of sexuality* (Vol. 3). New York: Pantheon Books.

Foucault, M. (1994). *Ethics: Subjectivity and truth.* (Vol. 1). (P. Rabinow, Ed.; R. Hurley, Trans.). New York: The New Press.

Frankena, W. K. (1963). *Ethics.* Englewood Cliffs, NJ: Prentice Hall.

Frederick, W. C. (1995). *Values, nature, and culture in the American corporation.* New York: Oxford University Press.

Gergen, K. (1991). *The saturated self.* New York: Basic Books.

Gergen, K. (1994). *Realities and relationships: Soundings in social construction.* Cambridge, MA: Harvard University Press.

Gert, B. (1988). *Morality: A new justification of the moral rules.* New York: Oxford University Press.

Giddens, A. (1979). *Central problems in social theory.* Berkeley: University of California Press.

Giddens, A. (1984). *The constitution of society: Outline of the theory of structuration.* Berkeley: University of California Press.

Giddens, A. (1990). *The consequences of modernity.* Stanford, CA: Stanford University Press.

Giddens, A. (1991). *Modernity and self-identity.* Stanford, CA: Stanford University Press.

Gilbert, M. (1996). *Living together: Rationality, sociality, and obligation.* Lanham, MA: Rowman & Littlefield Publishers.

Gilligan, C. (1982). *In a different voice: Psychological theory and women's development.* Cambridge, MA: Harvard University Press.

Gilligan, C. (1999). *In a different voice: Sixteen years later.* Address to Utah Valley State College, Orem, Utah, November 1999.

Goffman, E. (1959). *The presentation of self in everyday life.* New York: Doubleday Anchor.

Goffman, E. (1974). *Frame analysis: An essay on the organization of experience.* Cambridge: Harvard University Press.

Goldman, A. (1988). *Moral knowledge.* London: Routledge.

Gottfried, H. (1994). Learning the score: The duality of control and everyday resistance in the temporary-help service industry. In J. Jermier, D. Knights & W. Nord (Eds.), *Resistance and power in organizations* (pp. 102–127). London: Routledge.

Habermas, J. (1979). *Communication and the evolution of society.* (T. McCarthy, Trans.). Boston: Beacon Press.

Habermas, J. (1984). *Theory of communicative action.* (T. McCarthy, Trans.). Boston: Beacon Press.

Habermas, J. (1990). *Moral consciousness and communicative action.* (C. Lenhardt & S. Weber Nicholsen, Trans.). Cambridge, MA: MIT Press.

Hardy, C., & Clegg, S. R. (1996). Some dare call it power. In S. R. Clegg, C. Hardy, & W. Nord (Eds.), *Handbook of organization studies* (pp. 622–641). London: Sage Publications.

Hare, R. M. (1995). Foundationalism and coherentism in ethics. In W. Sinnott-Armstrong & M. Timmons (Eds.), *Moral knowledge? New readings in moral epistemology* (pp. 190–199). New York: Oxford University Press.

Harman, G. (1977). *The nature of morality: An introduction to ethics.* New York: Oxford University Press.

Harman, G. (1995). Moral relativism defended. In S. C. Cahn & J. G. Haber (Eds.), *20th-Century ethical theory* (pp. 519–530). Englewood Cliffs, NJ: Prentice-Hall.

Harman, G., & Thomson, J. J. (1996). *Moral relativism and moral objectivity.* Cambridge, MA: Blackwell.

Harré, R. (1986). An outline of the social constructionist viewpoint. In R. Harré (Ed.), *The social construction of emotion.* London: Blackwell.

Harré, R. (1991). The discursive production of selves. *Theory and psychology, 50,* 51–63.

Harré, R. (1992). Introduction: The second cognitive revolution. *American Behavioral Scientist, 36,* 5–7.

Harré, R. (1995). Agentive discourse. In R. Harré & P. Stearns (Eds.). *Discursive psychology in practice* (pp. 120–136). London: Sage Publications.

Harrison, B. (1991). *Inconvenient fictions: Literature and the limits of theory.* New Haven, CT: Yale University Press.

Hawes, L. (1999). The dialogics of conversation: Power, control, vulnerability. *Communication Theory, 9,* 229–264.

Hegelsen, S. (1990). *The female advantage: Woman's ways of leadership.* New York: Doubleday.

Heidegger, M. (1996). *Being and time: A translation of Sein und Zeit.* (J. Stambaugh, Trans.). Albany, NY: State University of New York Press.

Hobbes, T. (1921/1651). *Leviathan Part I.* New York: Hafner.

Hume, D. (1748/1961). *An enquiry concerning human understanding.* New York: Anchor.

Jackall, R. (1988). *Moral mazes: The world of corporate managers.* New York: Oxford University Press.

Jacobs, J. (1995). *Practical realism and moral psychology.* Washington, DC: Georgetown University Press.

Jacques, R. (1996). *Manufacturing the employee.* London: Sage Publications.

James, G. G. (1988). *Stolen legacy.* San Francisco: Julian Richardson Associates.

James, W. (1890). *The principles of psychology.* New York: Henry Holt.

Jermier, J. M., Knights, D., & Nord, W. R. (1994). Resistance and power in organizations: Agency, subjectivity and the labour process. In J. M. Jermier, D. Knights, & W. R. Nord (Eds.), *Resistance & power in organizations* (pp. 1–24). London: Routledge.

Johnson, M. (1987). *The body in the mind: The bodily basis of meaning, imagination, and reason.* Chicago: University of Chicago Press.

Kagan, S. (1998). *Normative ethics.* Boulder, CO: Westview Press.

Kamm, F. M. (1988). Ethics, applied ethics, and applying applied ethics. In D. M. Rosenthal & F. Shehadi (Eds.), *Applied ethics and ethical theory* (pp. 162–187). Salt Lake City: University of Utah Press.

Kant, I. (1785/1959). *Fundamental principles of the metaphysic of morals.* (L. W. Beck, Trans.). New York: Liberal Arts Press.

Katz, J. H. (1978). Racism as a white problem: Theoretical perspectives and overview. In J. H. Katz (Ed.), *White awareness.* Norman, OK: University of Oklahoma Press

Knights, D., & Vurdubakis., T. (1994). Foucault, power, resistance and all that. In J. Jermier, D. Knights, & W. Nord (Eds.), *Resistance and power in organizations* (pp. 167–198). London: Routledge.

Knights, D., & Willmott, H. (1985). Power and identity in theory and practice. The *Sociological Review, 33,* 1, 22–46.

Knights, D., & Willmott, H. (1989). Power and subjectivity at work. *Sociology, 23,* 4, 535–558.

Kuhn, T. (1970). *The structure of scientific revolutions.* (2nd ed.). Chicago: University of Chicago Press.

Kymlicka, W. (1989). *Liberalism, community and culture.* Oxford: Clarendon Press.

Lacan, J. (1968). *The language of the self; the function of language in psychoanalysis.* (A. Wilden, Trans.). Baltimore: Johns Hopkins Press.

Lacan, J. (1977). *Écrits: A selection.* (A. Sheridan, Trans.). New York: Norton.

Laclau, E. (1990). *New reflections on the revolution of our time.* London: Verso.

Laing, R. D. (1971). *The politics of the family and other essays.* New York: Vintage Books.

Laing, R. D. (1982). *The divided self.* New York: Pantheon Books.

Lakoff, G., & Johnson, M. (1988). *Metaphors we live by.* Chicago: University of Chicago Press.

Lanigan, R. L. (1990). Is Erving Goffman a phenomenologist? In S. H. Riggins (Ed.), *Beyond Goffman: Studies on communications, institution, and social interaction* (pp. 99–112). New York: Mouton de Gruyter.

LaNuez, D., & Jermier, J. (1994). Sabatoge by managers and technocrats: Neglected patterns of resistance at work. In J. Jermier, D. Knights & W. Nord (Eds.), *Resistance and Power in Organizations* (pp. 219–251). London: Routledge.

Latour, B. (1987). *Science in action.* Cambridge: Harvard University Press.

Lazega, E. (1992). *The micropolitics of knowledge: Communication and indirect control in workgroups.* New York: Aldine De Gruyer.

Lears, T. L. J. (1985). The concept of cultural hegemony: Problems and possibilities. *American Historical Review, 90,* 567–593.

Lehrer, K. (1974). *Knowledge.* Oxford: Clarendon Press.

Lehrer, K. (1990). *Theory of knowledge.* Boulder, CO: Westview Press.

Levin, D. M. (1985). *The body's recollection of being: Phenomenological psychology and the deconstruction of nihilism.* London: Routledge.

Levin, G. (1992). *Constructions of the self.* New Brunswick, NJ: Rutgers University Press.

Luhmann, N. (1990). *Essays on self-reference.* New York: Cambridge University Press.

Lukes, S. (1974). *Power: A radical view.* London: Macmillan.

Lyotard, J-F. (1984). *The postmodern condition: A report on knowledge.* (G. Bennington & B. Massumi, Trans.). Minneapolis: University of Minnesota Press.

MacIntyre, A. (1988). *Whose justice? Which rationality?* Notre Dame, IN: University of Notre Dame Press.

Manning, P. K. (1992). *Organizational communication.* New York: Aldine de Gruyter.

Martin, J. (1993). *Cultures in organizations: Three perspectives.* New York: Oxford University Press.

Martin, J., & Nakayama, T. K. (1999). Thinking dialogically about culture and communication. *Communication Theory, 9,* 1–25.

Martin, L. H., Gutman, H., & Hutton, P. H. (1988). *Technologies of the self: A seminar with Michel Foucault.* Amherst: University of Massachusetts Press.

Martin, R. (1977). *The sociology of power.* London: Routledge & Kegan Paul Ltd.

Maturana, H. R., & Varela, F. J. (1980). *Autopoiesis and cognition: The realization of the living.* Dordrecht: D. Reidel Publishing Company.

Maturana, H. R., & Varela, F. J. (1992). *The tree of knowledge: The biological roots of understanding.* Boston: Shambala.

Mayo, E. (1945). *The social problems of industrial civilization.* Cambridge, MA: Harvard University Press.

McPhail, M. L. (1998a). From complicity to coherence: Rereading the rhetoric of Afrocentricity. *The Western Journal of Communication,* 114–140.

McPhail, M. L. (1998b). Passionate intensity: Louis Farrakhan and the fallacies of racial reasoning. *Quarterly Journal of Speech,* 84, 416–429.

Mieth, D. (1997). The basic norm of truthfulness: its ethical justification and universality. In C. G. Christians (Ed.), *Communication ethics and universal values* (pp. 87–104). Thousand Oaks, CA: Sage Publications.

Mill, J. S. (1897). *Utilitarianism.* London: Longmans Green.

Mills, A. J. (1993). Organizational discourse and the gendering of identity. In J. Hassard & M. Parker (Eds.), *Postmodernism and organizations* (pp. 132–148). Thousand Oaks, CA: Sage Publications.

Mintzberg, H. (1973). *The nature of managerial work.* New York: Harper & Row.

More, T. (1516/1964). *Utopia.* New Haven, CT: Yale University Press.

Morgan, G. (1997). *Images of Organizations.* Thousand Oaks, CA: Sage Publications.

Mumby, D. (1987). The political functions of narrative in organizations. *Communication Monographs,* 54, 113–127.

Mumby, D. (1988). *Communication and power in organizations: Discourse, ideology, and domination.* Norwood, NJ: Ablex.

Mumby, D. (1996). Feminism, postmodernism, and organizational communication: A critical reading. *Management Communication Quarterly,* 9, 259–295.

Mumby, D. (1997a). Modernism, postmodernism, and communication studies: A rereading of an on-going debate. *Communication Theory,* 7, 1–28.

Mumby, D. (1997b). The problem of hegemony: Rereading Gramsci for organizational communication studies. *Western Journal of Communication,* 61, 343–375.

Nicolson, P. (1996). *Gender, power and organisation: A psychological perspective.* London: Routledge.

Nietzsche, F. (1967). *The will to power.* (W. Kaufmann & R. J. Hollingdale, Trans.). New York: Random House.

Nietzsche, F. (1969). *On the genealogy of morals.* (W. Kaufmann & R. J. Hollingdale, Trans.). New York: Random House.

Nöth, W. (1990). *Handbook of semiotics.* Bloomington: Indiana University Press.

Pearce, W. B., & Cronen, V. E. (1980). *Communication, action and meaning: The creation of social realities.* New York: Praeger.

Peirce, C. S. (1960). *Collected papers* (Vol 2; C. Hartshorne & P. Weiss, Eds.). Cambridge, MA: The Kelnap Press of Harvard University Press.

Perrow, C. (1986). *Complex organizations: A critical essay.* New York: Random House.

Philipsen, G. (1975). Speaking "like a man" in Teamsterville: Culture patterns of role enactment in an urban neighborhood. *Quarterly Journal of Speech, 61,* 13–22.

Popper, K. R., & Eccles, J. C. (1977). *The self and its brain.* New York: Springer International.

Potter, J., & Wetherell, M. (1987). *Discourse and social psychology: Beyond attitudes and behavior.* London: Routledge.

Quinn, R. E., Faerman, S. R., Thompson, M. P., et al. (1996). *Becoming a master manager: A competency framework* (2nd ed.). New York: John Wiley & Sons.

Rabinow, P. (1994). Introduction: The history of systems of thought. In M. Foucault, *Ethics: Subjectivity and truth* (Vol. 1). (P. Rabinow, Ed.; R. Hurley, Trans.). (pp. xi–xlii). New York: The New Press.

Rachels, J. (1993). *The elements of moral philosophy* (2nd ed.). New York: McGraw-Hill.

Railton, P. (1996). Moral realism: Prospects and problems. In W. Sinnott-Armstrong & M. Timmons (Eds.). *Moral knowledge?* (pp. 49–81). New York: Oxford University Press.

Rainwater, M. (1996). Refiguring Ricoeur: Narrative force and communicative ethics. In R. Kearney (Ed.), *Paul Ricoeur: The hermeneutics of action* (pp. 99–110). Thousand Oaks, CA: Sage Publications.

Rasch, W. (1995). Immanent systems, transcendental temptations, and the limits of ethics. *Cultural Critique, 30,* 193–221.

Rasmussen, D. (1996). Rethinking subjectivity: narrative identity and the self. In R. Kearney (Ed.), *Paul Ricoeur: The hermeneutics of action* (pp. 158–172). Thousand Oaks, CA: Sage Publications.

Rawlins, W. K. (1987). Gregory Bateson and the composition of human communication. *Research on Language and Social Interaction, 20,* 53–77.

Rawlins, W. K. (1992). *Friendship matters: Communication, dialectics, and the life course.* New York: Aldine de Gruyter.

Rawls, J. (1954/1995). Two concepts of rules. In S. M. Cahn & J. G. Haber (Eds.), *20th-Century ethical theory* (pp. 273–290). Englewood Cliffs, NJ: Prentice-Hall.

Rawls, J. (1971). *A theory of justice.* Cambridge, MA: Harvard University Press.

Rawls, J. (1999). *A theory of justice* (2nd ed.). Cambridge, MA: Harvard University Press.

Raymond, D. B. (1991). *Existentialism and the philosophical tradition.* Englewood Cliffs, NJ: Prentice Hall.

Ricoeur, P. (1991). *From text to action: Essays in hermeneutics,* II. Evanston, IL: Northwestern University Press.

Ricoeur, P. (1992). *Oneself as another.* (K. Blamey, Trans.). Chicago: University of Chicago Press.

Ross, P. J. (1994). *De-privatizing morality.* Brookfield, VT: Ashgate Publishing Co.

Sackmann, S. J. (1991). *Cultural knowledge in organizations: Exploring the collective mind.* Newbury Park, CA: Sage Publications.

Sartre, J-P. (1956). *Being and nothingness.* New York: Philosophical Library.

Sayre-McCord, G. (1996). Coherentist epistemology and moral theory. In W. Sinnott-Armstrong & M. Timmons (Eds.), *Moral knowledge? New readings in moral epistemology* (pp. 137–189). New York: Oxford University Press.

Schoening, G., & Anderson J. A. (1995). Social action media studies: Foundational arguments and common premises. *Communication Theory, 5,* 93–116.

Scott, C. E. (1990). *The question of ethics: Nietzsche, Foucault, Heidegger.* Bloomington: Indiana University Press.

Scott, J. C. (1990). *Domination and the arts of resistance.* New Haven, CT: Yale University Press.

Scott, W. G., & Hart, D. K. (1989). *Organizational values in America.* New Brunswick, NJ: Transaction Publishers.

Searle, J. R. (1969). *Speech acts, an essay in the philosophy of language.* New York: Cambridge University Press.

Searle, J. R. (1995). *The social construction of reality.* New York: The Free Press.

Sheets-Johnstone, M. (1994). *The roots of power: Animate form and gendered bodies.* Chicago: Open Court.

Shotter, J. (1993a). *Conversational realities.* London: Sage Publications.

Shotter, J. (1993). Becoming someone: Identity and belonging. In N. Coupland & J. F. Nussbaum (Eds.) (1993). *Discourse and lifespan identity* (pp. 5–28). Newbury Park, CA: Sage Publications.

Sigman, S. J. (1987). *A perspective on social communication.* Lexington, MA: Lexington Books.

Spivak, G. C. (1988). *In other worlds: Essays in cultural politics.* New York: Routledge.

Sterba, J. P. (1995). Reconciling conceptions of justice. In J. P. Sterba, et al. (Eds.), *Morality and social justice: point/counterpoint* (pp. 1–38). Lanham, MD: Rowman & Littlefield Publishers.

Taylor, C. (1982). Rationality. In M. Hollis & S. Lukes (Eds.), *Rationality and relativism* (pp. 87–105). Oxford, UK: Basil Blackwell.

Taylor, C. (1989). *Sources of the self: The making of the modern identity.* Cambridge, MA: Harvard University Press.

Taylor, F. (1911). *Principles of scientific management.* New York: Harper.

Taylor, M. C. (1980). *Journeys to selfhood: Hegel & Kierkegaard.* Berkeley: University of California Press.

Thoreau, H. D. (1849/1960). *Walden: Or life in the woods.* Garden City, NY: Dolphin Books.

Tompkins, P. K., & Cheney, G. (1985). Communication and unobtrusive control in contemporary organizations. In R. McPhee & P. K. Tompkins (Eds.), *Organizational communication: Traditional themes and new directions* (pp. 179–210). Newbury Park, CA: Sage Publications.

Toulmin, S. (1950). *The place of reason in ethics*. New York: Cambridge University Press.

Traber, M. (1997). Conclusion: An ethics of communication worthy of human beings. In C. G. Christians (Ed.), *Communication ethics and universal values* (pp. 327–343). Thousand Oaks, CA: Sage Publications.

Vangelisti, A. L., & Daly, J. A. (1997). Gender differences in standards for romantic relationships. *Personal Relationships, 4,* 203–219.

Van Maanen, J. (1991). The smile factory: Work at Disneyland. In P. Frost, et al. (Eds.), *Reframing organizational culture* (pp. 58–76). Newbury Park, CA: Sage Publications.

Varela, F. J., Thompson, E., & Rosch, E. (1991). *The embodied mind: Cognitive science and human experience*. Cambridge, MA: MIT Press.

Volosinov, V. N. (1973). *Marxism and the philosophy of language*. New York: Seminar Press.

Volosinov, V. N. (1976). *Freudianism: A Marxist critique*. New York: Academic Press.

von Bertalanffy, L. (1968). *General systems theory*. New York: George Braziller.

Vygotsky, L. S. (1978). *Mind in society: The development of higher psychological processes*. Cambridge, MA: Harvard University Press.

Wade, J. (1996). *Changes of mind: A holonomioc theory of the evolution of consciousness*. Albany: State University of New York Press.

Walker, M. U. (1998). *Moral understanding: A feminist study in ethics*. New York: Routledge.

Walker, R. C. S. (1989). *The coherence theory of truth*. London: Routledge.

Weber, M. (1909/1947). *The theory of social and economic organization*. (T. Parsons, Trans.). Oxford: Oxford University Press.

Werhane, P., & Doering, J. (1995). Conflicts of interest and conflicts of commitment. *Professional Ethics, 4,* 47–81.

West, C. (1982). *Prophesy deliverance! An Afro-American revolutionary Christianity*. Philadelphia: Westminster.

Weick, K. (1987). Theorizing about organizational communication. In F. M. Jablin, L. L. Putnam, K. H. Roberts, & L. W. Porter (Eds.), *Handbook of organizational communication* (pp. 97–122). Newbury Park, CA: Sage Publications.

Wilber, K. (1993). *The spectrum of consciousness*. Wheaton, IL: Quest Books.

Wilson, J. Q. (1993). *The moral sense*. New York: Free Press.

Wong, D. (1984). *Moral relativity*. Berkeley: University of California Press.

Wood, J. (1997). Clarifying the issues. *Personal Relationships, 4,* 221–228.

Wrong, D. (1979). *Power: Its forms, bases and uses*. Oxford: Basil Blackwell.

Zagzebski, L. T. (1996). *Virtures of the mind: An inquiry into the nature of virtue and the ethical foundations of knowledge*. Cambridge: Cambridge University Press.

Zimmerman, M. J. (1996). *The concept of moral obligation*. Melbourne: Oxford University Press.

INDEX